Leonard Woolf

Twayne's English Authors Series

Kinley E. Roby, Editor

Northeastern University

TEAS 352

Leonard Woolf
c. 1933
Photograph from *Virginia Woolf:
A Biography* by Quentin Bell,
reprinted by permission of Harcourt Brace Jovanovich, Inc. and
the Hogarth Press.

Leonard Woolf

By Selma S. Meyerowitz

Stanford University and
San Jose State University

Twayne Publishers · Boston

Leonard Woolf

Selma S. Meyerowitz

Copyright © 1982 by G. K. Hall & Company
All Rights Reserved
Published by Twayne Publishers
A Division of G. K. Hall & Company
70 Lincoln Street
Boston, Massachusetts 02111

Book Production by Marne B. Sultz
Book Design by Barbara Anderson

Printed on permanent/durable acid-free
paper and bound in the United States of
America.

Library of Congress Cataloging in Publication Data

Meyerowitz, Selma S.
   Leonard Woolf.

   Twayne's English authors series ; TEAS 352]
   Bibliography: p. 221
   Includes index.
   l. Woolf, Leonard, 1880-1969—Criticism and
interpretation.   I. Title.   II. Series.
PR6045.068Z77 1982   828'.91209   82-9334
ISBN 0-8057-6838-6   AACR2

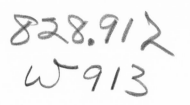

To Hari, Nila, and Anjali

Contents

About the Author
Preface
Acknowledgments
Chronology

Chapter One
Perspectives on a Life   1

Chapter Two
Early Writings on
Imperialism and Civilization   30

Chapter Three
Increasing Social Consciousness: Studies on War,
International Government, and Imperialism   62

Chapter Four
Studies on Socialism and Cooperation,
and Responses to Barbarism   93

Chapter Five
Contributions to Journalism and the Hogarth Press   117

Chapter Six
Perspectives on the Past: The Autobiography   163

Chapter Seven
Conclusion   198

Notes and References   207
Selected Bibliography   221
Index   229

About the Author

Selma Meyerowitz is a lecturer in English at Stanford University and San Jose State University. She received the Ph.D in English from Wayne State University in 1975.

She has published book reviews and articles on Virginia Woolf, Leonard Woolf, and Bloomsbury for the *Virginia Woolf Miscellany, New Feminist Essays on Virginia Woolf, San Jose Studies,* and *Jewish Currents.* At present she is working on coediting an anthology of critical essays on Leonard Woolf.

Preface

This study attempts to provide an overview of Leonard Woolf's life, thought, and work. Its primary focus is a critical analysis of Woolf's published writings which are discussed in a roughly chronological order. Although there is no new biographical material, biographical details have been provided to create a framework for the development of Woolf's career in literature and politics. In the past, biographical studies have examined Woolf's life in relationship to Virginia Woolf, with only general comments on his writing. While Duncan Wilson's political biography of Woolf provides a more comprehensive view of Woolf's life and work, its main concern is Woolf's contribution to political journalism and practical politics, and thus the literary works are only briefly discussed.

Woolf's political work and political journalism are indeed a central concern when assessing his place in British society; however, his literary works also provide important insights into twentieth-century British life and thought. Several critical analyses of these works exist, but they focus mostly on Woolf's first novel, *The Village in the Jungle*, and on the autobiography. This study, then, hopes to emphasize his other literary works: his second novel, *The Wise Virgins*; his four short stories and his only play; and his literary essays. Several important areas have been omitted. First, no attempt has been made to interpret the personal or literary relationship between Leonard and Virginia, except to provide some of their comments about each other and their marriage, and to note that there are striking correspondences between their literary and political writing and thought. Second, Leonard's role and influence as a critic of Virginia's work have not been considered, as that would involve analysis of Virginia's diary and of the manuscripts and revisions of her work. These areas are undoubtedly of great interest, and should be investigated in other studies.

LEONARD WOOLF

An examination of Woolf's published works in relation to his personal life and to the practical political work he did reveals that he believed that rationalism should be the basis of thought and action because it could lead to civilized behavior. He acted on this belief in all stages of his life: as a Cambridge University undergraduate and a British civil servant in Ceylon, as a member of the circle of writers and artists known as the Bloomsbury Group, as Virginia Woolf's husband, and then as an editor and publisher, as well as a writer of fiction, political journalism, literary criticism, drama, and social, political, and philosophical commentary. Woolf was most interested in the relationship between individual and communal values and actions on the one hand, and social, economic, and political systems on the other. This became the subject of all his writings. Moreover, he argued that the writer and artist, as well as the man of practical politics, plays an important role in society—that of presenting the general public with a rational perspective for evaluating both individual and social values, and social, political, and economic systems. It was Woolf's belief that if the values of civilization could be recognized, they could be adopted. This was the goal he set for himself as a member of society who engaged in literary and political work throughout his life; and in turn, this is how his life and works can best be evaluated.

Selma S. Meyerowitz

*Stanford University and
San Jose State University*

Acknowledgments

I would like to thank the following people for their interest in and critical response to my work: Professors Lucio Ruotolo, Beverly Schlack-Randles, and Robert Schulzinger. Also, Mr. William Allen and Mr. George Spater were helpful in making copies of Leonard Woolf materials more readily available. Finally, I would like to thank the English Department of San Jose State University for partial financial support of this project.

Chronology

1880   Born in Kensington, London, 25 November.

1892   Death of father, Sidney Woolf.

1899   Graduates from St. Paul's School; enters Trinity College, Cambridge.

1900   First meets Virginia Stephen.

1902   Joins the Apostle Society.

1904   Graduates Cambridge; joins the Ceylon Civil Service (assigned to Jaffna, 1905 to 1907; Kandy, 1907 to 1908; and Hambantota, 1908 to 1911).

1911   Returns to England; meets Virginia Stephen, 3 July; moves into 38 Brunswick Square where Virginia lives, 4 December.

1912   Proposes marriage to Virginia, 11 January; she refuses; consults Virginia's doctor, Sir George Savage, about her health, 21 March; resigns from the Civil Service, 7 May; Virginia agrees to marriage, 29 May; marriage to Virginia takes place on 10 August; honeymoon to Spain and Italy.

1913   *The Village in the Jungle*; meets Beatrice and Sidney Webb, 12 July; begins work for the Fabian Society and the *New Statesman*.

1914   *The Wise Virgins*.

1915   Purchase of Hogarth House in Richmond.

1916   *International Government*; exemption from military service, 30 May.

1917   Founding of the 1917 Club; founding of the Hogarth Press; publication of short story "Three Jews."

1918   Editor of *International Review* (until 1919).

1919   *Co-operation and the Future of Industry*; purchase of Monks House, 1 July.

1920   *Empire and Commerce in Africa, Economic Imperialism, International Economic Policy,* and *Mandates and Empire*; founding of the Memoir Club, 4 March; offered nomination as Labour candidate for the Combined English University Constituency for the 1922 election for Parliament, 11 May.

1921   *Socialism and Co-operation.*

1922   Stands for Parliament, 7 July—defeated; editor of foreign affairs for *Contemporary Review.*

1923   Accepts literary editorship of the *Nation*, 23 March; travels to Spain.

1924   Sale of Richmond House; lease taken for 52 Tavistock Square.

1925   *Fear and Politics.*

1926   Resigns as literary editor of the *Nation*, 24 March.

1927   *Hunting the Highbrow* and *Essays on Literature, History, Politics, Etc.*

1928   *Imperialism and Civilization*; travels to France (to Cassis, where the Bells and Duncan Grant are staying).

1929   Travels to Germany; moves to 37 Mecklenburgh Square.

1930   Founding of *Political Quarterly*; Woolf becomes joint editor with W. A. Robson.

1931   *After the Deluge, Volume I*; travels to France; gives a series of six radio broadcasts.

1932   Travels to Greece with Roger and Margery Fry.

1933   Travels to France.

1934   Acquires a pet marmoset, Mitz, 25 July (died 24 December 1938).

1935   Travels to Holland, Germany, Italy.

1936   *Quack, Quack!* and *The League and Abyssinia.*

1937   Period of poor health.

1938   *The Hotel;* John Lehmann becomes a partner in the Hogarth Press, 1 March.

1939 *After the Deluge, Volume II* and *Barbarians Within and Without;* death of his mother, 2 July.

1940 *The War for Peace.*

1941 Death of Virginia Woolf. (After Virginia's death, Leonard became involved in editing and publishing Virginia's remaining manuscripts as follows: *The Death of the Moth and Other Essays*, 1942; *A Haunted House and Other Stories*, 1943; *The Moment and Other Essays*, 1947; *The Captain's Death Bed and Other Essays*, 1950; *A Writer's Diary*, 1953; *Virginia Woolf and Lytton Strachey: Letters*, 1957; *Granite and Rainbow*, 1958; *Contemporary Writers*, 1965; *Collected Essays, 4 Volumes*, 1966–67.)

1944 *The International Post-War Settlement.*

1946 John Lehmann withdraws as partner of the Hogarth Press; Woolf allows the press to become a subsidiary of Chatto & Windus, Ltd.

1947 *Foreign Policy: The Labour Party's Dilemma.*

1953 *Principia Politica.*

1957 Travels to Israel.

1959 Resigns as joint editor of *Political Quarterly.*

1960 Travels to Ceylon; *Sowing: An Autobiography of the Years 1880–1904.*

1962 *Growing: An Autobiography of the Years 1904–1911.*

1963 *Diaries in Ceylon.*

1964 *Beginning Again: An Autobiography of the Years 1911–1918.*

1967 *Downhill All the Way: An Autobiography of the Years 1919–1939.*

1969 Death at Monks House, 14 August; posthumous publication of *The Journey Not the Arrival Matters: An Autobiography of the Years 1939–1969.*

Chapter One
Perspectives on a Life

Leonard Woolf is generally known either as the husband of Virginia Woolf[1] or as part of the writers and artists in England known as the Bloomsbury Group. Yet a study of Woolf's life and work reveals that he had a considerable influence on his society as an important writer, one whose literary and political work reflected the history of his times. Early in life, through family and ethnic background, and through intellectual training, Woolf developed a perspective based on rational thought and humanist values. This perspective developed into a moral standard against which he evaluated historical, social, and political events, literary works, personal relationships, and, ultimately, the accomplishments of his life. Moreover, through his study of history and in response to contemporary social experiences, he became sensitive to man's conflicting impulses toward civilization and barbarism in both personal and social life. He believed that through rationalism, man could develop positive moral values and a civilized society. Thus, he felt that the role of the writer and political thinker was to present a rational view of historical and political events, and of social and economic systems, to the general public. As a result, he often took a didactic approach in his writing, directing many of his works to the general public, in an attempt to lead people to a rational understanding of history, politics, and economics.

Woolf's five-volume autobiography presents an overview of the events of his life and of personal relationships set against the events of the times and an account of his literary and political work. Another view of Woolf, however, is available through a study of his works on history, literature, and politics. These works reveal Woolf's commitment to rationalism, and they are characterized by a synthesis of political consciousness, social conscience, and personal morality. Woolf developed an early interest in the relationship of economics, political systems, and social structure to communal psychology, which he defined as individual and communal consciousness. This interest appears most clearly in his political and historical studies on imperialism, war, international government, socialism, and the Co-operative Movement. Woolf's literary work, however—as a writer of fiction, drama, autobiography, and literary criticism, and as an editor and publisher—was also shaped by his political consciousness and social conscience. His fiction, for example, criticizes imperialism in general and British imperialism in Ceylon in particular, as well as anti-Semitism and class discrimination in England. Similarly, political commitment dominated his publishing work. Thus, as cofounder of the Hogarth Press, he sought unusual works in literary and political areas, and he helped to establish such important political journals as *International Review* and *Political Quarterly*. In addition, he wrote review articles, editorials, and literary reviews regularly for over fifty years for the *New Statesman*, the *Nation*, and *Political Quarterly* on many areas of history, literature, and politics. Finally, Woolf's personal life also reveals his lifelong commitment to positive moral values. He was a devoted friend and husband, a man who loved both animals and nature, and who tried to build positive values into interpersonal relationships and relationships with nature.

From Kensington to Cambridge and Ceylon

Leonard Sidney Woolf was born on 25 November 1880, the third of ten children. His father, Sidney Woolf, a barrister, made a comfortable salary and was able to support a large household. Although Leonard Woolf rejected formal religious belief at the early age of fourteen, he developed a strong sense of Jewish tradition. He identified with a universal racial heritage of Semitic ancestors, and adopted both his father's respect for learning and instinctive sense of morality. Woolf claimed that his father lived according to the message of Micah—"do justly and love mercy"—and Woolf accepted this moral standard as his own. Later, Woolf learned practical lessons about economics when his father's sudden death in 1892 left the family in a state of near poverty. This experience shaped Woolf's understanding of the important influence of economic factors on individual and social life.

The sense of being an outsider, first because of religion and class position and then because of his personal inclination toward a strict morality and a desire for learning, dominated Woolf's early years of education in English public schools. When he graduated from St. Paul's School with a sound knowledge of the classics, he was awarded a scholarship to Trinity College, Cambridge, which he entered in 1899. Cambridge represented his first satisfying intellectual experience. There he also developed friendships with Saxon Sydney-Turner, Lytton Strachey, Thoby Stephen, and Clive Bell, and with these young men he joined the Apostles in 1902. This secret society was devoted to intellectual discussion of literary and philosophical topics. At this time, the most important influence on the Apostles was G. E. Moore, a fellow of Trinity College. Moore's philosophy emphasized moral judgment in terms of defining the nature of "the good." Although Moore stressed personal relationships and aesthetic pleasure as "good," Woolf extended this philosophy to include an understanding of the moral consequences of one's actions. For Woolf, man is a social being and therefore also a political being; thus, social and political action had to be included in a philosophy of life. This synthesis of intellectual and aesthetic theory with political practice was the beginning of a commitment to practical politics which Woolf maintained throughout his life.

At the end of five years at Cambridge, Woolf joined the Ceylon Civil Service. He was assigned to Jaffna (1905–1907), Kandy (1907–1908), and Hambantota (1908–1911). During these years, he learned Tamil and Sinhalese and gained valuable judicial, business, and administrative experience. Although he became increasingly critical of imperialism and imperialists, he fulfilled his responsibilities faithfully and efficiently and was promoted regularly to positions of increasing responsibility. An extraordinary, detailed account of his duties as Assistant Government Agent in Hambantota exists in *Diaries in Ceylon,* the official government records he kept. These diaries reveal that Woolf was constantly involved in essential aspects of village life: health and sanitation of the villagers and livestock, methods of salt collection, agriculture and irrigation, and education.

In Ceylon, Woolf's experiences with other British civil servants and with the Ceylonese revealed to him the influence of cultural and economic factors on individual and social life. He particularly observed the rigid class hierarchy of the British and their isolation from the natives. Slowly the life of the Ceylonese became fascinating to him, and he later expressed his understanding of Ceylonese culture and village life in his first novel, *The Village in the Jungle.* This work, written in 1912 after Woolf returned to England, is considered a classic in Ceylon. In the novel, Woolf reveals the relationship of the villagers to nature, particularly the jungle. At the same time, he analyzes village life, focusing on the destructive effects of superstition, class and racial prejudice, and an economic system of debt. This work of fiction is complemented by three short stories on the East, which reflect the antiimperialist attitudes Woolf developed during his years in Ceylon. "A Tale Told by Moonlight" explores the theme of romantic love, portraying how it is destroyed by caste and racial differences. A similar political theme is developed in "Pearls and Swine," which uses imperialism to examine moral values and to comment on the power of human greed and the remorse of conscience, and the final tale, "The Two Brahmans," like *The Village in the Jungle,* portrays how the caste system creates social antagonisms and a rigid system of social conventions which can destroy individual fulfillment.

After seven years in the Civil Service, Woolf returned to England on a year's leave. The work in Ceylon had been challenging and rewarding at times, but also frustrating and depressing. In his letters to Lytton Strachey, Woolf commented on his emotional and psychological states, how he would struggle to overcome the difficulties of, and sense of futility about, his position. These letters also reveal that Woolf often thought about his Cambridge friends and was especially interested in their love affairs, particularly if they involved Thoby Stephen's two sisters, Vanessa and Virginia, whom Woolf first met in 1900 and found to be very beautiful and talented young women.[2] When Woolf returned to England, he slipped back into his Cambridge circle of friends, which had extended to include Vanessa and Virginia Stephen. As months passed, Woolf found himself falling in love with Virginia. He decided not to return to the civil service but to attempt to make his living as a writer. Virginia refused Woolf's first proposal of marriage, but later agreed, and they were married on 10 August 1912.

Politics and Literature: A Life's Work

In the years following his marriage, Woolf's political and literary interests broadened. He became involved with the Co-operative Movement, the Fabian Society, and the Labour party. At the same time, he began his career in journalism, and then, in 1917, along with Virginia, he founded the Hogarth Press. These interests were to shape his work for the rest of his life.

After completing *The Village in the Jungle* in 1912, Woolf attempted a second novel. This time, however, his focus was on English society. *The Wise Virgins* was published in 1914, but it did not sell well and went out of print.[3] It has only recently been republished, perhaps because of interest in its portrayal of Woolf's life after he returned to England from Ceylon. In this novel, Woolf criticizes racial and class prejudice, revealing how such prejudice creates alienation and unhappiness. Class barriers and antagonisms exist between the characters in the novel representing a wealthy family, the Lawrences, which is modeled after Virginia Woolf's family, and a lower-middle-class Jewish family, the Davises, which parallels Leonard Woolf's family. Woolf emphasizes the importance of individual fulfillment, spiritual love, and physical passion, which are threatened by alienation and prejudice. A similar theme is developed in Woolf's remaining work of fiction, a short story entitled "Three Jews," which was included in *Two Stories*, the first publication of the Hogarth Press in 1917. This story uses Jewish characters and a cemetery setting to comment on the deathly nature of a class system which fosters intensive class, racial, and religious intolerance.

Woolf's Ceylon experiences had given him valuable insights into administrative and judicial work. They had also brought him from a state of political naiveté and irresponsibility to a commitment to personal political responsibility, and they had completed his conversion from imperialist to anti-imperialist. In London, he soon became interested in analysis of the class system and capitalism through practical political work in the East End. As he became more critical of capitalism because of the poverty and personal destruction it caused, socialism seemed to represent a positive alternative. His interest soon focused on the Co-operative Movement, a working-class system of manufacturing, retail trade, and banking, and his work for the Co-operative Movement culminated in two studies, *Co-operation and the Future of Industry* (1919) and *Socialism and Co-operation* (1921). These works examine the economics and communal psychologies of capitalism and socialism, evaluating to what degree each system fosters civilized values. Woolf's basic premise is that the social and economic system of a society affects social psychology. A class system, for example, fosters alienation of individuals by class and allows a minority to exploit the majority. In contrast, socialism, which breaks down class hierarchies, fosters respect for equality and individualism, which constitute the basis of civilization. *Co-operation and the Future of Industry* traces the development of the Co-operative Movement and describes its goals and functioning. The Co-operative Movement represents a democratic economic system which provides communal control of property and money and establishes the organization of production on the basis of consumption, not profit. Woolf explored the role the Co-operative Movement might have in a Socialist society in *Socialism and Co-operation,* and his studies led him to conclude that socialism was the means to a prosperous and civilized society.

In 1913, Woolf's work with the Co-operative Movement brought him to the attention of Beatrice and Sidney Webb, leaders of the Fabian Society who had an important influence on Woolf's political and literary work. Under sponsorship of the Fabian Society, Woolf began his study of international government and war. In 1916, he completed *International Government,* which discussed the different types of international disputes and the failure of treaties and international conferences to resolve them. Woolf argues that national interests have become international; thus, there must be an international organization to regulate international relations in order to prevent war. This work established Woolf's reputation as an authority on war and international government, and was so well respected that it influenced the British proposals for the League of Nations and the Versailles Conference. During this time, while Woolf was working on *International Government*, the Webbs helped launch Woolf's career in journalism. They had created the journal the *New Statesman* for the Fabian Society, and they persuaded Woolf to write for this publication. Finally, the Webbs brought Woolf into political work with the Labour party. When Sidney Webb became a member of the Labour Party Executive, he appointed Woolf secretary of two advisory committees on international and colonial affairs. Later, Woolf's political involvement with the Labour party developed further when he stood for Parliament in 1922 as a candidate of the Seven Universities Democratic Association, which was affiliated with the Labour party. His platform was based on international government and an end to imperialism, as well as on equality of education, equity of taxation, and a cooperative system for industry.

Thus the early years of Woolf's marriage were creative in terms of political and literary work. These years, however, also were troubled by Virginia's illnesses, particularly a nervous breakdown lasting many months of 1914 and 1915. During this time, Woolf had to provide constant attention and care for her. It was a difficult period, yet both Virginia and Leonard managed to survive the months of illness and strain and return to creative work. In 1917, a new stage in Leonard Woolf's career, and in Virginia's, began when the Woolfs purchased a printing press and decided to adopt printing as a hobby. The first publication of the Hogarth Press, as they named their new venture, was *Two Stories*, an edition of Virginia's "The Mark on the Wall" and Leonard's "Three Jews." Publishing their own work was a rewarding experience, yet the Woolfs also intended to use the press for publishing literature by new writers which would not be acceptable to commercial presses. Soon they became the publishers of such important writers of literature as Katherine Mansfield, T. S. Eliot, and E. M. Forster, and such important social writers as John Maynard Keynes and Freud.

Between 1917 and 1920, Woolf became engrossed in political work which centered primarily around the Labour party. Post–World War I society was moving steadily closer to war. Woolf's work toward the prevention of war and the development of international government and his study of imperialism dominated his efforts in the Labour party advisory committees on international and colonial affairs, and he produced several full-length studies. After *International Government* in 1916, Woolf's thoughts on war and international government were developed in *The Framework of a Lasting Peace* and *The Future of Constantinople,* both written in 1917. *The Framework of a Lasting Peace* analyzes various peace proposals and emphasizes the need for an organization of international authority. In *The Future of Constantinople,* Woolf argues about the need for an international policy to resolve the tensions resulting from the strategic geographic position of Constantinople. He proposes that an international administrative body, similar to the European Commission of the Danube, should control Constantinople and thus assure that the area would not be in the hands of a single power and continue to be a source of political unrest and war. Somewhat later, Woolf focused on the problems of imperialism in Africa and Asia, and he developed several studies on this area. *Empire and Commerce in Africa* (1920) examines the role of European expansion in Africa from the 1870s to the present, as Woolf also analyzes how the dominant ideologies of imperialist expansion are false. Arguing that European economic imperialism has had a destructive effect on the Africans, he suggests how through a mandate system Europeans can develop a constructive policy in Africa. Similarly, *Economic Imperialism,* written in 1920, emphasizes the false assumptions imperialism is based on and contrasts the patterns of imperialist control in Africa and Asia.

Woolf again urges the institution of a mandate system as an alternative to economic imperialism. Later, in his final study on imperialism, *Imperialism and Civilization* (1928), Woolf reasserts his negative views of imperialism as he analyzes imperialist domination in Asia and Africa and again examines the role that the League of Nations could have in solving the problems of imperialism by instituting a mandate system.

In the 1920s, other new stages in Woolf's work were beginning. Although he had reservations about the quality of journalists and journalism work, he was writing for the *Nation* under the editorship of H. W. Massingham. In 1923, he accepted the position of literary editor, which he held for three years. Through his work for the *Nation,* Woolf came into contact with key literary and political figures of the time. Before this, Woolf's journalism work was mostly documentary journalism, or reporting on contemporary social and political issues and events. He had contributed to the *Co-operative News,* the *New Statesman, International Review* (of which he was editor from 1918 to 1919), and *Contemporary Review* (of which he was editor for foreign affairs in 1922). Later, he continued this type of journalism work in major articles for *Political Quarterly*; he had helped to found this journal in 1930, and held the position of joint editor with W. A. Robson from 1930 to 1959. His remaining journalism work consisted of literary reviewing, first as literary editor of the *Nation* and then as writer and reviewer for both the *New Statesman and Nation* and *Political Quarterly.* Although many of Woolf's literary reviews focus on the arts—literature, music, and painting—the majority cover such social and political issues as war, international government, politics, statesmen, fascism, and nazism. Yet whether he was discussing the arts or history and politics, his prose style is clear and his high standards of value for both individual and social life are evident. These characteristics, typical of all Woolf's works, become the most distinctive and impressive features of more than fifty years of journalism work.

During the years Woolf was literary editor of the *Nation,* he did not publish many works of his own, only two literary essays, *Fear and Politics* (1925) and *Hunting the Highbrow* (1927), and a collection of literary essays from his journalism work, *Essays on Literature, History, Politics, Etc.* (1927). *Fear and Politics* reveals Woolf's mastery of the art of satire. In this short essay, Woolf draws on literary conventions of the fable and debate to present a commentary about human nature. *Hunting the Highbrow* is also an excellent example of Woolf's sense of humor and satire, yet his subject is serious as he examines the alienation of intellectual and artistic highbrows from the rest of society. Woolf argues that the role of the artist and intellectual in society is to set standards by challenging conventions and working against prejudice, passion, and unreason. In contrast to these two satirical works, *Essays in Literature, History, Politics, Etc.* reveals Woolf's views of writers, diplomats, aristocrats, politicians past and present, foreign policy and international morality, old age, death, and nature. Like Woolf's many book reviews and editorials for journals, these essays indicate his standards for literary criticism and political morality, at the same time that they reveal his wide range of knowledge, his understanding of human nature, and his respect for nature.

World War I had been a shattering experience for people like Woolf who worked for social progress and the values of civilization. Woolf's post–World War I studies on war had focused on the need for an international organization to prevent war. Yet he realized that even if an external force could prevent war, it could not eliminate the inclination toward war which seemed inherent in the communal psychology of nations throughout history. Woolf became fascinated with man's conflicting impulses toward the communal psychologies of civilization and barbarism, and the relationship of social, political, and economic institutions to these psychologies. He devoted many years, particularly those between the wars, to the study of this aspect of history and human nature, and several key works resulted. *After the Deluge, Volume I* (1931) and *Volume II* (1939) were the first two parts of Woolf's study of the psychology of man as a social being. Woolf explores the development of political ideas which have motivated men to wage war throughout history, and he examines these ideas in relation to social and economic structures. This study was not completed until 1953, when *Principia Politica* was published. This was Woolf's final full-length political work, and his focus was on the modern totalitarian state and its political ideologies, in contrast to the democratic state and its ideologies. Continuing his examination of communal psychology beyond *After the Deluge,* Woolf focused more specifically on nazism and fascism in his study *Quack, Quack!* (1936), which Virginia described as likely to "get him into hot water with all classes, as it is a very spirited attack upon human nature as it is at present."[4] In *Quack, Quack!*, Woolf analyzes the role of magic in primitive cultures and how civilizations have consistently abandoned reason for belief in the supernatural and absolute truths. To Woolf, the growth of fascism represents a similar rejection of reason and an acceptance of primitive passions, and he parallels this barbarism to twentieth-century man's acceptance of unreason in religion and philosophy. Woolf pursued this analysis further in *Barbarians Within and Without* (1939), surveying the development of the conflict between civilization and barbarism throughout history, and pointing out how a class system destroys the possibility of establishing a civilized society. He also discusses the social, political, and economic factors of twentieth-century Europe which led to war, particularly to the Nazi rise to power. This analysis of World War II Europe continues in his only work of drama, *The Hotel* (1938). Woolf draws on Christian and Hebraic traditions to represent contemporary social and political ideologies, but he also dramatizes the continuing historical conflict between civilization and barbarism. Although Woolf portrays twentieth-century man's acceptance of barbarism in this play, he nevertheless implies that man can struggle against individual moral decadence and social tyranny to assert the values of civilization.

During the war period, Woolf again addressed the problems of international government. *The League and Abyssinia* (1936) points out how Mussolini's attempt to take over Ethiopia in 1935 was a test case for the League of Nations. Woolf counters criticisms of the League, asserting that it represents the world's best choice for a system of international relations based on peace.

Later, in *The War for Peace,* written in 1940, Woolf argues further that peace is not a utopian notion, and that war is not inevitable. Moreover, Woolf surveys the psychological roots of war and the development of war throughout history. He argues that reason, rather than emotion, and a system of consent and cooperation must be the basis of the relations between nations. A few years later, Woolf published several pamphlets on the role of the Labour party. *The International Post-War Settlement* (1944) and *Foreign Policy: The Labour Party's Dilemma* (1947) both argue that Britain will profit from peace, which can be achieved only through international trade, cooperation, and international government. At this point, Woolf believed that Britain was a second-class power which could not participate in an atomic war and therefore should end its attempts to be a world power through imperial policies and atomic-weapons research.

Personal life during the 1930s was marked by loss and destruction. First, there were a number of deaths of friends and family— Lytton Strachey, Dora Carrington, Francis Birrell, Leonard's mother, and Julian Bell. In addition, destruction of the Rodmell countryside at this time deeply upset the Woolfs. They watched the area around Monks House, which had afforded them beautiful views and a peaceful refuge from city life, being destroyed by real-estate and commercial development. Finally, there were constant threats of a Nazi invasion of Britain, and the Woolfs considered suicide as an alternative to being taken prisoners by the Nazis.[5] At this time, it was not unusual for them to hear planes bombing London and the Sussex countryside. During one of the London bombings, the house in Mecklenburgh Square which housed the Hogarth Press was destroyed. The Woolfs returned to salvage the materials that survived, and they moved the equipment of the press to Letchworth and many of the books to Monks House.

Despite the personal losses and international tensions of the 1930s, the Woolfs continued their literary and political work, trying to create in spite of the chaos of war and its threat to civilized values. At the end of 1940, Virginia seemed on the verge of another nervous breakdown. This time Leonard was unable to help her. She committed suicide by drowning on 28 March 1941. Months after this devastating loss, Woolf returned to his work as joint editor of *Political Quarterly* and as director of the Hogarth Press. The press had survived the war years well; however, John Lehmann, who had bought out Virginia's share in the press in 1938, had become increasingly unhappy about Leonard's editorial and business policies and decided to withdraw as partner in 1946. Woolf then let the press become a subsidiary of Chatto and Windus, Ltd., but he continued to direct the press's editorial decisions. At this time, Woolf also continued his position as secretary of the Labour party advisory committees, and, drawing on the judicial experience he acquired in Ceylon, he participated as a member of the Civil Service Arbitration Tribunal.

The last two decades of Woolf's life were devoted to those activities he enjoyed most: travel, gardening, and writing. He took two important trips—to Israel in 1957 and Ceylon in 1960. At home, he carefully tended the Monks House garden and was president of the Rodmell Horticultural Society. Yet writing appears to have been his most constant activity. In the last years of his life, he continued to write review articles for *Political Quarterly* and the *New Statesman and Nation*, and he undertook and completed his five-volume autobiography. This final work provides a perceptive overview and assessment of personal, social, and historical events of the period 1880 to 1969, as well as important insights into Virginia Woolf's life and works, and unusual portraits of the major literary and political figures Woolf knew. The last volume of the autobiography was completed before his death on 14 August 1969.

A Personal Portrait

Although a partial picture of Leonard Woolf can be constructed from the events of his life and a study of his work, one also needs to understand Woolf's personality and psychology. This can be approached by correlating his life and self-portraits with comments by those closest to him: Virginia and his friends. Considering Leonard's strong moral sense and his dedication to learning and knowledge, it is not difficult to picture him as he frequently describes himself in his autobiography, as a serious young man, an introspective intellectual. Virginia emphasizes this aspect of Leonard when describing her first impressions of him while he was still a Cambridge undergraduate:

He was as eccentric, as remarkable in his way as Bell and Strachey in theirs. He was a Jew. When I asked why he trembled, Thoby somehow made me feel it was a part of his nature—he was violent, so savage; he so despised the whole human race....Most people, I gathered, rather rubbed along, and came to terms with things. Woolf did not.... I was of course inspired with the deepest interest in that violent trembling misanthropic Jew who had already shaken his fist at civilisation and was about to disappear into the tropics.[6]

Virginia's description also identifies two other characteristics which set Leonard apart from others—his Jewishness and his intolerance of human folly. Woolf's ethnic background alienated him from upper-middle-class English society, of which he had never been a part because of economic position.[7] This sense of being an outsider may well have fostered some of his personality traits. Leon Edel comments: "Leonard's ambition and tenacity, his law-enforcing character, his ability to treat emotions as an army treats its recruits—all this was the measure of an anxious man who clings to cleared land beside a jungle."[8] Indeed, this sense of anxiety might also have accounted for Woolf's unusually careful, perhaps unnecessarily careful, keeping of accounts, whether of his work in Ceylon, Virginia's illnesses, their expenses, or the expenses of the Hogarth Press; perhaps he wanted to be sure of facts and thus able to defend himself with objective proof against possible errors of memory or action.

Leonard's Jewishness and lower economic background were important factors to those closest to him, including Virginia. When announcing her engagement to Leonard, Virginia described him to her friends Violet Dickinson and Janet Case as a "penniless Jew."[9] Frequently throughout their marriage, she referred to Leonard's Jewishness and ridiculed stereotypical Jewish physical traits and behavior, particularly in Leonard's family. Although her social class fostered and accepted verbal attacks on Jewishness, her love for Leonard somewhat altered this attitude. In 1930, for example, she wrote: "How I hated marrying a Jew—how I hated their nasal voices, and their oriental jewelry, and their noses, and their wattles—what a snob I was: for they have immense vitality, and I think I like that quality best of all."[10] Here Virginia's focus on vitality indicates her recognition of Leonard's commitment of time and energy to the literary and political work he believed was important.

As for Leonard's intolerance of human folly, he himself states that he was difficult to work for because he was very demanding and had a high standard of values. For example, he failed to understand irrationality, particularly in intelligent people. Thus, he was shocked at Beatrice Webb and T. S. Eliot's religious beliefs. George Spater and Ian Parsons comment on Leonard's intolerance in general: "Leonard was not content to hold to his own disbelief and to allow others to believe; he had a missionary's zeal to destroy the belief of others and to convert them to the Truth: that is, to his way of thinking."[11] Similarly, Woolf could be critical of people's views in print. In his literary reviews, he never refrained from expressing scorn for ideas he felt were irrational or illogical, or for use of language or literary style which he considered poor. Again, as Spater and Parsons suggest, Leonard's intolerance may have been a defensive reaction due to his sense of a hostile world to which he never belonged, because he was an outsider in caste and class.[12]

Yet what Virginia, as well as other friends, respected were Leonard's intelligence and his broad range of interests. After many years of marriage, Virginia described Leonard as "a most cultivated man."[13] She consistently commented in her diary and letters about his intelligence and often compared her intellectual and literary abilities to his, stating that she is "outdistanced" by him, or that Leonard could be "more impressive with much less pains."[14] Often, she wrote that he was much more knowledgeable about politics and economics than she was.[15] But despite this recognition of differences, Virginia could identify with Leonard's attitude toward his work. When, for instance, Leonard was depressed about his work, Virginia could sympathize: In 1915, she wrote:

L's melancholy continues, so much so that he declared this morning he couldn't work. . . . When I analyse his mood, I attribute much of it to a sheer lack of self confidence in his power of writing; as if he mightn't be a writer after all; & being a practical man, his melancholy sinks far deeper than the half assumed melancholy of self conscious people like Lytton & Sir Leslie & myself.[16]

In contrast to her sympathy with Leonard's doubts, Virginia also expressed excitement and pleasure about his successes. In her diary of 1921, she wrote: "To add to Leonard's trophies, the Webbs have asked him to edit a book; the League of Nations Union offer to reprint Inl. Government; & The Village in the Jungle is sold among other rare first editions at 6/-. All very good." Later in 1922 she records: "America wishes him to write a monthly article—New York Times that is; which increases our income & proves him at the tree top. People write little articles about him, saying he is selfless in his work for the public, & the most brilliant of our writers, & leader of the younger school."[17] In addition, Leonard's success with journalism brought in enough money to allow Virginia to give up, gratefully, her journalism writing, which she had grown to dislike. She commented: "To have broken free at the age of 38 seems a great piece of good fortune—coming in the nick of time & due of course to L. without whose journalism I couldn't quit mine. But I quiet my conscience with the belief that a foreign article once a week is of greater work, less labour & better paid than my work."[18]

Although Virginia wrote enthusiastically about all of Leonard's writing she was a little less enthusiastic about his position as literary editor of the *Nation*, commenting that it took up time that could be spent on more important work. Like Leonard, she had reservations about the literary merit of journalistic writing. Nevertheless, she recognized Leonard's editorial talents and wrote that even though she didn't "want to see Leonard engulfed in wretched little chatter about new novels...he is a masterly man: in two days he does what a thoroughly good editor spreads over a week."[19] Virginia also expressed doubts about some of Leonard's political work. At the same time that she frequently attended Labour party meetings with Leonard and even toured factories in Manchester with him, she distrusted and disliked politicians and feared that Leonard would become one. In her diary, she wrote: "Mrs. Webb told me it was wrong to prevent L. from going into Parliament; we want men of subtle intellect &—But what is 'right' & who are 'we.'...One deals with the situation more easily, but the horror of it increases with familiarity. Shall we become like that too?"[20] Leonard never became the conventional politician Virginia disliked. Indeed, he never held office, but he did continue to contribute to practical politics through his writing and his Labour party advisory committee work.

Despite differences of personality, talent, and interests, there are striking similarities in the works of Leonard and Virginia Woolf, which suggest that they influenced each other. They were concerned with social and political factors in their fiction and nonfiction, as they both explored the close relationship between social experience and individual consciousness. Virginia, however, developed this relationship in terms of the artist's vision and his art form, while Leonard focused on individual and social behavior in relationship to political thought and economic systems. In their earliest novels—Virginia's *The Voyage Out* and *Night and Day,* and Leonard's *The Wise Virgins*—they present their views of love, both spiritual and physical, marriage, and individual fulfillment as they portray twentieth-century English society. They both emphasize the important effects of class conventions on psychology and behavior. These works also incorporate autobiographical elements of the Virginia-Leonard relationship and aspects of the Bloomsbury circle. Around this time, in their respective journalism work, they were writing about the same authors, and, with their founding of the Hogarth Press, there must have been continued exchanges of opinion about new manuscripts, new authors, finances, and the literary and political philosophy of the press.

Other areas of common political concern for both Leonard and Virginia were the Co-operative Movement and women's rights. They became involved in the Working Women's Guild of the Co-operative Movement through Margaret Llewelyn Davies. Leonard was particularly impressed by the Women's Guild and believed that the emancipation of women might prove to be one of the greatest social revolutions in history. Virginia, who also was impressed with the Women's Guild, conducted monthly meetings of a branch of the guild and wrote an introductory essay, "Memories of a Working Women's Guild," to a collection of essays by the Guildswomen entitled *Life as We Have Known It.* Although of a class different from that of the workers and their wives, the Woolfs recognized the importance of the workers' protests against the inequalities of the class system.

In the 1920s and 1930s, Leonard and Virginia were analyzing the connection between the structure and ideology of the class system and fascism and war. Leonard viewed man's acceptance of tyranny and authoritarian social rule as a reversion to barbarism. Political beliefs were for Leonard an indication of social and personal life, and he protested the rejection of reason and the turn toward religion and intuition in philosophy, science, and art in *Quack, Quack!* and *Barbarians Within and Without.* Like Leonard, Virginia claimed that the political world was an indication of the private world. Both *A Room of One's Own* and *Three Guineas* explore this point. *Three Guineas* can be seen as a companion piece to Leonard's *Quack, Quack!,* as both analyze the communal psychology of barbarism and link it to fascism and war. Virginia had first identified the psychology of male domination that a class system creates in *A Room of One's Own.* In *Three Guineas,* she associates male domination with nationalism and militarism and, hence, with war. Moreover, in a short essay, "Thoughts on Peace During an Air Raid," written in 1940, she argues further that the patriarchal system creates a subconscious desire to dominate and enslave. Clearly, Leonard and Virginia believed that individual freedom is related to social structure and social institutions, and they argued that if those institutions deny freedom and fulfillment to individuals, they should be changed. Thus, their works examine and support the values and modes of life which lead to peace and civilization. This common outlook generated a literary and political compatibility that, no doubt, created a substantial bond in their marriage.

The traditional view of the Leonard-Virginia marriage relationship casts Leonard in the role of devoted husband: he catered to Virginia's emotional needs and preserved her sanity by providing a balance of rationality and discipline to her temperament and life-style, especially when she seemed close to another nervous depression; and he respected her intellect and artistic genius and did everything possible to encourage her literary work, as well as publication of her work, both while she was alive and after her death. This view emerges in Leonard's autobiography, Quentin Bell's biography of Virginia Woolf, and Spater and Parsons's biography of Leonard and Virginia.[21] Leonard's letters to Virginia before their marriage reveal his love for her. In Ceylon, Woolf had come to realize that relationships with women were dissatisfying and humiliating if they did not involve love. His affection for Virginia, serious and strong, seems to have been based on great respect for her. After his proposal of marriage, he wrote:

I am selfish, jealous, cruel, lustful, a liar & probably worse still. I had said over & over again to myself that I would never marry anyone because of this, mostly because, I think, I felt I could never control these things with a woman who was inferior and would gradually enfuriate me by her inferiority & submission.... It is because you aren't that the risk is so infinitely less. You may be vain an egoist untruthful as you say, but they are nothing compared to your other qualities magnificence intelligence wit beauty directness. After all too we like one another, we like the same kinds of things & people, we are both intelligent & above all it is realities which we understand & which are important to us.[22]

Some months later, he wrote:

God, the happiness I've had by being with you & talking to you as I've sometimes felt it mind to mind together & soul to soul. I know clearly enough what I feel for you. It is not only physical love though it is that of course & I count it the least part of it, it isn't only that I'm only happy with you...: It's that I want your love too. It's true that I'm cold & reserved to other people; I dont feel affection even easily: but apart from love I'm fond of you as I've never been of anyone or thing in the world.[23]

His feeling was reciprocated, as Virginia's letters to Leonard on the occasions when they were separated reveal. In these letters she wrote: "I think of you and want you. . . . I get happiness from seeing you."[24] She also wrote that without him, life seemed "all rather pointless and secondrate,"[25] and that he had given her the best things in her life.[26] Moreover, the compatibility of their marriage seems to have been noticed by others. In 1917, Virginia wrote to Leonard that their friend Saxon Sydney-Turner had commented that "our marriage seemed the best of any he knew, and how coming to see us one night, he had understood for the first time the advantages of being married, which I thought a pretty compliment."[27] Finally, when Virginia committed suicide in 1941, she wrote to Leonard: "You have given me the greatest possible happiness. . . . I don't think two people could have been happier. . . . I owe all the happiness of my life to you. You have been entirely patient with me and incredibly good."[28] Thus, Virginia's expressions of affection for, and happiness with, Leonard are indications of the fulfillment provided by many aspects of their marriage, particularly their similar intellectual, literary, and political interests, and the friends and the love of travel and of nature that they shared.

Nevertheless, the Woolfs faced many periods of stress during their married life. Virginia's conflicting feelings about her illnesses reveal more about the Woolfs' marriage relationship. At times, Virginia deeply appreciated Leonard's constant care when she was ill, and she wrote, "I should have shot myself long ago in one of these illnesses if it hadn't been for him";[29] however, she also chafed at the restrictions Leonard placed on her when she began to show signs of illness. Even a headache, she wrote, "makes Leonard gloomy and tightens my ropes—I mustn't walk or do anything but sit and drink milk."[30] After another period of illness she wrote: "I'm really better, only mustn't, as Leonard says, think of writing so for another 10 days: when I say now I'll begin to think of a book, he puts a shade over me just as I used to shut up my canary."[31] Virginia most resented being isolated and often turned her anger against Leonard, who had instituted the regime of isolation. During one spell of illness, she wrote to Ethel Smyth: "That Friday when I was alone in bed, I could hardly keep myself from cursing Leonard for being so positive, against you, or any visitor."[32] Her anger also came out in harsh comments about her marriage when she associated it with the onset of her illnesses: "Marriage—yes?—What about marriage? I married Leonard Woolf in 1912, I think, and almost immediately was ill for 3 years."[33] Thus, the periods of illness generated tension and ambivalent feelings about the marriage relationship, just as aspects of the marriage relationship may have generated, in part, the illnesses.

Periods of illness and tension, however, did not limit the full life the Woolfs led, which included close relationships with friends and family, fairly frequent travel, and an unusually large amount of literary and political work. Again, insights into the dedication and energy Leonard gave to his work are provided by Virginia. For example, she comments to a friend that "Leonard is as usual writing away at about 6 books, and he has now trained himself to compose straight on to a typewriter without a mistake in sense or spelling."[34] She also indicated the diversity of Leonard's interests and talents in his literary and political work in a letter to Violet Dickinson: "Leonard is in the middle of a new novel; but as the clock strikes twelve, he begins an article upon Labour for some pale sheet, or a review of French literature for the Times, or a history of Co-operation."[35] Furthermore, Virginia recognized Leonard's abilities in the practical activities of their daily life: "nursing his wife, advising his maids, digging his garden, and printing books. (Here he is with an apple tree in his hand)."[36] Caring for Virginia when she was ill, managing the responsibilities of at least two households, and maintaining the extensive Monks House Garden—these areas alone could have absorbed all Woolf's time and attention and given him a sense of purpose and accomplishment. Yet because he was unable to ignore social and political events, he continued to balance personal responsibilities with his commitment to bettering society through literary and political work.

A Fable of Personal and Political Vision

One of Leonard Woolf's books, *Fear and Politics,* provides insights into his thought and work. This essay reveals Woolf's understanding of human nature and social and political institutions, as well as his dedication to rationalism and socialism. As his autobiography reveals, Woolf, in addition to being a perceptive observer of people and their psychology, was interested in animals and their behavior.[37] An animal lover, he had several dogs and a pet marmoset, Mitz, which he describes in his autobiography.[38] These animals were often important, even helpful, companions. In Ceylon, for example, his dog Charles was able to bring him fame and respect in Jaffna, when, by killing a cat and a large snake within ten minutes, Charles raised the reputation of his master.[39] Similarly, many years later, while on a trip through Nazi Germany in 1935, his marmoset Mitz attracted everyone's attention and affection, and this allowed Leonard and Virginia to travel pleasantly through a country of militant anti-Semitism.[40]

Woolf's respect for animals was extensive. Striking descriptions of animal life in the jungle which appear in his Ceylon novel *The Village in the Jungle,* in his essay "The Gentleness of Nature,"[41] and in his autobiography[42] reveal his reverence and awe. He believed that one could learn a lot about a country and its people from watching animals, and he found himself drawn to the zoo as he traveled to different cities.[43] The Ceylon Zoo, for example, was full of tropical vegetation, which provided a natural environment for the animals. In contrast, in Israel, the animals in the zoo appeared to Woolf to be a reflection of the city's melancholy mood. Dismayed by the Orthodox Jews in Jerusalem, Woolf commented: "The long-haired monkeys gazed at one, it seemed to me, with the self-satisfaction of all the orthodox who have learned eternal truth from the primeval monkey, all the scribes and pharisees who spend their lives making mountains of pernicious stupidity out of molehills of nonsense."[44]

Woolf also often saw animal life in relationship to human life. In his autobiography, he wrote:

When in Ceylon I for the first time saw in the jungle what nature was really like in the crude relation of beast to beast, I was shocked and at first even disgusted at the cold savagery, the pitiless cruelty. But when I contemplate the jungle of human relations, I feel that there are savageries and hatreds—illuminated by Zeus, Jupiter, Jehovah, Christ, or Dr. Freud—which make the tiger and the viper seem gentle, charitable, tenderhearted.[45]

Woolf draws on this analogy in an unusual satirical essay, *Fear and Politics: A Debate at the Zoo,* written in 1925, as this beast fable examines the ideologies of twentieth-century man, the political animal Woolf studied throughout his life.

Though the narrative voice of *Fear and Politics,* Woolf comments with heavy sarcasm on the way conventions of thought and behavior are established by the upper classes. In a society where "civilization consists in acting and thinking like the ordinary man ... or woman of the upper middle classes,"[46] the constraints on anyone who wishes to think or live differently can destroy all natural impulses. This is also true of animals in the zoo, where solitary confinement and imprisonment destroy the vitality of the animals, causing them to adopt an attitude of "sombre melancholy and dingy respectability" (6) like the upper middle classes of England. By drawing this comparison, Woolf sets the context for his fable in which animals represent the thoughts and behavior of men.

The animals in Woolf's fable have become so "civilized" that they form a debating society. Woolf seems to be satirizing both the Apostle Society, to which he belonged as a Cambridge undergraduate, and the League of Nations, which he worked so hard and long to establish because he believed that international government could be a means of preventing war. Like the Apostle Society and the League—indeed, like any society run by the elite classes—this debating society of animals excludes certain groups or classes. Members are:

> Only those ... whose spirits are completely tamed by confinement and civilization: experience has shown the necessity of excluding, for instance, those animals, natives of Asia and Africa, who are not yet able to stand by themselves under the strenuous conditions of the modern world and whose personal habits are offensive, and also the lower classes of even European animals whose smell is naturally unpleasant. (6)

Outsiders are thus the poor, the powerless, the "uncivilized," and those of ethnic background. The topic of debate is man. Woolf presents the development of different beliefs about man's relation to his universe. The animals first believed that men, the keepers of the zoo, were like gods, because they had the power to give or withhold food and drink and reward and punishment, and to create day and night. Then a new belief developed which claimed that there was one central, omnipotent Man, addressed as "Secretary to the Zoological Society," who is the God. This belief, however, was challenged by one of the snakes, known as "Russell's Vipers" or "Bertie" (an obvious reference to Bertrand Russell and to the rational agnostic or atheistic view of the universe which Woolf accepted), who argued logically that there was no such godlike Man, only men. Finally, there was the theory of the orang-outang, "a cynical and savage pessimist" (7), which argued that men and animals are the same.

As the fable progresses, the animals begin to debate the state of international affairs, focusing on the war, with its "struggle between right and wrong, between the ideals of militarist tyranny and democratic freedom" (9). Soon, however, discussion turns to the Bolsheviks, or the "new species of animal in the world" (10). Speaking for the Conservatives is the Rhinoceros, who is shortsighted, hard of hearing, and "rarely conscious... of what was going on about him" (10); he believes that "everything new is terrifying and spells disaster" (10), and he argues that the rest of the animals should refuse to recognize the Bolsheviks. The genteel Ostrich, who follows the hereditary tradition of his race by burying his head in the sand to cope with change or fear, supports this view.

The conservative view of the Rhinoceros holds the floor. He argues that as a species, man "is suffering from a kind of malignant disease of mutability" which began in 1789 with "the French revolutionaries, terrorists, or democrats" (11). In addition, when confronted with something new or fearful, men act irrationally, either talking at once, or quarreling, or philosophizing, or doing all of those together. Satire accumulates through the Rhinoceros's use of language: the French Revolution is "abominable"; the revolutionaries and democrats "infect" other nations; the Germans are a new "malignant" species (11). According to the Rhinoceros, the Germans have terrified other men for almost fifty years until men began "shooting Germans happily and contentedly" (this appears to be Woolf's satirical description of World War I). Nevertheless, this did not successfully solve "the German menace." Moreover, "another new species of human animal, the most terrible and horrible the world has ever known" (13)—the Bolsheviks—has emerged. The Rhinoceros, who earlier announced that he agreed with "the King... the ever-to-be lamented Tsars, and all the other Conservative species of human animal" (10), believes that the human animals should "shoot the Bolsheviks and all the workers and strikers here who support and copy them" (13). He also scorns the illogical actions of human animals: "The upper classes here are only too ready to shoot the lower classes in Russia who have already shot their own upper classes, while the lower classes here have not yet been sufficiently frightened of the lower classes in Russia to agree to go and shoot them there" (14).

The Rhinoceros then proceeds, as Woolf's satire borders on the offensive, to use his own illogical reasoning to point out how the brain of the English pig, i. e., the Englishman, resembles the brain of the rhinoceros, and he comments that Baldwin and the Conservatives "have learnt a good deal of their political wisdom from the pigs" (14). Woolf further describes this wisdom as based on "a judicious mixture of fear, blindness, and deafness" (14). Here Woolf consistently ridicules the Conservative Party and its leader Baldwin. This is not surprising, since Woolf was a member of the Labour party, and the Conservatives had won the general election of 1924. Woolf's work for the Labour party emphasized internationalism, not protectionism, which was the Conservative party's position, as well as reinforcement of the League of Nations to help ease the international tensions which lead to war, and an end to imperialism, which would give nations greater autonomy and equality.

Woolf's animal debate continues as the Mandril speaks. He first announces that he is a Bolshevik who belongs to the "intelligentsia" but who identifies with the proletariat. In contrast to the Rhinoceros, who had commented how fear is the beginning and end of political wisdom (14), the Mandril believes that inspiring fear produces power, while feeling fear makes one powerless. This has been the basis of all religious and elite class and power relationships. The revolution in Russia, however, has reversed class relationships through a change in control over fear, and "for the first time in history the upper classes became more afraid of the lower classes than the lower of the upper" (17). Unlike the Rhinoceros and the Conservative party position that he represents, the Mandril feels that this change is good.[47]

Language and inversion of logic continue to create satire as the next debater, the Owl, speaks. He expresses surprise that the species known as "the human animal," which he describes with Woolf's typical mixture of scorn and exaggeration as a "savage and unbalanced creature," has not destroyed itself: "Man appears to be a most dangerous animal, so clever that he would have destroyed every living thing on the earth, including himself if he had not been repeatedly saved by long lucid moments of extreme stupidity" (18). Having studied the political history of man since the French Revolution, the Owl has come to see "that when men talk about justice and reason and patriotism, they often really mean panic and terror" (19). Patriotism among human animals, the Owl claims, is impossible to maintain, unless they are terrified of some other nation. As a result, they have "invented a special class of men, called statesmen and diplomatists, who are paid very large salaries . . . to make the rest of the people afraid of some other nation (or preferably nations) and so keep up their patriotism" (19). Thus, it is not surprising that Bolshevism, since it is based on internationalism or the lack of fear between nations, would frighten those who wished to maintain the status quo. In many ways, the Owl points out important concerns of Woolf's. He too had studied the history of man with a particular focus on the development of communal psychology before the French Revolution and up to the present.[48] In addition, Woolf had a very poor opinion of the role of statesmen, which he expressed in his autobiography, his play *The Hotel,* and many of his essays, particularly "Statesmen and Diplomatists," "Please, Sir, it was the other Fellow," and "Politics in Spain" (see Chapter 5), and, finally, he consistently supported a policy of internationalism.

The debate continues as the animals comment further on the role of fear in the life of the human animal. Another debater, the Elephant, explains that fear dominates the human animal's relationship with other human animals:

Everyone is terrified that his neighbour will cut his throat or shoot him in the back or blow him up with high explosive shells or drop a bomb on his head or destroy his lungs with poison gas or steal his wife or conquer a bit of his native land or a bit of land that he has conquered, or filch his watch or his money, or get better pay than he does, or climb over his head in society. (22)

Woolf's use of language, particularly repetition and extended sentence structure, communicates the emotional tension such a relationship based on fear fosters. The Elephant recalls life in the jungle, where there is freedom, but there is also perpetual fear and killing. In captivity, however, the animals are "peaceful, happy, unafraid, civilized" (24). Thus, the Elephant believes that the only way for human animals to achieve civilization will be to confine each human animal in a separate cage. The Elephant's comments win the applause of his friends, and the essay ends.

Clearly, Woolf's voice is present throughout his fable. He views class society throughout history as the source of economic and social inequalities which create fear, hostility, and destruction among men. The study of history has not helped man to recognize or maintain the values of civilization. Human nature uninhibited, like animals in the jungle, will not lead to civilization. In addition, progressive changes in social and political systems, such as those created by the French and Russian Revolutions, are both feared and subverted; thus, even if these revolutions are based on civilized values and attempt to reorganize society so that equality and justice dominate, they will be undermined, and man will revert to the barbarism of jungle life. Woolf argues that if such barbarism exists, then men will lose their freedom, and fear and violence will dominate. The animals in *Fear and Politics* frequently use the term "political wisdom," yet, according to Woolf's satire, man lacks political wisdom, particularly if he resists change and chooses fear as a means of maintaining social, national, and international relationships. Woolf's zoo is indeed a microcosm of society, past and present. For without the values of a civilized society—freedom, justice, equality, reason—men will live like animals in the zoo: isolated behind the bars of a cage.[49]

The values of civilization stressed in *Fear and Politics* dominated all of Woolf's thought and work. The ending of the fourth volume of the autobiography describes how he was planting some flowers during the late summer of 1939 before the outbreak of World War II:

Suddenly I heard Virginia's voice calling... 'Hitler is making a speech'. I shouted back: 'I shan't come. I'm planting iris and they will be flowering long after he is dead.' Last March, 21 years after Hitler committed suicide in a bunker, a few of those violet flowers still flowered under the apple-tree in the orchard.[50]

This anecdote captures the essence of Woolf's aspirations for man and society: that what is beautiful and natural should survive and be the basis of civilization, while what is destructive should be destroyed. Woolf, however, was quite pessimistic about how much he had influenced society. In the last volume of his autobiography, he questions the success of his efforts. Although he considered himself well suited for the political and literary work he did, and although his work on international government and for the Labour party advisory committees did influence people and policies, he wrote that he had "achieved practically nothing,"[51] and he believed that his efforts to change man's social and political history for the better were "mainly ineffective" (170). Undoubtedly, Woolf's faith in the power of ideas, particularly in rationalism, and his position as an advisor to those who held political power rather than as the person who wielded that power, limited his ability to achieve his goals.[52] Nevertheless, the title of this last volume of the autobiography, "the journey not the arrival matters," a paraphrase of a comment by Montaigne, whom Woolf considered to be "the first civilized modern man" (172), indicates that Woolf believed it was important to work toward a goal—that of constructing a civilization based on justice and mercy—even if that goal could not be achieved during his lifetime. An overview of Woolf's life and work suggests that perhaps Woolf can be compared to Leslie Stephen, whom he admired and described as "not great enough or original enough to alter the social history of his time," but whose intellect and character made him "contemporarily an...'influence'...in the intellectual and social history."[53] For Leonard Woolf did help to shape public opinion, even though his countrymen were adopting only in the 1960s the kind of behavior he proposed in the 1920s,[54] and with these changes in public opinion and behavior, the social changes which Woolf worked for might still occur.

Chapter Two
Early Writings on Imperialism and Civilization

Leonard Woolf's literary and political career did not actually begin until after he graduated from Cambridge University. A few of his writings before this period survive, however. On 4 August 1889, at age eight, he produced "The Leonard Paper," which reported the day's events,[1] and some years later, he contributed to a family newspaper, the *Zoological News,* produced from 1897 to 1900.[2] Still over a decade later, as a Cambridge undergraduate, he read a paper to the Apostle Society entitled "George or George or Both?", which discussed the choice between a life of contemplation, typical of George Moore, or a life of action, typical of George Trevelyan. In his paper, Woolf argued that contemplation and action should be merged,[3] and this became the philosophy he followed the rest of his life.

Ceylon Years

The end of Leonard Woolf's years at Cambridge University represented a turning point in his life. When he finished his undergraduate degree, his academic record was not particularly distinguished; thus, his career choices were either to become a schoolmaster or to go into government service. He chose the latter and was accepted by the Ceylon Civil Service. The seven years Woolf spent in Ceylon—in Jaffna, Kandy, and Hambantota—influenced much of his writing: the second volume of his autobiography; an official Ceylonese government record, *Diaries in Ceylon,* which he kept during 1908–1911 while assistant government agent in Hambantota District; his first novel, *The Village in the Jungle;* and several short stories.

Diaries in Ceylon is perhaps the central work of this period. When Woolf revisited Ceylon in 1960, copies of the diaries he kept were presented to him. Along with letters to Lytton Strachey, these records helped him to remember the experiences he later described in *Growing,* the second volume of the autobiography, which was published in 1961. Woolf comments in *Growing* that the diaries were sent each month to the secretariat in Colombo. Anything in these official records which was critical of the government would be shown to the colonial secretary or the governor. Woolf remembers being "severely rapped over the knuckles by His Excellency"[4] for criticizing the government agent who was his superior. Nevertheless, Woolf maintains that he wrote the diaries "fully and frankly" and felt that they would "show up the iniquities of the ancient imperialists' regime" (200). Therefore, he was surprised when the Prime Minister of Ceylon informed him that the diaries would be printed and published by the government in the *Ceylon Historical Journal.*

Woolf's dedication to his responsibilities as assistant government agent is clear throughout these diaries. His duties involved agricultural, judicial, educational, and health matters. Special attention was given to reorganizing the system of salt collection and the method of chena cultivation, and to combating periodic rinderpest outbreaks among the cattle. Woolf apparently regarded the diaries as public documents which would serve the administrators who succeeded him. Thus, his personal thoughts, such as his sense of futility about his work or his criticism of other Englishmen in the service, emerge more in the autobiography than the diaries. Moreover, he felt that the diaries would be especially interesting to the historian of imperialism, and respecting their historical nature, he appears to have left them unrevised for publication; he did, however, include a preface which comments on the basic changes in Ceylonese life that he observed fifty years after the diaries were written, most notably the increased pace of life caused by self-government, the advent of the car, and an increase in the general standard of living.

Much of *Diaries in Ceylon* presents facts and figures, yet this kind of documentation is typical of Woolf's writings. Sections of the autobiography, for example, present careful accounts of the income and expenses of the Woolf household and the Hogarth Press. Woolf himself admits to having a natural inclination toward details and record-keeping. Similarly, in volume two of the autobiography, Woolf comments that he was unpopular among the Tamils and Sinhalese and had the reputation of "being a strict and ruthless civil servant,"[5] because of his emphasis on efficiency and organization. Many of his techniques of organization were learned from F. H. Price, his superior government agent in Jaffna. Woolf comments that Price taught him "very valuable lessons and methods in administration, lessons and methods which are applicable to all *business*" (106). It is therefore not surprising that the same dedication and businesslike organization and efficiency, and the same difficulties of working with subordinates typical of his work in Ceylon, later characterized his direction of the Hogarth Press.

In the Ceylon Civil Service, the government agent had an unusual amount of power which resulted from performing executive, legislative, and judicial functions.[6] Yet there was little abuse of this power due to the tradition of the service which made it "well-disciplined and free of corruption" with "liberal humanitarian and utilitarian ideals" (xiv). To ensure dedication to these ideals, the civil servant was paid well and, as a result, was not inclined to seek ways of exploiting the country through planting or trade. Moreover, social "purity" was emphasized; the civil servant was not to mix with the Ceylonese but to associate only with Englishmen in social clubs and expensive hotels in order to maintain British cultural values and acceptable social behavior. Woolf became a perceptive observer of the strict class divisions among the English in Ceylon, as comments in the autobiography reveal.

Although the autobiography was written retrospectively with a mature political vision, it is likely that Woolf had a basic awareness of social and economic hierarchies during his years in Ceylon, even though he describes himself as politically naive. The boat trip to Ceylon was Woolf's first introduction to a rigid class milieu. It seemed to Woolf, as he wrote in *Growing*, that "the world and society of the boat are a microcosm of the macrocosm" (15), providing a shocking lesson in the "gratuitous inhumanity" and "spontaneous malevolence" which were part of the "class war and hatred between Europeans" (16) characteristic of British imperialism in the East. Of the four levels or classes—civil servants, army officers, planters, and businessmen—the civil servants were the most respected, the best paid, and the most powerful. Acute awareness of this social hierarchy created the same "snobbery, pretentiousness, and false pretensions" (17) among white Europeans in India and Ceylon that existed in English suburban life.

Woolf also comments in the autobiography on the rituals of British social life in Ceylon. Long hours of work were followed by drinking whiskey and soda with the other men in the service, as well as a regular round of tennis each night. This rigid routine, along with separation by race, since no natives were members of the British clubs, seemed to Woolf to place the British in an "imperialist isolation" (44) from the society they ruled. He described the colonial government servants as "displaced persons" (46) who had the "psychology of people whose lives had suddenly been torn up by the roots and, in a foreign country, had therefore become unreal, artificial, temporary, and alien" (47).

In the preface to *Diaries in Ceylon,* Woolf comments that when he arrived in Ceylon, he was "in a state of political innocence," never having "really considered what my relations would be with the inhabitants."[7] He attributed his political naiveté to the lack of concern with political issues typical of his generation in pre–World War I England. While in Jaffna, Woolf learned to speak Tamil, and when he was assigned to Kandy, he learned Sinhalese. An unusual closeness to the people and a deep concern for improving the conditions of their lives characterized his work in Ceylon. Yet Woolf soon came to see himself as being "in the position of empire-builder and imperialist" (lxxvi), and eventually he developed antiimperialist feelings.

Two incidents seemed to characterize Woolf's position as imperialist ruler. The first occurred in Jaffna when a well-known Ceylonese lawyer, Mr. Sanderasekara, registered a complaint that

Woolf had deliberately hit him in the face with his riding whip.
Woolf remembered that he had been using his whip to point out a
road as the lawyer passed nearby. Analyzing the incident in
Growing, he comments:

It shocked me that these people should think that, as a white man and a
ruler of Ceylon, I should consider the brown man, the Tamil, to be one of
"the lesser breeds" and deliberately hit him in the face... to show him
that he must behave himself and keep in his place... perhaps... Mr.
Sanderasekara... [was] right in feeling that my sitting on a horse
arrogantly in the main street of their town was as good as a slap in the
face. (113–14)

The second incident, which occurred when Woolf returned to
Ceylon in 1960, and which is described in the last volume of the
autobiography, again revealed the antagonism between the ruling white class and the Ceylonese. The former Mudaliyar or
Headman of East Giruwa Pattu in Hambantota District con-
fronted Woolf at a hotel and claimed that Woolf had unfairly
settled a dispute fifty years earlier. Woolf recalled that during a
rinderpest outbreak he had killed a buffalo with the disease,
fining the owner ten rupees for breaking the law that required
destroying any infected animal. Since the owner happened to be
the village headman, Woolf fined him another ten rupees "for
not carrying out his duties, i. e. reporting and prosecuting the
offender (himself) for breaking the law."[8] Fifty years later, the
Mudaliyar bitterly claimed that Woolf's actions were unfair
because he had had to pay one of the ten-rupee fines for the
headman. For Woolf, this incident represented the unpleasant
nature of imperialism: imposing a system of justice on people
who view that system as injustice.

   In *Diaries in Ceylon,* Woolf defines colonial administration as
"the control of headmen, the enforcement of ancient customs and
the development of cultivation" (14). The headman was thus
recognized as an essential part of the native administration of the
district. This local official, however, often caused trouble; in fact,
Woolf had to institute disciplinary administrative action against

one of the revenue collectors and chief native officials whom he found to be irresponsible in his duties despite warnings. Woolf saw the headman as having an important position in the caste hierarchies of Ceylonese life, and he was wary of the headman's misuse of his social, political, and economic power. He believed that the headman must set a good example: "when a headman is slack...the headmen under him become slack and the sins of the headmen are frequently and unfortunately necessarily visited upon the villagers" (42). A serious example of a headman's mismanagement would be if he did not enforce proper application for chena permits among the villagers, who would therefore be in danger of losing chena rights and, consequently, their means of subsistence farming. Woolf was to portray the headman's misuse of power in his novel about Ceylon, *The Village in the Jungle.*

In addition to comments on political aspects of village life, the diaries reveal that although Woolf was sensitive to the beauty of the Ceylonese countryside, he was also aware of the difficulties of life there. During the drought of July 1910, he wrote: "The heat during the day makes life intolerable...one sits in a perpetual sandstorm waiting for the sun to go down and for the mosquitoes to come to take the place of the eyeflies" (166). Yet instead of despairing about improving conditions or despising the natives for their lives, Woolf set about to improve conditions as much as possible, basing his actions on an understanding of and respect for the intellectual and emotional attitudes of the villagers.

Entries in *Diaries in Ceylon* indicate that Woolf was constantly concerned with essential aspects of village life: health and sanitation of the villagers and livestock; methods of salt collection; agriculture and irrigation; and education. For example, during one inspection of a school, Woolf noticed that the children looked "most unhealthy, most of them with swollen spleens" (24). Their condition reminded Woolf that the health and sanitation problems of the island needed to be regarded as "a form of war, requiring money, discipline, organization and thought" (24). He also tried to apply this insight to the periodic outbreaks of the rinderpest disease among the cattle. After some time, he recognized that the government was mishandling the inoculation of cattle by charging the villagers one rupee for each shot:

The people are ignorant and hopelessly conservative. They positively hate anything new. They are therefore prejudiced against inoculation. Now anyone who has had any experience with this class of native knows that the one thing which . . . would finally determine him not to allow inoculation is for him to find that he has to pay one cent for it. If you tell him you will do it for nothing, though he disapproves of it, he may consent just in order to get something done for nothing. (51)

Woolf solved the problem of the villagers' resistance to inoculation by paying for the shots; he thereby ensured that the inoculation effort, the best method for controlling the rinderpest epidemic, would succeed. His understanding of human nature, and particularly of the villagers' mental and emotional attitudes, thus allowed him to pursue the practical, effective solution to a persistent problem.

Many of the diary entries describe Woolf's dissatisfaction with the methods of salt collection and his attempts to change them. Woolf records how he found that the weights were inaccurate when he went to the salt stores to check the receipt of salt. Attributing this to the checkers and headguard, whom he suspended from government service for a year (35), and having "very little faith in the accuracy with which Government salt is weighed anywhere" (36), he decided that those responsible should be held accountable for their jobs; otherwise, he believed, the dishonesty would be uncontrollable (36). Under the present system, moreover, a large amount of the salt collected was kept unweighed for years; as a result, no one could be held responsible for any wastage (60). Woolf was intent on changing the system so that the salt was weighed immediately. Similarly, when he discovered corruption in the system of issuing stamped tickets entitling the salt collectors to payment, he instituted a new system of issuing tickets which involved immediate payment (104). Gradually, the methods of collecting salt and distributing payment for it were improved, and Woolf was able to announce proudly that record collections were achieved.

Woolf also tried to improve the system of cultivation by introducing the plow. At first, the villagers rebelled against any change in methods, but Woolf used personal influence by going to talk to the landowners. He also requested instructors from the Agricultural Society to teach the people to use the machinery and to stay with the villagers throughout the cultivation period to help settle any problems (94). Woolf believed that resistance to the new method of plowing would crumble if benefits were evident. He reported how "the Hambantota carters, who all said that Hambantota bulls would never be able to pull these English ploughs, are now quite won over after seeing the ploughs being used" (103). In addition, he experienced personal pleasure in learning more about cultivation and commented that "it is a most fascinating occupation at the same time to teach two bulls and oneself to plough" (103).

Another aspect of agricultural practice which Woolf tried to improve was land ownership. He believed in giving small cultivators land and "advancing seed paddy to help them eventually to get out of the middleman's hands" (75). He also attacked the problems of the chena system of agriculture, which involved burning and clearing a portion of the jungle and cultivating seed on it as long as the land remained fertile. Since water for cultivation other than seed was not available five years out of six (117), a lack of chenas would cause hardship for the villagers. Despite the difficulties of agriculture, the village population was rooted to the land. The people would rather own land, even if they could not support themselves, than leave their villages and seek work in the cities. Woolf realized that if the government limited the number of chena permits, it would mean the gradual extinction of some villages. This would also happen unless some land were set aside and given to the villagers without demanding payment in advance. The present government policy of requiring advance payment made the villagers accept credit on "ruinous terms" (86). In addition, Woolf suspected that if chena cultivation were curtailed, there would be an increase in crime. This proved to be true in one area of the district, where, he wrote, "the people... having no chena crop eat only meat and prey upon one another and one another's cattle" (178). The government accepted Woolf's suggestions about revising chena permit procedures and payment, but since Woolf understood that the government's new procedures would be very difficult to carry out, he decided "to inspect every village personally and to enquire into its circumstances... with regard to chenas" (136). Again, this incident reveals Woolf's willingness to take on responsibility and extra work to make progress in improving the lives of the villagers.

Thus, Woolf was interested in bettering Ceylonese village life through control of disease, more efficient production and collection of salt, and better agricultural methods. He was, however, also interested in improving the level of education. In several diary entries, he comments on visits to schools. For example, he wrote: "Inspected the new school at Bundala. There were 50 children there which was excellent, as my visit was quite unexpected, nobody knowing I was coming" (150). He also worked toward starting a new Tamil school in Hambantota, "the first Sanitary Board School in the Island... a mixed vernacular school" (182), which was to be financed through grants-in-aid. Woolf hoped the school would keep the children from roaming the streets, and would thus curtail the "colossal laziness of the people" by having the school teach the children "something other than obscenity, ill manners, and the torturing of animals, which at present are the three things which make up the education of most of the children in Hambantota" (182).

In the autobiography volume *Growing,* Woolf describes much of the work—particularly in regard to census-taking, salt-collecting, introducing the plow, and controlling rinderpest outbreaks—that he recorded in *Diaries in Ceylon.* Yet there are additional insights into Woolf's thoughts and his relationships with the Ceylonese. For example, about his promotion to assistant government agent of Hambantota, Woolf comments that he felt inspired "to make the Hambantota District the best administered in the island" (81). While the diaries revealed how his determination to run the district efficiently required both good administrative ability and shrewd insight into human nature, the autobiography provides further insights into how Woolf cleverly met the challenges involved in administering a district. For example, he describes the way he pressured a contractor to accept his offer of 1.80 rupees per ton of salt. His strategy consisted of taking the contractor, who was not a good walker, on a long walk. The contractor capitulated to Woolf's terms when faced with two uncomfortable alternatives: continuing the walk, which would be beyond his physical strength, or turning back without Woolf, which would be embarrassing (184–85).

In addition to providing complementary details about Woolf's work in Ceylon, *Diaries in Ceylon* and *Growing* reveal how Woolf used those experiences as material for his fiction, particularly *The Village in the Jungle,* published in 1913. This work was translated into Sinhalese and has been considered by the Ceylonese as "the finest imaginative work based on life in this country."[9] In *Growing,* Woolf comments on his awareness of the jungle: its beauty, and its ugliness and cruelty. Having lost his way twice in the jungle, he could attest to its fearsomeness and its treachery, which, he claimed, obsessed his memory and imagination after leaving Ceylon, and thus became the theme of *The Village in the Jungle* (212). Another aspect of the novel, religion, particularly the beliefs of Buddhism, is discussed in *Growing.* Woolf considered Buddhism to be superior to all other religions, "a civilized and humane dream of considerable beauty and it has eliminated most of the crude anthropomorphic and theological nonsense which encrusts other religions" (159). He admired the emphasis on solitude and contemplation, and the preaching of a way of life which is "extraordinarily gentle, unaggressive, human" (162). Woolf, however, also recognized that the practice of Buddhism was susceptible to corruption and perversion. For example, he writes about a pilgrimage to the temple at Kataragama, which he supervised while in Hambantota. This pilgrimage is described as a "Ceylonese Lourdes" by Woolf, who found much of it cruel and grotesque. At the same time, he realized that "the people believed what they believed simply and purely. The beliefs were deplorable, no doubt, but the purity, simplicity, and motives for taking the terrible journey to the temple I respected" (230). It was this same ability to accept the beliefs of the Ceylonese as valid for their way of life, although alien and unacceptable for the European, which enabled Woolf to write about peasant life in *The Village in the Jungle* from the perspective of the native.

The Village in the Jungle portrays not only the physical level of village life, but also the mental and emotional life of the characters, the rhythms of rural speech, and the relationship of the villagers to nature. Woolf understood the way the jungle dominated village life and was able to recreate its unique physical environment. Yet he also presents the jungle as symbolic geography; it represents evil and destruction, which Woolf parallels with the equally destructive human evil, or greed. Woolf then explores man's reaction to evil, both his struggle against it and his passive acceptance of it. He himself was susceptible to the duality of the jungle, commenting in the preface to *Diaries in Ceylon:* "I was fascinated... by the perpetual menace of nature, the beautiful and... savage life of the jungle." Similarly, he was "deeply moved by the lives of the villagers and their psychology" (lxxviii). His sympathetic understanding of the villagers as individuals increased as he perceived the destructive nature of the economic system, how the headman and the money-lender controlled the survival of the villagers through their personal whims, and through the machinery of the debt system and chena cultivation.

The novel is written in third-person narration, which is appropriate to both charcterization and theme. The external narration allows Woolf to present the story as a tale, to fill in details of location and customs for the non-Ceylonese reader. Moreover, it sets a narrative frame for the stories told by the characters, indicating that storytelling is basic to the culture, both as a means of communication and of transmitting experience. Finally, none of the characters develop enough self-consciousness to be the source of an internal narration. This parallels their relationship to experience; they are controlled by external forces—nature, the caste economic and social system, mysticism, and individual greed—rather than being in control of their lives.

The opening pages of *The Village in the Jungle* identify Woolf's view of the jungle as fearful and evil. In contrast to the jungle, the village is vulnerable. Survival is based on chena cultivation, but "hunger and the fear of hunger always lay upon the village"[10] because of poor cultivation. In addition, there is the threat of starvation caused by debt, for "the villagers lived upon debt" (30), owing part of their crop to the headman and the money-lender. Knowing the power of the headman, the villagers show their deference to him. For example, Silindu, Woolf's main character, brings the best meat of a slain deer to the headman to gain his favor, for he knows that the headman controls the issuing of government permits for clearing the jungle for a chena. Since the headman dislikes Silindu, he causes difficulties, such as reporting the lack of a gun permit and refusing to lend grain. As a result, Silindu will have to go to town to borrow from the money-lender, "who knew him too well to give anything but ruinous terms" (41).

In addition to economic caste difficulties, Silindu's family faces social caste alienation in the village. As his two daughters grow up, he takes them into the jungle and they learn the ways of hunters. The women in the village scorn the girls, calling them *vedda,* the word for the aborigines of Ceylon who are hunters and are often identified with devils (27). Similarly, when the headman's brother-in-law, Babun, later decides to marry Silindu's daughter Punchi Menika, the headman's wife insults Silindu's daughters, calling them *Rodiyas,* the name for the lowest Sinhalese caste, and "daughters of a dog" (54). Nevertheless, Babun is willing to defy village prejudice and caste barriers to marry Silindu's daughter.

Woolf further develops a theme of racial alienation in the novel by juxtaposing Sinhalese and Tamils. When the headman's wife curses Silindu's daughters, she also calls them *Tamils,* a form of abuse among the Sinhalese. Moreover, the village doctor, Punchirala, an ugly man with the scar of a bear's claw on his face, is described as "black as a Tamil" (81). Like Punchirala, Fernando, the money-lender who comes to the village, is a man of low character, "cunning, unscrupulous" (45), who lends money at more than the usual rate, and he, too, is said to be a Tamil (144). This interpersonal racial alienation is reinforced by the religious mythology. When Silindu and the others go to the Beragama temple, they hear that the god does not allow Tamils to serve him. In the mythology, he was originally a Tamil god, but the Tamils refused to serve him, while the Sinhalese served willingly (105).

After Punchi Menika's marriage to Babun, Silindu's life becomes more troubled by adversity. Here Woolf explores the role of religion and magic in the villagers' lives. When the vederala, or village doctor, Punchirala, desires Silindu's second daughter, Hinnihami, Silindu refuses, although he knows "the vederala is a dangerous man to offend" (79). As a result, "the slow sapping of his life by a spell" of Punchirala begins. Although Silindu goes to the temple in Beragama and prays to the god to free him from evil, the god does not aid him. A sanyasi, or holy man, tells him that only the sacrifice of a daughter will release the spell of the evil spirit from the jungle. Hinnihami gives herself to Punchirala but leaves him. Later, she bears and raises his child while nurturing a fawn from the jungle which she regards as "the mysterious gift and pledge of the god" from Beragama (137). When the villagers scorn her attachment to the deer, however, and vent their anger by killing the animal, Hinnihami's spirit is destroyed and she dies.

Just as Hinnihami's death is caused by human evil—jealousy and viciousness—similar factors cause further misfortunes to strike Silindu. A money-lender named Fernando comes to live in the headman's compound in order to ensure that the chena cultivation of the village will yield enough profit to the villagers for them to repay their debts to him. Although this is illegal, the headman allows it, since his "consent was purchased by the cancellation of his debts, by a private arrangement with Fernando" (146). The man soon desires Silindu's daughter Punchi Menika. Angered by the woman's refusals, Fernando persuades the headman to withhold Silindu's chena permit, which will mean starvation for them within a month. In addition, Silindu and Babun are charged with robbing the headman in a frame-up, and they are taken away to the town to court. These events break Babun's spirits, but Silindu sees "at last the malignity of the headman and how his life had been ruined by it" (185).

The court scenes reveal Woolf's criticism of the colonial justice system. Silindu and Babun are locked in a wooden cage. The judge, a white Englishman, communicates to the prisoners through a Sinhalese interpreter. The men understand nothing of the procedures, except that Babun realizes he is being destroyed by the caste system which gives power to certain individuals and leaves him powerless: "How can I have witnesses? No one will give evidence against the headman" (196). Even though the judge realizes that aspects of the case are hidden, the facts point to Babun's involvement in the robbery, and since Babun is unable to refute the accusations, he is sentenced to six months in prison.

Once Silindu understands that the evil in the village is caused by the headman and Fernando, he is not a passive victim; his anger against the headman and money-lender increases, and he shoots both men. When Silindu is brought to court, the white judge "noted the helplessness and suffering in Silindu's face" (240–41). Because the judge understands the law of the jungle and of the village caste system, he sees that Silindu is a poor man who wanted to be left alone, like the animals in the jungle, but if disturbed, he would kill in anger. The novel does pose an alternative to the European justice system and the caste antagonism of village life, that of Buddhist philosophy, which is stated by an old beggar: "[it] seems foolish to kill a man because he has killed. If it is a sin, will he not be punished in the next birth?" (264). He also comments that killing in the jungle is wrong, because "the Lord Buddha said, 'It is a sin to kill' " (266). Silindu accepts this view of the jungle and attains inner peace. When he is sentenced to death, he looks "forward to the day as the end of some period of evil, as the beginning of something happier and better" (279). Yet Woolf's novel ends with a focus on the village and the destructive power of the jungle. Several of the huts have been abandoned, and as time passes, the village disappears "into the jungle from which it had sprung" (204).

The Village in the Jungle is an impressive work because it focuses on a mode of existence rarely portrayed in fiction. Moreover, Woolf presents the lives of the villagers without sentimentality or condescension. His experiences in Ceylon account for the startling authenticity of character, situation, and setting; however, through the narrative technique, Woolf creates intellectual distance allowing the reader to observe a foreign culture set against the powers of nature. Woolf presents similar material in *Stories from the East,* which, along with *The Village in the Jungle,* was written after his return to England. The three short stories—"A Tale Told by Moonlight," "Pearls and Swine," and "The Two Brahmans"—reveal aspects of Eastern culture, but also emphasize the role of the British in the East and the effects of class and caste barriers, common to both British and Ceylonese society, on human behavior.

The theme of love in the first story, "A Tale Told by Moonlight," may well have been influenced by Woolf's relationships with women in Ceylon. In the autobiography volume *Growing,* he records a brief involvement in 1906, in Jaffna, with a young Englishwoman named Gwen, whom Woolf describes as "pretty, lively, sweetnatured." He remembers their relationship vividly: "After the fierce heat of the day...we would lay on the seaweedy sand platonically...in each other's arms" (102). Moreover, Woolf claims to have had a romantic, even sentimental attitude toward women. He comments in *Growing:* "I have always been greatly attracted by the undiluted female mind, as well as by the female body.... The minds of most women differ from the minds of most men.... Their minds seem to me to be gentler, more sensitive, more civilized" (152). This seems to have been his view of another young woman, Rachel Robinson, with whom his relationship "reached the maximum intimacy...allowed by the extraordinary etiquette and reticencies of the age...I had for her a real affection without ever falling in love with her" (153). When he met her two years later, he sensed, uncomfortably, that he was being tempted, that Rachel, as well as her parents, expected an offer of marriage (155) which he could not extend. Thus, despite these involvements with young British women in Ceylon, Woolf left the civil service unattached.

In "A Tale Told by Moonlight," the theme of romantic love is explored, but it is set against the reality of caste and racial differences. The double narrative presents a first, unidentified narrator who describes the second narrator, Jessop, as an outsider to British upper-class society because he rejects sentimental notions of reality and confronts others with the truth.[11] As the narrator establishes a romantic setting in nature for the tale, he comments that he is becoming sentimental. Similarly, when all the men in the group respond to the sight of a couple embracing by telling stories of their first loves, the narrator describes the group as "passionate in our belief in it, love, the great passion, the real thing" (256). Again, Jessop is the outsider; he shatters their romanticism and sentimentality by describing love as "just a flicker of the body it will be cold, dead, this time next year" (256). Rejecting the idea that the average person experiences intense passion, Jessop states that most people consider the desire for physical affection to be love.

Jessop proceeds to tell the others about one case of love, an acquaintance whom he calls Reynolds. Detecting "some power of feeling" in Reynolds, despite the shyness and nervousness which have kept Reynolds isolated from emotional relationships, Jessop comments: "He knew a good deal about how other people think...but he didn't know how they felt; I expect he had never felt anything himself, except fear and shyness" (258). When Reynolds expresses a desire "to see life, to understand it, to feel it" (259), Jessop introduces him to the life of a brothel in the native quarter. Despite some initial discomfort and alienation in the brothel, Reynolds is attracted to a Sinhalese village woman with "the delicate innocent beauty of a child" and "an air of slowness and depth and mystery of silence and of innocence" (260). This young woman stimulates in Reynolds what Jessop defines as "the power to feel, the power that so few have, the flame, the passion, love, the real thing" (261). Although he

desires the woman physically, Reynolds also wants her to return
the depths of his passion. Jessop, however, doubts that the girl is
anything more than "a nice simple soft little animal like the bitch
at [his] feet" (262), but he urges Reynolds to buy the woman's
freedom to see if he can live out his illusion of a life together.
Soon after Reynolds follows Jessop's advice, he becomes aware of
the woman's limitations and the impossibility of her being able to
fulfill his needs and, through Jessop's influence, Reynolds decides
to leave. Although he provides for the woman's comfort, she
drowns herself, and it is Jessop who identifies her body. As he
tells this tale, Jessop expresses his sense of responsibility for
influencing Reynolds, but he does not seem to feel responsible for
destroying the woman's life. Indeed, he is scornful of her, comparing her to a female dog and characterizing her love and
devotion to Reynolds as "another sort of love... the love of dogs
and... of those slow, big-eyed women of the East" (263). Thus,
Woolf suggests that class and racial barriers destroy the possibility of emotional fulfillment.

Woolf's second story, "Pearls and Swine," which also develops
themes about imperialism and moral values, generated positive
response when it was written. Woolf reports in his autobiography that as a result of a review by Hamilton Fyfe in the *Daily Mail*
which stated that " 'Pearls and Swine' will rank with the great
stories of the world,"[12] Henry Holt, a literary agent in New York,
requested the story for publication. After reading it, Holt wanted
Woolf "to tone it down a bit" (89), but Woolf refused to make any
changes. The story was then sent to the well-known literary
agent Ann Watkins, who thought it "a masterpiece" but commented that the realism would be unacceptable to the American
reading public, which was still provincial and wanted to "veer
from the shocking, the revolting—the truth" (89).

The truth that Woolf probes in this story is the power of
human greed and the remorse of conscience. As in "A Tale Told
by Moonlight," the setting is the East, his narrator is British, and
his characters are members of the upper classes.[13] Again, Woolf's
narrator is alienated from his countrymen; he scorns their intellectual and moral values, as suggested by his criticism of their

appearance. For example, he describes the Colonel as having "kind choleric eyes bulging out on a life which he was content never for a moment to understand" (265). Later, as the men talk in "fat, full-fed assured voices" (265), the narrator is surprised by their sentimental comments on the East. At first he comments, "Well, I expect one is sentimental about it, having lived there," but later he states more strongly, "How one hated it and how one loved it!" (265), thus expressing the tensions of the racial and cultural conflicts created by imperialism. Moreover, at the beginning of the story, Woolf uses his characters to raise questions about British involvement in the East. At first, he criticizes the British for their arrogance in thinking that they can understand the East. Sarcasm pervades the narrator's comment: "But they knew all about it, they had solved, with their fat voices and in their fat heads, riddles, older than the Sphinx, of people remote and ancient and mysterious whom they had never seen and could never understand" (266). Woolf seems to be commenting that the characters within his story who represent the British colonial rulers, are not aware of the realities of Eastern life. The tale within the story is thus intended to enlighten them.

"Pearls and Swine" also probes conflicting views of British imperialism. The character of an archdeacon raises the issue of the movement for colonial independence, commenting that "it seems . . . a good sign, this movement, an awakening among the people" (266). He condemns violence, however: "Nothing can condone violence, the taking of human life, it's savagery, terrible, terrible" (266). A different view of colonialism is voiced by a stock jobber, whom Woolf describes as "plump and comfortable . . . with a loud voice and shifty eyes" (266). The jobber criticizes administrators in the British civil service for being too liberal: "Rule 'em, I say, rule 'em . . . let 'em know you are top dog. That's the way to run an eastern country. I am a white man, you're black; I'll treat you well, give you courts and justice; but I'm the superior race, I'm master here" (266–67). The archdeacon accepts the principle behind this comment, that the white man has a duty to "spread the light" (267) to set an example for the colonial people to follow, and through a "message of hope and comfort," he feels the white man gains the Easterner's respect. His concept of the superiority of one race, the white race, over another reveals both the corruption of Christian doctrine and the similarity between the church and the political and financial sectors of British society.

As the narrator listens critically to the archdeacon and the stock jobber, his alienation from their conventional views is paralleled by another character, the Commissioner, who expresses his annoyance at the pompousness and ignorance of the others. When the Commissioner is challenged by the men to support his views, he tells a story about his experiences in India as administrator over a district as big as England with a population of 20 million natives, most of whom had not seen a white man. The main industry exploited in that area was gathering pearls from oysters. Although the Indians have been gathering the pearls for centuries before British rule, the British government takes two-thirds of the oysters and gives one-third to the divers. Administering the camp along with the Commissioner is a young Englishman, Robson, who "had been educated in a Board School, won prizes, scholarships, passed the Civil Service 'Exam' " (270). The Commissioner finds Robson ignorant and arrogant: "He was going to run India on new lines laid down in some damned manual of Political Science.... He hadn't seen anything, but he knew exactly what it was like" (272). In his self-satisfied intellectual ignorance, Robson resembles the Britishers listening to the Commissioner's tale. Like the archdeacon and the stock jobber, Robson believes that the white man is superior to the nonwhite and can improve the life of the Easterners "by reason, arguing them out of their superstitions, false beliefs; by education, by science, by example" (272). Moreover, Robson pompously expresses criticism and intolerance of the present methods of British administration: "You've none of you got clear plans out here.... The result is ... instead of getting hold of the East, it's the East which gets hold of you" (272). The Commissioner also describes another man at the fishery, a planter named White who was "unhealthily fat for the East," with bloodshot eyes and hands that shook, indicating his alcoholism (271). White agrees with

Robson's view of the white man's rule in the East, but believes in more militant methods. Moreover, White seems obsessed with India's wealth in gold, coal, iron, and even radium, which could be obtained were it not for restrictions by the British government. Thus, through Robson and White, Woolf dramatizes both the simplistic ideas about East-West relations and rule and the elemental greed of the British imperialists.

By telling his tale, the Commissioner attempts to give the British upper class facts about the East, since they "seem so far from life...doing things...according...to systems, views, opinions" (275). In contrast, in the East, one lives "so near to life....And things happen slowly, inexorably by fate and...you feel it there in everything" (274). Struggling to administer the Pearl Fishery Camp and obtain the British government's share of the oysters, the Commissioner recognizes that it is difficult to apply reason to control the two thousand divers almost single-handedly; thus, he is not surprised when a riot breaks out. Robson, however, is overcome; the riot shatters his belief that he knows effective methods of government. As the men riot and Robson breaks down because he is disillusioned, White becomes ill and has an attack of madness. Amidst this chaos, the Commissioner states:

One does one's work—forty-eight hours at a stretch doesn't leave one much time or inclination for thinking....If you can prevent people from killing one another or robbing one another, or burning down the camp, or getting cholera or plague or small-pox, and if one can manage to get one night's sleep in three, one is fairly satisfied. (275)

The Commissioner's mental and physical strength thus indicates that he has the moral discipline which Robson and White lack.

White's illness and death dominate the last part of the narrative. As White goes through the final stages of *delirium tremens,* he begins to see "things which had happened to him, and things which he had done—they weren't nice either" as if "the memory of his sins came upon him" (276). The Commissioner comments that he "couldn't stomach" the details of White's life, as it

becomes evident that White lived a life of pure greed, exploitation, and moral corruption: "It wasn't only that he had robbed
and swindled himself through India up and down for fifteen
years.... But it was what he had done when he got away 'among
the natives'—to men, and women too, away from 'civilization,'
God! the cold, civilized corrupted cruelty of it" (277). White's
remorse is terrible because it grows out of "fear of punishment, of
what was coming of death, of the horrors, real horrors and the
phantom horrors of madness" (277). His screams draw the
fishers to him, as if they seem to be judging him. To White, the
men appear to be "devils of Hell sent to plague and torture him"
(278). But in contrast to White, who writhes and screams in fear,
the native fishermen are quiet and look "calm, impassive, stern"
(277). When the men sympathetically move away from White,
the Commissioner feels "they understood" (278). As a further
contrast to the corruption of White's life and the horror and
torment of his death, the Commissioner describes an Arab fisherman who died suddenly while diving and whose body is brought
to shore. The Arab sheik or leader of the boat pronounces the
dead man's eulogy: he "had lived, had worked... had died working, without suffering as men should desire to die" (278–79). The
silent, dignified manner of the Arab men comments on the
degenerate manner of White's death, which is an appropriate end
to his corrupt life.

When the Commissioner finishes his tale, the narrator
observes the men. The Colonel is asleep and the stock jobber is
"looking bored." The archdeacon, who is "put out," rejects the
message of the tale, commenting that it involves "exceptional
circumstances, because it is an "out of the ordinary case" (279).
The Commissioner recognizes the limitations of his listeners:
they are narrow-minded and unlikely to realize that their views
are not fact. Woolf has created characters to represent the different institutions of society—government, military, church, and
finance; each seems locked into rigid mental attitudes. The tale
should provide an insight into human experience and moral
values for the characters, and for the reader. Woolf's double
narrative thus both comments on the importance of communi-
cating an understanding of human nature, political action, and

moral values, and stresses that, in order to achieve this understanding, it is essential to break through conventional social
values and mental attitudes.

Apparently, Woolf again drew on personal experience for
"Pearls and Swine." In *Growing,* he describes his work at a Pearl
Fishery Camp, eighty miles from Jaffna, where the methods for
running the camp seemed "antidiluvian, primordial" (88), and
the system for extracting the pearls was "primitive and unsani-
tary" (90). Woolf's duties seemed to him "onerous and exhaust-
ing" (90). He comments further:

> It is merely coolie work supervising this and the counting and issuing of
> about one or two million oysters a day, for the Arabs will do anything if
> you hit them hard enough with a walking stick, an occupation in which I
> have been engaged for the most part of the last 3 days and nights. (91)

Despite chaotic, crowded conditions and a large amount of valuable property (the pearls), there was no problem maintaining
law and order. Moreover, an interesting aspect of Woolf's work at
the Pearl Fishery was observing the Arab divers. He writes that
"the Arab is superb, he has the grand manner, absolutely satur-
nine, no fuss or excitement" (93), and he further comments that
the Arab's self-respect allowed him to treat the European politely
but with an "attitude of human equality" (93), which Woolf
valued. Woolf's descriptions of the Arab divers in "Pearls and
Swine" capture these qualities, as does the scene of the Arab
diver's death, which was a direct rendering of a death that
occurred during Woolf's stay at the Pearl Fishery. For the reader,
"Pearls and Swine" is a powerful story. Along with an exotic
setting, Woolf develops the theme of the exploitation of Eastern
labor and wealth by British imperialism. Through the contrasts
among White, the Commissioner, and the Arabs, Woolf comments on the mental and moral corruption which imperialism
often creates while also portraying the possibility that individual
and cultural integrity can be maintained by the natives.

The final tale in *Stories from the East,* "The Two Brahmans,"
is again set in Ceylon. Although in *The Village in the Jungle*
Woolf revealed the caste antagonisms of small village life, indi-

cating how jealousy and greed, engrained in a system of social and economic hierarchies, caused destruction, he understood the powerful attraction of a stable social structure. In "The Two Brahmans," the main characters belong to the highest of all castes, which maintains strict codes. Brahmans "could not eat food or touch or marry into any other caste, nor could they carry earth on their heads or work at any trade, without being defiled or losing caste" (280). Their society is cohesive; they live together in order to have their children marry into the same caste, and their way of life perpetuates customs of the past. Against this background of stability of life-style and mental attitudes, Woolf explores the way inner desires conflict with the conventions of social caste.

Woolf first develops his theme through the character of Chellaya, a forty-five-year-old Brahman who had "lived happily the life which all good Brahmans should live" (281). A passion for fishing, however, causes him to "hate his compound and his fat wife and the interminable talk in the temple" (282). Even though the fisher caste is a low caste and a Brahman would be defiling his caste if he were to fish, Chellaya persuades a fisherman to teach him to fish. Although torn by guilt over being "the first Brahman to pollute his caste" (283), he continues fishing each night. As word spreads about Chellaya's activity, he becomes an outcast among the Brahmans. Woolf's second character, Chittampalam, also illuminates the theme of individual passion versus social convention. A "taciturn man and a miser" (284), Chittampalam seeks to avoid paying someone to dig a well for him, even though he knows it would pollute his caste if he did the digging and carrying of the earth himself. His greed overwhelms his pride, however, and he breaks caste conventions and becomes an outcast like Chellaya.

The reaction of the community further develops Woolf's theme. Although the other Brahmans refuse to admit to strangers that these breaches of caste codes have occurred, they shun the two men and consider them caste pariahs. Moreover, the Brahmans take "an oath that their children's children should never marry with the grandsons and granddaughters of Chellaya and Chittampalam" (284). Throughout the years, the stigma of the social alienation of these two families survives, each family having to go to distant villages to marry. Yet Woolf also suggests that this prejudice is linked to greed and pride. For when many generations have passed and the great-great-great-grandsons of Chellaya and Chittampalam consider marriage between their son and daughter, their marriage negotiations break down over the question of the dowry. Each man reveals his greed, and their talk degenerates into name-calling—"fisher, low caste dog, pariah" (286)—thus reviving the old social caste discrimination and alienation which cannot be broken.

Return to England

Stories from the East and *The Village in the Jungle* reveal that when Woolf returned to England, his views about British rule in the East, about the conflict between emotions and social conventions, and about class and caste barriers continued to be important to him. He incorporated these concerns, attacking racial and class prejudice of Christians and Jews alike and portraying the way such prejudice leads to alienation and unhappiness, into his only other short story, "Three Jews," written in 1917, and published in one of the earliest Hogarth Press publications, *Two Stories*. In "Three Jews," Woolf again presents a double narrative. The first narrator describes a Sunday, the first day of spring, when the air has an "inevitable little touch of sadness."[14] The narrator also describes himself as "restless" with "nowhere to go," because all his friends are out of town. Since he wants to have closer contact with nature, he goes to Kew Gardens. There he observes the English people. Couples and families seem "happy in their quiet orderly English way" (6). Soon, however, he notices a man with a "dark fat face and . . . sensual mouth . . . a clever face, dark and inscrutable" (7), who is sitting at a table drinking tea. The man comes to the narrator's table, and the narrator realizes they have something in common: "You knew me at once and I knew you. We show up don't we, under the appleblossom and this sky. It doesn't belong to us, do you wish it did?" (8) The man agrees with the narrator and comments on their alienation: "We belong to Palestine still" (9). He then proceeds to tell the narrator a story about another Jew.

On a cold November day, the anniversary of his first wife's death, the second Jew goes to the cemetery to visit her grave. This, he reveals to the first Jew, is "sentiment.... No one can say we Jews haven't got that, and family affection. They're among our very strongest characteristics" (11). At the same time, he comments on anti-Semitism: "They don't like us.... We're too clever, perhaps, too sharp, too go-ahead.... But they can't deny us our other virtues—sentiment and family affection" (10). At the cemetery, the cemetery-keeper, also a Jew, approaches. In their conversation about death, the cemetery-keeper reveals his skepticism about belief in God. He attributes his free-thinking to a change in the times: "One don't have to believe everything now; it was different when I was young. You had to believe everything then; you had to believe everything they told you in Schul. Now you may think for yourself" (13). The second Jew is sad about this loss of tradition and faith; he comments: "We're Jews only externally now, in our black hair and our large noses, in the way we stand and the way we walk. But inside we're Jews no longer" (14).

The following year, when the second Jew again visits the cemetery, the cemetery-keeper is in mourning for his wife, but he still expresses pride in his two sons. Before the two Jews part, the second Jew gives the cemetery-keeper a shilling. Another year passes, and when the narrator again meets the cemetery-keeper, he notices him looking "seedy through and through ... gone all to bits. And yet ... there was something in him that still stood up and held him together, something like a rock which, beaten and buffeted still held out indomitable" (16–17). The cemetery-keeper reveals his misfortune to the second Jew; he has disowned his son for marrying a Christian serving girl. This is beyond his dignity, as he claims he could have accepted a Christian, but not a servant girl. This sense of pride and class discrimination the narrator cannot condone. Unable to offer the cemetery-keeper a shilling, the second Jew leaves the third Jew "brooding over his son and his graves" (18), an ending which suggests that Woolf links death with class and racial prejudice.

Woolf's second novel, *The Wise Virgins,* published in 1914, is probably his least-known work, for it has been out of print and largely unavailable. In his autobiography, Woolf commented on the reception to the book, that "the war killed it dead and my total earnings from it were £20."[15] This apparently indicated to him that he would not be able to earn a living as a writer of fiction, so he turned his energies toward social work and journalism. *The Wise Virgins* portrays Woolf's view of English society after he returned from Ceylon. Although it was exciting for him to be back in the atmosphere of Cambridge, he noted some changes:

What was so exhilarating in Cambridge . . . was the sense of profound intimacy with a number of people whom one liked and who were passionately interested in the same things and pursued the same ends . . . . What was so new and so exhilarating to me in the Gordon Square of July, 1911 was the sense of intimacy and complete freedom of thought and speech, much wider than in the Cambridge society of seven years ago, and above all including women.[16]

Woolf immersed himself in Gordon Square society, soon becoming involved with Virginia Stephen, whom he married in 1912.

The Wise Virgins is based on aspects of Woolf's life. Some critics consider it to be "a poem in praise of his wife, and the literary expression of his love for her,"[17] while other critics feel the novel reveals Woolf's fears of love and marriage.[18] Perhaps both elements are present, but it is interesting that what connects this work with Woolf's experiences in Ceylon and his earlier fiction is his examination of social, economic, ethnic, and intellectual barriers in a class society. In the novel, Woolf portrays class barriers and antagonisms between a wealthly Kensington family, the Lawrences, modeled after Leslie Stephen and his family, and a Jewish family in Richstead, the Davises, representing Woolf's family. Woolf himself characterized the difference in economic situation and outlook between the two families: "I learnt by experience as a child and a youth to be insecure and comparatively

poor," whereas "Virginia's experience had been very different
and had had a very different effect upon her. Her family belonged
to the Victorian professional upper middle-class which was
financially as impregnably secure as (almost) the Bank of
England."[19] Aside from economic differences and in regard to the
question of Woolf's ethnic consciousness, Duncan Wilson writes
that *The Wise Virgins* indicates that a young man "could be very
sensitive about his Jewishness when courting . . . a brilliant girl . . .
from an established English family."[20] Yet since Woolf has not
written elsewhere about racial prejudice in his personal relationships, he seems to have portrayed religious and ethnic difference
and discrimination in both "Three Jews" and *The Wise Virgins*
primarily as part of his examination of the effects of social
structure in a class society on individual and communal psychology.

Through the narrative voice in the opening pages of the novel,
Woolf comments that, behind the facade of civilization, modern
man is still an animal with possessive and animalistic sexual
urges; also, despite conformity in taste, man maintains a strong
sense of individuality.[21] In contrast to this view of modern man,
Woolf describes the quiet, comfortable suburban life of Richstead
through two families, the Garlands and the Davises; however, all
is not placidity and contentment. One of the Garland daughters,
Gwen, yearns for adventure. As she reads fiction, she feels "not a
bit like the people in books—they're so superior" (17). She is
attracted to Harry Davis, who is "rather foreign looking and
artistic" (18), and who rebels against the conventional living and
thinking of the middle classes. Harry has a look of "discontent,
discomfort, almost suffering" (37). When his mother complains
about a servant who has left them, he comments angrily on the
oppression of the working classes: "They won't stay . . . because
they're not treated like human beings" (31). He also challenges
the anti-Semitism prevalent among the middle classes by
expressing his feelings outwardly about his sense of alienation
because of ethnic discrimination.

When the Garlands discover that the Davises are Jews, only
Gwen is eager to learn what they are like. Her sister May is

annoyed and thinks that "it was rather a bore that these Jews should come and dump themselves down at Richstead and her set" (21). Even more hostile is May's comment, "I hate Jews" (48). Harry, in turn, is aware of their dislike, covert or overt. He later comments on his sense of powerlessness as an outsider in society to one of the young men visiting the Lawrence household: "You can glide out of the room and I can't: I envy you that! But I despise you...I admire your women, your pale women with their white skins and fair hair, but I despise them...there's no life in you, no blood in you, no understanding. Pale hair, pale soul" (77). Later, Harry defines his Jewishness in terms of intense feeling and a need for action in a conversation with Camilla Lawrence: "We aren't as pleasant or as beautiful as you are. We're hard and grasping, we're out after definite things, different things, which we think worthwhile" (157). He also comments that having ideals distinguishes Jews from non-Jews, who "don't know what they're after; they haven't got the imagination for it" (159).

A young friend of the Lawrence family, Arthur Wodehouse, also reveals racial hatred, claiming to Harry that his not having been in love is "a characteristic of your race—they've intellect and not emotion; they don't feel things" (133). Later, at the Lawrences', more anti-Semitic remarks are made behind Harry's back by another visitor, Wilton, who refers to Harry as "that Jew fellow" (140) and comments that "there has never been a good Jew artist, and there never will be...they're too like Davis—too cold and clammy. They're just like crabs or lobsters. They give me the creeps" (141). Harry feels this racial hatred keenly; he dreams of "standing up on some raised platform above a crowd, a hostile crowd threatening him. Stones were thrown, there was blood on his face" (142). He becomes discouraged about the possibility of developing close relationships: "The only bonds between human beings seemed to be dislike and scorn and jeering and envy; otherwise, completely isolated, they staggered and strayed through life" (143). Similarly, he later thinks that the rigidity of the class system in Richmond is stronger than the caste system in India. Harry's sentiments are reinforced by other characters. For example, Gwen realizes the nature of class barriers when she meets Camilla Lawrence and recognizes that "it was Camilla she hated, and she envied her for all the graces, beauty, cleverness, and culture with which she endowed her" (187). Finally, Camilla also comments on class barriers as she calls the young women of Richstead "poor wretches" (190), because "they are bored to death... they are lost and they know it" (191). At the same time, she is critical of her own class, wondering if the people of Richstead whom she scorns do not have more nobility than those of her own class, with their "vanities and frills, intellectual and moral" (200).

Despite Harry's Jewish intensity of intellect and emotion, he is drawn to simplicity; thus, the "freshness and prettiness" of Gwen Garland appeals to him: "It would be pleasant to be like that—to have what is called a simple outlook. Complexity—that's the curse of human existence. Life must be so simple to a creature like that, so free of desires and difficulties. And wasn't it really just as good?" (98) Nevertheless, Harry needs the intellectual and emotional stimulation of a more complex temperament. Thus, he urges Gwen to learn more about life and sets her on this course by encouraging her to read Dostoevski and Ibsen. At the same time, his relationship with Camilla Lawrence develops.

Camilla is a young painter who finds Harry intriguing: "He was so different from the other boyish students... so obviously hard and clever, and there seemed under the crust to be something intricate and perhaps violent. She wanted—it was purely curiosity—to see, if possible, what it might be" (56). Harry, in turn, finds Camilla attractive; she is "romantic, mysterious," and he notes "the purity of her face and her voice: the remoteness of a virgin" (56). Since he was a child, Harry has needed something romantic, yet he also longs for a "certain fierceness of love, mental and bodily" (62). He has to confront the possibility of a lack of feeling in Camilla. One of her suitors comments: "She's a woman and a virgin.... They simply don't know what desire is" (137). To Harry, Camilla seems remote, like a fine lady, "something not to be touched" (154). Camilla also thinks about her temperament when she and her sister Katharine discuss love: "But I'm not cold, am I? I couldn't be so very attractive if I were.

I'm very affectionate... I like silk and kisses and soft things and strokings. I was told the other day that I was like the hills with virgin snow on them; but that's nonsense, isn't it?" (118)[22] Katharine believes that Camilla was not "made for marriage... for a husband and children and middle-aged domesticity" (121). She senses Camilla would not be satisfied with love, but would be "wanting to go on to something beyond" (122). As Harry realizes his deepening love for Camilla, he feels more manly, yet Camilla's remoteness prevents him from feeling at peace with his love. And when she rejects his declaration of love, he despairs, noticing only the physical defects in the people who pass him on the street, and seeing women as "ridiculous, grotesque, repulsive" (216).

When the two Richstead families, the Garlands and Davises, vacation together in Eastbourne, Gwen notices Harry's unhappiness. They are brought into a closer intimacy than in Richstead. After reading Ibsen's *The Master Builder*, which Harry has given to her, Gwen sees herself in a similar relationship to Harry as Hilda is to Solness. At first, however, she is frightened by Harry's emphasis on love and sexual experience as the key to meaning in life. Nevertheless, she longs "to prove herself by some daring act or noble passion" (277), and she declares her love for Harry. He rejects her, but soon a sense of responsibility for his actions develops, and he debates the possibility of happiness with her: "*Could* he marry her? After all, Camilla would never love him. It might be comfortable with Gwen—but God! how tired he would grow of that child's face.... And yet it was his fault. She might do anything" (293). Later, when Gwen comes to Harry's room, she appears to him "extraordinarily beautiful. A little movement of desire, cruel and beautiful ran through him" (299). After their lovemaking, he exults in having proved his manhood; at the same time, he is sick and faint at the thought of marrying her: "he despised, loathed himself, for not having seen what she was" (308). A sense of doom develops: "So ended dreams and the romance of life. The brave, wild words, the revolt of youth, the splendour of love" (310); his life would now be just like all the others in Richstead he has scorned. On the day of his marriage,

the smell of dead leaves blows in through the window of the
railway carriage and Harry thinks that "he had failed, failed,
failed." There was only a small "wave of happiness.... He had
known Camilla: he had loved her" (335).

The absence of a conventional happy ending to the Camilla-
Harry romance is surprising to the reader, particularly because
the fictional couple parallels Leonard Woolf and Virginia Stephen, who do marry. Yet while Woolf seems to have used
autobiographical elements as the material for fiction, his thematic concerns in the novel go beyond autobiographical experience. The narrator's comments at the beginning of the novel on
human nature and on the tendency of sentimentality and conventional behavior of suburban life to engulf one, establish a level of
realism about human experience which Woolf maintains through
characterization and plot. Still, to the literary critic, the novel has
structural weaknesses and stylistic awkwardness. For example,
Woolf frequently presents thematic points too obviously, indeed
almost didactically, through the narrator's voice as well as
through the speeches of the characters. Similarly, there are
descriptive sections in which details often become heavy-handed
symbols, and finally, some of the characters verge on stereotypes.
Nevertheless, there is compelling development of the three main
characters—Harry, Camilla, and Gwen—and some strikingly
poetic description.

After reading *The Wise Virgins*, Virginia Woolf wrote: "My
opinion is that its a remarkable book, very bad in parts; first rate
in others... I was made very happy by reading this: I like the
poetic side of L. & it gets a little smothered in Blue-books, and
organisations."[23] As Virginia Woolf's comment indicates, this
barely known novel, like *Diaries in Ceylon* and the short stories,
reveals an idealistic, poetic, even romantic side of Leonard
Woolf's temperament, which contrasts with the realistic, intellectual side. The former emphasizes the importance of individual
fulfillment, spiritual love, and physical passion, while the latter
analyzes the effects of social structure—class, racial and intellectual differences—on individual consciousness and interpersonal
relationships.

The Ceylon diaries and fiction of the years 1904 to 1918 represent the beginning of Leonard Woolf's political and literary work. His firsthand observations of British colonial rule in the East, recorded objectively and fictionally, continued to be of concern to him in his studies of war, international government, and imperialism, which dominate the years 1914 to 1929, and which are related to his analyses of civilization and barbarism, fascism, anti-Semitism, and World War II. Although Woolf never wrote fiction again, he remained involved with the craft of writing through his work with the Hogarth Press and his literary criticism for various journals. *Growing*, the title of the autobiography of this early period, thus aptly emphasizes this continuity of the personal, social, and literary concerns which began in this period and extended throughout Leonard Woolf's work and life.

Chapter Three

Increasing Social Consciousness: Studies on War, International Government, and Imperialism

Woolf's early political education, which was shaped in Ceylon by the social and class systems of the British and the Ceylonese, in turn influenced his view of social and economic life when he returned to England. Woolf first plunged back into the intellectual life of Cambridge associates and the circle of writers and artists later known as the Bloomsbury Group. After a few months of reestablishing friendships and reacquainting himself with various aspects of English society, he settled down to write *The Village in the Jungle*. At this time, he was living on the fourth floor of the house which Virginia and Adrian Stephen were renting. Woolf's close friendship with Virginia Stephen soon developed into a love relationship. Although Virginia was not ready to commit herself to marriage, Woolf decided to apply for an extension of his leave from the civil service. When his request was denied, Woolf resigned. Some months later, however, Virginia agreed to marry him, and after their marriage in August 1912, Woolf continued to work on *The Village in the Jungle* while Virginia was writing *The Voyage Out*. Since, as Woolf explained in *Beginning Again*, their writing did not provide a "regular or even probable means of earning the £400 or £500 which we needed to cover our expenditure,"[1] he decided to give up writing novels and to turn more to journalism. It was also at this time that he began his political work.

Woolf's experiences in Ceylon led him to comment about political responsibility that "once one has been personally concerned with communal affairs and has felt personally responsible for them, one can never again escape the feeling of political responsibility" (49). This sense of personal political responsibility grew as he studied the social and economic system of England. His first political efforts developed through a cousin of Virginia's, Marny Vaughan, and involved working with the Care Committee of the Charity Organization Society. The poverty of the East End of London was appalling, and Woolf commented that "I would rather have lived in a hut in a Ceylon village in the jungle than in the poverty stricken, sordid, dilapidated, god-forsaken hovels of Hoxton" (11). He found the Care Committee's efforts to deal with such poverty paternalistic and ineffectual, and thus realized that the only solution would be a social revolution. This insight turned him "from a liberal into a socialist" and led to his involvement with the Co-operative Movement (11). Although Woolf felt the Co-operative Movement embodied the drab and dreary aspects of working-class life, he also realized that the workers had an important, "passionate belief in a social ideal" (104). Later, his work for the Co-operative Movement led to two full-length studies, *Co-operation and the Future of Industry* and *Socialism and Co-operation.*

An article Woolf wrote for the *New Statesman* in June 1913 about the Newcastle Congress of the Women's Co-operative Guild, which discussed a possible alliance among the Co-operative Movement, the Trade Unionists, and the Labour party, attracted the attention of Sidney and Beatrice Webb, the leaders of the Fabian Society. Woolf soon became a member of the Fabian Society and a writer for the *New Statesman*, which the Webbs had founded as a weekly publication. Neither the Webbs nor other Fabian Society members were particularly knowledgeable about foreign policy. Woolf was therefore able to provide valuable expertise in the area of international affairs, and when George Bernard Shaw suggested a thorough study for the Fabian Society on the need for a system of international law to prevent war, Woolf was asked to undertake the project. The report, entitled *International Government*, was first produced in installments, then discussed thoroughly by the Fabian Society Research

Department, and finally published as a supplement to the *New Statesman*.

International Government

In *Beginning Again*, Woolf states his position on war: "I have never been a complete pacifist; once the war had broken out it seemed to me that the Germans must be resisted and I therefore could not be a conscientious objector" (177). Yet, Dr. Maurice Wright, who had treated him for his problem of trembling hands, advised him that his induction into the army would be likely to affect Virginia's mental health adversely, so Woolf received a complete medical exemption from military service. As a result, he channeled his antiwar energies directly into political work. In his study for the Fabian Society on international government, Woolf sought to dismiss certain commonly held beliefs which he felt were barriers to international government: that national interests are opposed; that international politics is like the Darwinian struggle of survival of the fittest; and that international government involves a sacrifice of sovereignty. Moreover, Woolf recognized that many "apparently well-informed people" believed that arbitration was the way to prevent war (185). In contrast to these views, Woolf's study, based on extensive research of such original sources as "Blue Books and White Books and annual reports dealing with... vast international organizations" as well as interviews with civil servants and representatives to international conferences (187), emphasized the importance of international law.

International Government soon established Woolf as an authority on the problems of peace and war, and such respected editors as H. M. Massingham of the *Nation* and Clifford Sharp of the *New Statesman* asked him to write on foreign affairs. Woolf commented in *Beginning Again* that *International Government* also had an important effect on world affairs, by influencing the committees which developed proposals for the League of Nations (189). Part II of the study, which describes the existing types of international cooperation, has been considered "the most original as well as the most influential part of Woolf's work on international organizations,"[2] and Part III has been described as a "direct ancestor of the Covenant of the League of Nations and the Charter of the United Nations" (71).

International Government begins with Woolf's comments that World War I revealed both how men had not ceased to desire war, and how social progress can be destroyed by a relapse into barbarism which war represents. To prevent war, Woolf argues, there must be laws and rules of conduct, as well as peaceful methods of settling disputes. Woolf defines four types of international disputes, those arising from legal, financial, political, and social relationships. Laws to maintain peace must be made consciously, not developed through custom. If no such laws exist, then nations try to regulate their relations by individual contracts or treaties. Treaties have developed in the past as the primary means to ensure peace, but they pose two problems: how to guarantee that they will be carried out, and how to alter them.[3] Moreover, Woolf points out that "the great treaties which were designed to introduce a millennium of peace have been precisely those which turned out to be the most dangerous threateners of war" (19–20). Similarly, congresses, such as the Congress of Vienna and the Holy Alliance, which were supposed to develop a Federation of Europe with a constitution and a legislative assembly, became "merely the meetings of diplomatists negotiating to maintain the agreement and alliance of a few powerful States" (32). Nevertheless, Woolf believed that the international conferences which settled the question of the Greek revolt for independence from Turkey in 1821 "were the central point of a new, if rudimentary, international system" (42). The participating states, which did not include Turkey and Greece, studied the facts and presented a basis for reconciliation. Similarly, during the Balkan wars in 1876–89, states met at the Conference of Constantinople and presented proposals to Turkey, even agreeing to send an international police force into the Balkan Peninsula. In a sense, this conference acted not as a mediator but as an international legislative organ, and was treating Turkey as a member of a community of European states.

The Hague Conference, established in 1899, was intended to be an international organization to maintain peace. As a lawmaking body, it faced two problems in settling disputes—arbitration methods and voting power. On the question of arbitration, Woolf comments that two types exist: in the first, the arbitrator bases his decision on law; in the second, on his judgment of a reasonable decision. The first method poses a problem, since international law is not comprehensive enough to cover all aspects of international relationships. Woolf asserts that the important aim of international government is not to establish "an imposing permanent tribunal, but to make an agreement to arbitrate operative by providing a court in which that agreement can be carried out" (91). Although the Hague Tribunal does provide the basis for settling judicial questions, it is up to the member nations to consider the tribunal's decisions binding. Woolf argues further that a problem arises in the appointing of judges to the tribunal. If all constituent nations participate, agreement would be too difficult, yet if small states do not participate, "an absolute world-hegemony of the Great Powers" would develop (93). An appropriate plan to alleviate this problem would give each state the right to appoint a judge, and would allow "the judges appointed by the Great Powers to sit continuously" (94).

Included in Woolf's discussion of the prevention of war is an analysis of the psychology of crisis and war: "War between two nations under modern conditions is impossible unless you get a large number of people in each nation excited and afraid" (133). With an atmosphere of crisis, politicians can easily manipulate public opinion. An international conference, however, can counteract this atmosphere of crisis by providing a forum for calm, lengthy discussion, which would prevent fear and the exploitation of fear and ignorance, which "unreasonable excitement" fosters. Most important, though, the conference would assert that nations "have the right collectively to settle questions which imperil the peace of the world" (135).

Woolf also discusses and rejects those beliefs which are barriers to international government. For example, many people consider war to be a "natural and necessary corollary of the existence of States" (143), and they therefore believe that international government is impossible. Similarly, others contend that international hostility arises because individuals in one nation consider themselves to be different and, often, superior to individuals of other nations, or they believe that their national interests are threatened by another nation. Woolf counters this argument by claiming that in the last century, people have recognized that national interests are international interests (150). Continual contact between countries because of railways, steamships, and communications systems has established a "network of international intercourse" (155); as a result, a system of international government encompassing political relations, trade, finance, health, and other areas has developed. Thus, Woolf claims that "there is hardly a sphere of life in which a consciousness of international interests has not penetrated" (166). Woolf also traces in detail the growth and structure of international administration in the areas of communications, shipping, railways, and health. Agriculture, for example, is an international area because it involves international trade, international finance, exchange of scientific information, international health issues, and political relations. Similarly, a study of shipping reveals how "cosmopolitan law," or the "process of unifying the law over a wide stretch of territory under the jurisdiction of a number of independent States," is part of the growth of international government (268).

Discussing the relationship of labor to international government, Woolf points out that the interests of the small class of capitalists in each nation dominate the interests of the wage-earners. Often, industrialists protest against state regulations of industry, claiming that they will destroy a particular industry which is vital to national security (289). In addition, employers in one country frequently refuse to adopt particular measures if employers in other countries refuse to do the same. Woolf argues that capitalists realize that applying international government in the area of labor legislation is likely to strengthen the position of the working masses within each country in their struggle against exploitation. Thus, the capitalist and industrial classes actually oppose international government because they know it will weaken their power over their fellow citizens, rather than because it will weaken their position in relation to foreigners, as they argue. Woolf comments further that the first person to recognize the need for international labor legislation was Robert Owen in 1818. Although Owen's efforts were later continued by Daniel Legrand, it was not until the second half of the nineteenth century that a voluntary association for labor legislation was formed (291). This organization created two international treaties for unifying national laws. At the same time, industrial and commercial standardization had developed to control the quality of materials used in production.

Woolf's response to the remaining argument against international government—that it would endanger vital national issues—strongly restates his main points throughout *International Government*: "The most vital interests of human beings are hardly ever national, almost always international. The interests which most nearly affect a man's life are those of the international group—e.g., labor or capital, to which he belongs, not of his national group" (354). Woolf therefore argues that international government develops out of the mode of modern life, for the material benefit of the masses of individuals within each country, and for the purpose of assuring world peace. To support this last point, he insists that the territorial integrity of the national state will be respected, and that political independence will be fostered by an international government created to regulate international relations in order to prevent war.

Woolf was to return to the problems of international government and war several times more throughout his life. At this time, however, other political developments in the post–World War I period deepened his political consciousness. Among these were the events of the Russian Revolution in 1917. In *Beginning Again*, Woolf states that "all Labour people—nearly all people in England—hated the Tsarist régime" and were unhappy about being an ally of Russia during the war (211). A Labour party convention in June 1917 which Woolf attended gave its support to the Russian Revolution. Woolf, however, comments with historical hindsight that "the intelligent revolutionary knows... that all revolutions must disappoint him" (215); his analysis of the development of socialism and communism elsewhere in his autobiography, in *Barbarians Within and Without* and *Quack, Quack!*, and in his play *The Hotel*, reveals his disillusion with a social revolution which had overturned the destructive Tsarist regime but had failed to fulfill its promise of a new, civilized society.

At this time, Woolf also became involved with developing Labour party policy to enable it to compete with the Conservative and Liberal parties. When Sidney Webb was forming four or five advisory committees of people with expertise on policymaking, he asked Woolf to become secretary of the committee dealing with international and imperial questions; this committee later split into two, and Woolf remained the secretary of both for over twenty years. As Woolf continued to study international government issues and plans, he also became involved with Ceylon affairs. He writes in *Beginning Again* that civil rioting in Kandy and Colombo had led to martial law, and when a delegation from Ceylon was sent to England to appeal to the Secretary of State for the Colonies to examine the sentencing of civilians in Ceylon, Woolf worked with the delegation to present its case (229–30).

In 1917, Woolf published *The Framework of a Lasting Peace* as part of his work for the League of Nations Society, which he had helped Goldsworthy Lowes Dickinson to establish in 1915. This volume included an introductory essay which Woolf wrote for the March 1917 issue of *War and Peace*, and the drafts of the following peace proposals: Minimum Programme of the Central Organization for a Durable Peace, The Hague; The League of Nations Society; Proposals of Lord Bryce's Groups; The Fabian Society Draft Treaty; The Community of Nations; and Preliminary Draft of a General Treaty for the Pacific Settlement of International Disputes, by a Dutch Committee. As in *International Government*, Woolf addresses the problem of "the creation or development of political inter-state institutions for maintaining peace and preventing war," and again he argues that although war will not cease without "the will to peace," that will can be fostered by political institutions.[4]

Woolf's main aim in *The Framework of a Lasting Peace* is to analyze the various peace proposals, to demonstrate the similarities between them, and to indicate which areas are the most valuable. Each peace group recognizes that the relationships between nations can be regulated either by force or by general rules. Having stated their preference for international relationships being regulated according to rules, two problems arise: how to establish the rules, and how to apply them to particular cases. Woolf concedes that the existing rules of international law have developed through custom; very few have been made "deliberately and consciously at conferences called for the express purpose of international legislation" (26). To Woolf, rectifying this situation was of utmost importance in the post–World War I world.

Each of the peace groups proposes that a judicial tribunal exist which will impartially resolve justiciable disputes, or those international questions covered by general rules. As a result, any nation which refuses to follow the decision of the international tribunal will be rejecting the basic agreement to regulate relations by law. In addition, for those disputes not covered by international law, two alternatives exist: to extend the scope of international law so that more disputes will be subject to judicial settlement; or to provide other methods for settling nonjusticiable disputes. For the latter, nations will have to choose between conciliation and arbitration. Almost all the groups presenting plans for international government primarily propose conciliation as a method of resolving nonjusticiable disputes; however, the Fabian Society urges conciliation first and then arbitration. Woolf reasserts this emphasis on arbitration, which he defines as having an "independent body ... of reasonable and unprejudiced people to say what appears to be a just and fair decision" (231–32). This method had already been incorporated into the Hague Convention and had been used successfully to resolve the Dogger Bank incident between Russia and Great Britain.

On the question of an international legislature for making the rules, Woolf emphasizes the need for international conferences. This point is embodied in the plans of the League to Enforce Peace and the Fabian Society. As Woolf points out, the need for international government has developed so that "in recent years, where dangerous international disputes have arisen . . . the question of how the disputes should be settled, whether by conference or tribunal or other pacific machinery, has itself been a most prominent part of the controversy" (54). Establishing an international legislature would allow for a regular and immediate resolution of international conflict. The question of membership in the League, or in any body of international government, is the last important issue Woolf considers. The admission of small states to the Hague Conferences increased the difficulty of obtaining agreement among nations; moreover, the possibility of small states becoming an overwhelming majority presented a problem about voting power. Woolf emphasizes that this problem is best resolved by the Fabian Society plan, which gives the right of admission to all small states, but makes "elaborate provision as to separate International Councils and as to voting power" (56).

Throughout *The Framework of a Lasting Peace,* Woolf stresses that international government is not a utopian scheme. History has proven that international tribunals, commissions of inquiry, and international conferences have been effective in settling disputes and developing rules for international relations. International government for Woolf is thus the only choice for man, since regulating international relations by international law, Woolf maintains, will result in civilized behavior.

During the years that Woolf was working for the Labour party, the Ceylonese delegation to England, and the League of Nations Society, he was also writing *The Future of Constantinople* as part of his continuing study of the problems of war. Woolf focuses on Constantinople as "the chief European centre of international unrest,"[5] a "breeding-ground of hatred and covetousness and war" (12). To ensure peace, Woolf argues, the problem of Constantinople cannot be resolved along national and imperialist lines, but international lines. Constantinople has been dominated by the imperialist and nationalistic ambitions of France, Russia, Austria, Germany, and Britain; at the same time, it has been used to "oppress at least five European subject races" (14). To counteract this history of oppression, war, and imperialism, Woolf proposes an international policy, claiming that "international interests are often promoted better by international co-operation than by international competition" (16).

Woolf also points out that Constantinople has been politically important because of its geographical position between the Black Sea and the Mediterranean, one of the most strategic areas for commerce and trade. Although freedom of navigation on many waterways had been maintained by international government or by international guarantee since 1814, assuring international passage in the Bosphorus, Sea of Marmora, and Dardanelles would mean international control over the waters and the narrow strip of land on either side (26). Thus, Constantinople should not be controlled by a single state, but by an international government. Woolf claims that a similar need for international control of the Danube existed, and in order to ensure free right of way over the Danube, several states agreed to give up sovereign rights over the sections of the river on their territories (47). To support this, they established an independent administrative body, the European Commission, to supervise the river. Woolf traces the constitutional history of the European Commission to reveal how it may provide a model for an international administration of the Straits. He argues that the Danube was administered so efficiently that the number of shipwrecks decreased, the volume of river traffic increased, and the commission's revenue increased, even though the navigation dues were gradually reduced (67–69).

Woolf envisions an international administrative body similar to the European Commission of the Danube operating in Constantinople. In times of peace, it would maintain freedom of commerce and navigation, law and order, sanitation and public health; it would also levy taxes to meet its expenses and develop a judicial system for dealing with infringements of regulations. Considering a solution to Constantinople in times of war, Woolf points out that Russia must feel that no state will have the power to use Constantinople as part of an offensive strategy against her. This point supports the importance of having the International Commission "provide for the neutralization and disarmament of the territory" (92). All the powers signing a treaty to keep the Straits open in times of peace and war would also have to agree to take action against any state which attempted to violate the neutrality of the Straits (95). Finally, Woolf comments that "Constantinople is a test case of the success of the Allies' aims in the war" (97). If it is settled in a nationalistic and imperialistic manner, nations will be creating the same political environment which led to World War I. The alternative to this, which involves choosing international government, would ensure peace, for if Constantinople would not be in the hands of a single power, no nation would be aggressive or defensive, and thus could not instigate war.

Empire and Commerce in Africa

Woolf's next major work, *Empire and Commerce in Africa*, written in 1918, examined European expansion and control in Africa and established Woolf's anti-imperialist views. Although the Fabian Society position was basically in support of the Empire, well-known journalists such as J. A. Hobson, Norman Angell, and H. N. Brailsford were arguing that imperialism did not benefit the interests of the nation as a whole, and, moreover, that it led to international conflict which further undermined the nation's interests.[6] *Empire and Commerce in Africa* grew out of a Fabian society project. Woolf was asked by the Fabian Society Executive Committee to write a study of international trade, but when he discovered that the area was too broad, he attacked the problem of trade between an imperial power and its colonies, focusing primarily on Africa.

The study begins with Woolf's historical survey of the development of the state from a vested interest of the ruling family to a unified entity influenced by the ideologies of democracy, nationalism, and industrialism, which emerged in the nineteenth cen-

tury. In the twentieth century, Woolf argues, the main function of
the state is "the pursuit of national economic interests by means
of organized national power."[7] As a result, industry and commerce become "the greatest of political interests" (10) and dominate foreign policy, while material profit becomes the main
standard of value. Unlike imperialism before 1800, which was
"partly religious, partly dynastic, partly economic, and partly
sentimental" (22), nineteenth- and twentieth-century imperialism is primarily economic. Woolf emphasizes that economic
motives influenced traders, shippers, and financiers of the various European nations to expand into Africa.

Control of African territory and resources by European nations
began in the late 1870s. Although an international committee for
the purposes of science and exploration had already been established in 1878, one year later, the imperialist pattern of economic
penetration began when stations were established along the
Congo and treaties with native chiefs were signed. Britain then
sought to become involved in 1884 by having its ally Portugal
control the Congo. Even though the 1884 Congo Conference in
Berlin was seemingly called to establish international cooperation, rather than commercial competition (43), none of the
European nations acted in accord with the principles of the
conference. From this point on, European nations persisted in
economic penetration, so that by the early twentieth century
Abyssinia was the only portion of Africa not under complete
control of a European nation.

Part I of *Empire and Commerce in Africa* traces the history of
involvement by each European nation in Africa. At the same
time, Woolf is mainly concerned with revealing how the dominant ideas of imperialist expansion were false. He points first to
the notion that the possession of Algeria by France affected the
balance of power of European nations or the status quo in the
Mediterranean area. Although these fears also shaped British and
French foreign policy, they proved to have "no relation to existing facts or future realities" (80). For, as Woolf emphasizes in his
analysis of the French control of Tunis, economic motives were
the primary cause of action. In Tunis, French financiers estab-

lished an economic alliance with the ruling power, the Bey. As the Bey became heavily in debt to European money-lenders, he taxed the people to the point where they rebelled, and civil disorder in turn led to further European intervention. Woolf sums up these events as a predictable pattern: political power is used to acquire economic control; economic interests become a pretext for political control; and political control is used to promote economic interest (93–94).

Woolf analyzes similar patterns of action in the struggle between France and England for control over the valley of the Nile. Ethiopian Abyssinia was distinctive as the only African territory not under the control of a European state. Woolf attributes this to the dominance of Christian religion and ancient cultural traditions which foster national cohesiveness. Moreover, Ethiopia had had a history of strong central government, yet in the period 1868–1872, Ethiopia faced both internal struggle among native chiefs and external struggle with the advancing of troops from Egypt. This civil unrest and the aggression from Egypt were checked by 1880, just at the time that European nations began to play off their powers for control over the area, generating appeals to patriotism within their countries to eliminate foreign control. Woolf comments: "Neither France nor the British Empire had the slightest right to the possession either of Egypt or the Sudan or the Nile. The claims of each state, when they are stripped of the fig-leaves of diplomacy and patriotic journalism, are based upon economic imperialism and nothing else" (193). The conflict between France and England culminated in the Fashoda incident in the late 1890s, after which France withdrew, indicating that the major powers were acting in agreement with "the principle that the territory of Africa should belong to the European State which was strong enough to seize and to hold it" (195); thus, in the valley of the Nile, England had proven to be the stronger power.

Woolf's analysis of imperialism seems to assess the actions of European nations in terms of good and evil. He recognizes the "abominable cruelties" and "dishonest economic exploitation" of the African natives (258), and writes that these actions indicate

that "all European States, in different degrees, have shown themselves absolutely unfit to own African colonies" (259). For example, Woolf examines the course of imperialism in Eastern Africa,
commenting that the taking of slaves created a state of anarchy in
Africa which was "probably unparalleled in the history of the
human race" (229). Furthermore, the effects of economic imperialism have been overwhelmingly destructive for the Africans,
who were dispossessed of their land and forced to work for white
settlers in order to pay their taxes; as a result, white settlers came
to dominate African countries, controlling land and commerce by
virtue of having the armed forces of a European state at their
command. Woolf is similarly critical of the methods of exploitation by Germany and England in Eastern Africa. These countries
managed to get the Sultan of Zanzibar to give up half his territory, including the rich hinterland and the strip of coast land.
Although British historians of the time fostered the view that the
Sultan voluntarily gave up these territories to avoid possibility of
invasion, Woolf analyzes the official history of the British East
Africa Company by Sir William Mackinnon and Mr. McDermott,
and points out how the accounts by British historians are distor-
tions of historical reality.

Woolf further argues that the destructive effects of imperialism in Africa "can never be atoned for," yet he believes that
twentieth-century Europe must make "some amends to Africa
for the crimes and cruelties of the nineteenth" (259). The ideology or beliefs and desires which state that the power of a nation
can be and should be used to promote the economic interests of its
citizens—i.e., the doctrine of economic imperialism, as followed
by nineteenth-century European nations—is for Woolf a course
of action which destroys the idea of moral responsibility; thus,
"the right of Europe to civilize became the right of Europe to rob
or to exploit the uncivilized" (352–53). The amends Woolf considers suitable would be an end to the colonial system and the
development of a new system assuring integrity to the Africans.
In addition, European nations must recognize that imperialism
has not benefited Europe. Woolf comments that "it is extremely
doubtful whether the possession of an African Empire has added

to the power of any European State: it is certain that it has in no case added to their wealth" (314). Most European states, for example, had to commit more military energy to Africa than they received in return. Moreover, as capitalists and politicians pursued economic imperialism, they believed they were acquiring more resources and markets for the state, but Woolf again emphasizes that "the economic beliefs behind economic imperialism are dreams and delusions" (333). Although people have believed that, by controlling a foreign territory, a state could assure the raw materials for itself, European states have not succeeded in "reserving the raw materials in their African possessions for their own industries and industrialists," because "raw materials are mainly exploited by European capital" which sells them to the highest bidder (335).

Woolf's final concern focuses on how European nations can substitute a constructive policy in Africa for their pattern of economic exploitation with its devastating effects on African cultural traditions. The study concludes with his thoughts about the future of international relations between Europe and Africa. He believes that "no change for the better would be brought about by having the European State withdraw its control. Economic imperialism has itself created conditions in which that control must inevitably continue" (377). Similarly, instituting international control for national imperialism will not prevent the same economic exploitation from continuing. Instead, the policy of economic exploitation, which is based upon the capitalist belief in profit-making, must be eliminated for there to be significant change. Woolf himself admits that he cannot be certain human nature will change so that the beliefs of capitalism can be abandoned; however, he does believe that this change can be partially achieved through a system of trusteeship in which the white man does not "seek his own economic interests in Africa" but instead becomes "the trustee for the interests of Africans" (364). This system of trusteeship could be adopted either by making each state a mandatory of the League of Nations or by making the League an international trustee responsible for the administration of the territories (364).

Empire and Commerce in Africa is a detailed, methodical study with careful documentation. Woolf's focus on the history of European involvement in all areas of Africa is broad; however, he has developed his material in order to identify the beliefs and desires behind European economic imperialism in Africa, and to point out the fallacies of those beliefs and desires, so that men may modify their thinking and better control their destiny. Woolf argues that imperialism was morally wrong, culturally destructive, and economically impractical. In 1919, this position was radical. Yet events in Africa in the decades since Woolf's study have revealed that Woolf's analysis of the past and future relationships between Western imperialist nations and African territories was both historically perceptive and prophetic.

Woolf's next major work on imperialism, *Economic Imperialism,* restates many of the points presented in *Empire and Commerce in Africa*, as Woolf examines the relationship between European countries and the undeveloped countries of Asia and Africa. Written in 1920, the study was part of the International Handbooks Series edited by Goldsworthy Lowes Dickinson. In his foreword, Dickinson sums up Woolf's attitude toward international affairs when he writes that the main objective of the series is "to inculcate the international rather than the nationalist way" of regarding international relations.[8] Similarly, Woolf's belief that man is responsible for his own destiny, that history has "been mainly determined by man, by his beliefs and his desires" (10), is echoed by Dickinson's comment that the world can be saved "only by the creation, among the peoples of the world, of such a public opinion as cannot be duped by misrepresentation nor misled by passion" (8).

As in *Empire and Commerce in Africa*, Woolf analyzes how European countries have extended their control throughout the world within the last century. In Africa, the land and people "have been conquered and subjected to the direct and autocratic rule of European States" (13), whereas in China, Persia, and Turkey, European control has been organized to further European economic interests. Woolf examines the beliefs and desires that have produced European imperialism. The first belief, the concept of the moral nature and duty of imperialism, argues that the white man is superior to other races, and that it is "the white man's burden" to civilize the non-white countries. This moral argument, Woolf claims, played less of a role in motivating imperialist control of other countries than in maintaining that control. Similarly, the sentimental notion of the romantic passion for exploration and of the need to increase the glory of the European country through conquest, was also not a main force in instigating imperialist policy. And finally, Woolf counters the third belief in support of imperialism, that an Asian or African possession is a military necessity, claiming that this concept is less a cause of imperialism than a rationalization of it. *Economic Imperialism* reveals that, for Woolf, economic interests are the cause of European imperialist expansion. Industrialization in Europe created the need first for imports of food products and raw materials from nonindustrialized nations, and then for markets for industrialized products. Later, the policy of protectionism, established between 1870 and 1880, helped produce economic imperialism by implying that "the organisation of the State should be used as a weapon against the industrial and commercial interests of the citizens of other States" (30). Each European nation attempted to secure raw materials, food, and markets by shutting out rivals, and as a result, "the immediate impulse" toward imperialism "came from financiers or capitalist joint-stock companies" (33). At the same time he points to economics as the cause of imperialism, Woolf seeks to illuminate the fallacies behind the economics of imperialism. He first attacks the belief that Asian and African countries have great economic importance for the ruling country. In reality, the British African possessions have minimal economic importance to British trade and industry, particularly in comparison to other independent countries; for example, "as a market for British manufactures the Argentine Republic was nearly three times more important and as a source of British imports was six times more important" (56-57). This same fallacy applies to the idea that the imperialist possessions are more important sources of raw materials than independent nations.

In Chapter 2 of this study, Woolf examines the course of economic imperialism in Africa by presenting a more condensed form of the material developed in *Empire and Commerce in Africa*. In Chapter 3, however, he introduces new material in an analysis of the cause of imperialism in Asia. In Asia, "the same violent and sudden impact and penetration" occurred as in Africa (75), yet the policy of direct conquest and annexation was not pursued, so that much of Asia was not under the political control of Europe but under economic control. Woolf attributed the difference in the pattern of domination partly to the fact that in Asia, there were highly developed political and economic institutions which could not be dominated by European institutions. In addition, Japan proved to be a counterforce to European aggression, since it adopted the political, military, and economic system of Europe in order to remain free of control—and to become an imperialist power itself.

Asian imperialism began when France established a protectorate over Annan in 1884 whereupon each European imperialist power then began to establish "spheres of interest." As a result, China's interests were disregarded; her mineral wealth was exploited, and the revenue of the Chinese rulers was mortgaged to foreign financiers. When national rebellions began, the imperialist powers used military force to suppress them. Woolf comments that Europe now has two alternative paths to follow in China: either exploitation, by promoting only their economic interests; or cooperation, by helping "the Chinese to adapt their political and economic system ... to obtain their fair share of the wealth which the European system was capable of creating" (84). When they chose exploitation, European countries were merely applying capitalism and its principles of economic competition to international relations.

Woolf argues that alternatives to imperialism lie in the mandate system and in the administrative organization of the League of Nations. The mandate system would give the land to the natives, provide agricultural education, prohibit compulsory labor by natives for Europeans, provide social and political education, and give the natives local self-government. Woolf, however, realizes that "the League, as it exists to-day, and its Mandate System are both shams" (105), because the capitalist states refuse to give up their practices of competition and exploitation. Thus, as in *Empire and Commerce in Africa*, he argues that capitalistic beliefs would have to be rejected before the League or the mandate system could be an effective alternative to economic imperialism.

Later Writings on Economics and Politics

In the early 1920s, Woolf's political activities took a new turn when he was urged by the Seven Universities Democratic Association to become a candidate for Parliament in the 1922 election. Although he comments in *Downhill All the Way* that he considered the life of a member of Parliament to be "a vicious circle of unnecessary inaction or futile conversations,"[9] he agreed, "partly and rather pusillanimously, because there was really no chance of . . . being elected" (34). At this time, he considered his politics to be closest to those on the left in the Labour party. His platform was based on a foreign policy of international government through the League of Nations, disarmament, settlement of the reparations problem, recognition of Russia, close cooperation with the United States, and an end to imperialist expansion to provide independence and self-government for Asian and African nations. In addition, his domestic policy was based on equality of opportunity to obtain education, a more equitable system of taxation, and a cooperative system of industrial production (38-40). Woolf realized that these policies were not popular in 1922. Indeed, he lost the election, coming in third; however, when he wrote *Downhill All the Way*, he looked back over the years and commented that he believed his platform represented the policies which might have prevented the rise of fascism and nazism, and the disasters of World War II (40-41).

Between the years 1920 and 1939, Woolf was busy with the growing activities of the Hogarth Press and his writing and editing responsibilities for various journals. He also became engrossed in thinking and writing about the causes of war, and

about the psychologies of civilization and barbarism. Nevertheless, in his political writing, he returned to the subjects of international government and the prevention of war and to imperialism
and the problems of Empire, which had been most important to
him in the years immediately following World War I. During this
time, he completed several Labour party and Fabian Society
publications on these subjects, as well as three independent
studies entitled *Imperialism and Civilization, The League and
Abyssinia,* and *The War for Peace.*

Three essays—*International Economic Policy,* written for the
Labour party in 1920, *International Co-operative Trade,* written
for the Fabian Society in 1922, and "Labour and Foreign Affairs,"
written in 1924[10]—explore the national and international economic situation. In *International Economic Policy,* Woolf examines the Labour party's position on protectionism versus free
trade, continuation of the empire, and support of the League of
Nations. According to Woolf, the goals of the Labour party are
"maintaining and improving the standard of life of the non-
capitalist class" (2) through international peace and national
prosperity. Woolf points out that an international economic
policy of free trade works toward fostering an increase in wages,
equal distribution of income, a decrease in working hours, protection against unemployment, and an increase in the efficiency of
industry. Protectionism, or a system of embargoes and tariffs,
which "presupposes...a perpetual state of war and preparation
for war" (55), causes increases in prices and therefore in profits
for the capitalist class; it also protects war-related industries and
promotes international hostility. Woolf rejects protectionism
and supports free trade, which he considers to be similar to the
Co-operative Movement's aim of producing for consumption and
not for profit, and which would not allow any exploitation of
postwar shortages of goods.

In *International Economic Policy,* Woolf also urges the Labour
party to promote national efforts by cooperative societies to
expand and establish a system for international cooperative
trade. He develops this position further in another pamphlet,

International Co-operative Trade, arguing that economic reconstruction of Europe can occur only through the growth of international trade organized along the lines of the Co-operative
Movement. The English Co-operative Society became independent of the capitalist middleman in the import trade by establishing its own depot and forming a joint buying system with another
national cooperative movement (6). Woolf thus urged the extension of this system of exchanging goods on a nonprofit basis
between two or more national movements; he also commented
that there should be cooperation with cooperative agricultural
movements, as well as the development of an international
cooperative bank to mobilize economic resources (25). Moreover,
Woolf believed that the Labour party's support for national and
international socialism and cooperative trade was admirable. In
his essay "Labour and Foreign Affairs," he argues that the Labour
party is competent to deal with foreign affairs. Similarly, he
valued the Labour party's emphasis on a foreign policy of peace,
which involved opposing a postwar policy of retaliation against
the Germans, and its backing of the League of Nations, as well its
support for a national democratic policy by urging democratic
control of foreign policy.

In his next study, *Imperialism and Civilization,* written in
1928, Woolf returned to the problems of Empire, reemphasizing
his negative views of imperialism. For Woolf, imperialism was "a
menacing movement which ... has already caused great political,
economic, and social upheavals all over the world" and was
therefore "one of the most dangerous developments in human
history."[11] As in *Economic Imperialism,* Woolf analyzes the
stages of imperialist domination in Asia and Africa—economic
penetration, political control, and revolt. He points out the destructive effects of imperialism on non-European nations, and he
claims that the ruthless changing of the economic system to
adjust and assimilate it to that of European nations has destroyed
the bases of the non-European civilization. Thus, twentieth-
century imperialism represents the first time in history that
contact between nations "involved the destruction of one civiliza-

tion by another, or the permanent subordination of one to another" (52), which has been achieved through the "drastic revolution in the economic life of the subject peoples, and ... economic exploitation of their territory and labour on a large scale" (54).

Woolf points to Africa as an example of the destructive effects of European domination on a native culture. Europeans were interested only in the economic exploitation of Africa, which meant gaining possession of the land and having the natives work for Europeans. Yet in an agricultural society where people are dependent upon the land, taking away land makes the native an economic slave. In this way, European countries failed to protect the material interests of the African natives by preserving their rights to the land. Moreover, Woolf maintains, they failed to educate the natives to understand the changes in social and economic life and to be able to establish self-government.

Woolf considered the presence of a large number of Europeans in a non-European population, the situation produced by imperialism, as dangerous; similarly, he felt that the reverse situation, the presence of Asiatics or Africans in a European population, was equally dangerous. Analyzing the position of Negroes in America, he commented that such a large population will not "be satisfied to live in economic and political subjection within a modern State" (137), and he argued that the only solution would be "assimilation, which must involve political and economic equality, but need not ... involve physical assimilation" (137). He took a similar position on the problems of Asiatic immigration, especially of the Japanese, to America, and on the relationship between blacks and whites in South Africa.

Imperialism and Civilization concludes with Woolf's comments upon the role of the League of Nations in solving the problems of imperialism. The League supported a mandate system of rule which would establish international cooperation and respect for the natives of a country under imperialistic domination. Although Woolf recognized that the mandatory system had not been successful, he considered it a "remarkable and important international pledge" and an alternative policy to imperialism (159). Finally, Woolf viewed the League as providing the unique opportunity for a world society where "states, races and nations are not isolated," and where international conflict could be resolved peacefully (162).

With the rise of fascism and nazism in the 1930s and the imminence of war, Woolf again focused on the problem of international government as a means to prevent war. *The League and Abyssinia*, published in the Day to Day Pamphlet Series of the Hogarth Press, was written in 1936, but parts of the pamphet had appeared earlier in *Political Quarterly*. In this study, as in the beginning of *Downhill All the Way*, Woolf comments on how the "post-war world has adopted or accepted violence as a normal method of settling political and economic problems." [12] For example, "liquidation" has become a common term in both Fascist and Socialist countries, referring to a means of regulating social relations. Yet Woolf argues against the use of force because it represents barbarism and because it fosters national instability, for whenever there is violence among the population, the government is forced to counteract with violence.

Woolf believed that Mussolini's attempt to take over Ethiopia in the 1930s was a test case for the success or failure of the League and the system of collective security that it represented. Ethiopia was the only completely independent native state in Africa, although it had been divided up into "spheres of interest" by Italy, France, and Great Britain. In 1923, Ethiopia became a member of the League. Membership in the League should have been an assurance of peace; otherwise, the organization would have been unable to prevent world powers from conducting their relations with smaller countries "by the methods and moralities of tricksters, gangsters, and thugs" (10). Even though Italy was a League member, she was preparing for the conquest of Abyssinia. As Woolf points out, once a European nation has economic interests in a country, as Italy did in Ethiopia, it also attempts to gain political control of that country. Ethiopia brought the matter before the League in 1935, thereby warning every nation in the

League of the imminent violation of national boundaries. Nevertheless, Italy invaded Abyssinia, thus proving the League was unable to prevent aggression and ensure peace.

Woolf uses Britain to point out the problems preventing the League from maintaining peace. In terms of international relations, Britain's treaty and exchange of notes with Italy in 1906 placed it in a position of obligations to Italy, which would conflict with its allegiance to the League. Until October 1934, England seemed to be honoring its obligations to Italy, but when Mussolini invaded Abyssinia, Britain sided with the League. Immediately, other countries were ready to follow Britain and give their allegiance to the League. For Britain, this represented a departure from its anti-League actions. For example, previous to the Abyssinia issue, Japan had invaded Manchuria, but Britain did not move to prevent Japanese aggression. Similarly, national British political forces were jeopardizing support of the League. Although the Labour party had consistently supported the League, there was division of opinion over the Abyssinian issue. Still another force of opposition in England to the League was the political left. First, the left viewed the League as a group of capitalist states, and believed that "capitalism inevitably implies imperialism and imperialsim inevitably implies war; therefore, the League cannot prevent war" (31). On this point, Woolf admits that "in the long run, a world of capitalist states, with or without a League of Nations and a system of collective security, cannot eliminate war" (32); nevertheless, he asserts that the League can be effective in preventing war for a period of five to ten to even twenty years. He also acknowledges that even in a world of Socialist states, there would be differences in national interests which would cause conflicts and necessitate a "regular system of settling disputes and preventing war" (35). The left's second point of opposition to the League was that peace or war is "determined solely by economic causes" (33); Woolf, however, maintains that noneconomic causes are almost as important as economic causes in determining international events. Moreover, he reasserts his support for the League with his final comment that the League system presently poses a choice between peace or civilization on the one hand, and war or barbarism on the other.

In *The War for Peace* (1940), a later World War II study, Woolf challenges the idea that power must be the determining factor in human or international relations. He believes that although differences of power exist between individuals and nations, power can be "amenable to elimination and control."[13] Peace is not a utopian notion, he argues, and war is not inevitable. Woolf also explores the psychological roots of war and the development of war throughout history. Man has a divided mind and a divided soul; the conflict between reason or moral behavior and instinct or imagination thus constitutes the "dichotomy of the human being [which] makes his behaviour, particularly his collective behaviour, peculiarly erratic and unpredictable" (16). Instinct and imagination lead men into rituals which are maintained even when their meaning has long since become invalid. For example, in the past, the main objective of war was for one army to destroy another; this led to the science of warfare, a practice with elaborate rules, scrupulous training, and an aura of something sacred (19). Although during the medieval period war had been considered the "sport of kings," part game, part ritual, part profession, with the evolution of the state, it became an instrument of power, and the idea of killing became a "fixed and immutable element in human society" (22). In the early nineteenth century, Napoleon further changed the nature of war so that it affected everyone; as a result, it became a "universal catastrophe" (28) and thus the essence of the totalitarian war which we experience in the present century, which threatens all of civilization rather than only an isolated group or class.

Woolf next focuses on World War I. The aims of the war were peace, democracy, liberty, and the right of small nations to independence and self-determination. Although the war was won, these aims were not successfully achieved. In the postwar years, one of the main causes of the rise of fascism and the Nazi policy of aggression was the use of power and force to determine the relations of nations. Woolf thus believes that the occurrence of war is linked to the role of national power and force in social life. To eliminate power and force as a means of determining relations, individual and communal psychology must be changed so that reason rather than emotion will dominate actions. In addition, there must be a desire for a regular method of making rules to control international relations peacefully and efficiently, and to provide regular and functional procedures for settling disputes (72) between states.

In the nineteenth century, there were significant advances toward eliminating force as an "instrument of communal power" (83). This change in attitude and action developed from the concepts of democracy, liberalism, and humanitarianism, which differed from authoritarianism with its stress on hierarchies of power. Another part of the movement toward organizing social life according to consent and cooperation was a system of international government, particularly the concept of the League of Nations. Although the League assumes that there is a common interest in maintaining peace, its system for settling disputes takes into account the reality of international relations, which is that power is part of conflicting interests. For these reasons, Woolf maintains that a League system can be effective if nations adopt a psychology of consent and cooperation. Unilateral pacifism would not stop man's inclination toward violence, but "the communal control of power and force—which means that the community must enforce the law—is essential if we are to save ourselves from relapse into barbarism" (219-20). Thus, to Woolf, there is no evidence, no reason, why a successful international organization of law and collective security cannot exist.

Two Fabian Society pamphlets written in the 1940s reveal Woolf's continued participation in the Labour party and indicate that his views about socialism and international government at this time were consistent with his earlier political outlook in the years following World War I. In *The International Post-War Settlement* (1944) and *Foreign Policy: The Labour Party's Dilemma* (1947), Woolf argues that the Labour party's national goals of peace, security, independence, and prosperity can only be achieved through both national socialism and international socialism, the latter implying international government.

In *The International Post-War Settlement*, Woolf writes that Socialist principles or cooperation should be the basis of the postwar settlement. First, states must give up the idea of sovereign rights, since that sovereignty is no longer possible in the modern world. For Britain, particularly, internationalism is essential because of her dependence upon large imports of food and raw materials; thus, Woolf comments that Britain will profit from peace which can be achieved only through international trade, cooperation, and international government. Next, on the question of how to treat Germany, Woolf argues that breaking up German territory is sure to defeat peace efforts because "the last 100 years of European history prove that forcible subjection never destroys nationalism," but leads to international aggression.[14] Similarly, Woolf rejects economic sanctions for Germany, stating that "economic prosperity is internationally indivisible" (17); economic distress for Germany would therefore affect all other countries. Also, economic distress would thwart all attempts to reeducate the German people to accept a democratic ideology. To encourage the growth of democracy in Germany, Woolf proposes that efforts be made to revive trade unions, cooperative societies, and other democratic organizations, and to link these groups to local government.

The problem of Palestine is also analyzed from an international perspective. Woolf suggests that reconciliation between Arabs and Jews should be attempted through the United Nations and through an agreement between Allied nations "upon a Constitution for Palestine, restored to its original frontiers, and probably federative" (19). This constitution would safeguard the rights and liberties of both Arabs and Jews. Just as Woolf had focused on the response to Italy's invasion of Abyssinia by the League as a test case for international government in 1936, he points out that, in 1944, a peaceful settlement in Palestine will be the test case for the United Nations in the post-World War II period. Woolf's final point in *The International Post-War Settle-*

ment is that "the only hope for the future lies...in the application of democracy and socialism to the relations of states and peoples" (20), not just at the national level, but internationally as well. The Labour and Socialist forces, which played a major part in the resistance movements against fascism and nazism, should therefore be organized into a new international network for international socialism and world peace.

The second Fabian Society pamphlet, *Foreign Policy: The Labour Party's Dilemma*, examines Britain's role in postwar politics, which Woolf sees as being shaped by the cold-war opposition of the United States and the USSR. Woolf argues that Britain's socialist government must make the United Nations "the keystone of its long-term policy"[15] even though the United Nations is presently not effective. He further comments that if Great Britain is trying to set up a Socialist economy, which is the goal of the Labour party, it would be dangerous to be too closely aligned with the United States, and therefore to be dominated by United States capitalism, particularly since the United States sees economic aid to Europe in terms of political influence (12-13). Yet an alliance with Russia is not feasible. As Woolf points out, Russia has acted to divide itself from the West, and "there is...no evidence that the Soviet Government intends or wishes to co-operate with Great Britain" (12). Woolf also opposes an alliance with Russia because she has acted to make the United Nations ineffectual. Thus, he concedes that alignment with the United States is more appropriate than with Russia, but he urges Great Britain to pursue as independent a policy as possible.

On the question of Britain's role in world politics, Woolf argues further that Britain is a second-class power because it is unable to take part in a war fought with atomic weapons. As a result, Britain should reduce its armed services and "liquidate the empire and our imperial and imperialist responsibilities" (15). Finally, Britain should stop all research experimentation with atomic weapons, and should enter into "either bilateral or multilateral agreements to pool all knowledge connected with atomic research" (20).

Two other aspects of British foreign policy—Palestine and aid to Germany—are also analyzed. Woolf believes that Britain can no longer fulfill its obligations in Palestine and should notify the United Nations that it cannot be "solely responsible for the administration of Palestine after 1947" (23). The need for Palestine was military and economic. Palestine was considered to be a strategic base, particularly in a war against Russia; however, as Woolf argues, since Britain will no longer take part in a major war, there is no reason to maintain Palestine as a base. Similarly, Palestine was thought to be essential for oil supplies, yet Woolf points out that the need for oil in peacetime is much smaller than in war, and that peacetime oil supplies could be purchased on the world market.

Britain's relationship to Germany is a more problematic aspect of foreign policy. Withdrawal from Germany would save £120 million and millions of dollars per year and allow the armed forces to be reduced by 150,000 men. Nevertheless, Woolf urges Britain not to withdraw from Germany because withdrawal would mean allowing the United States to assume Britain's responsibility for food imports to Germany and would involve agreeing to United States foreign policy in Europe to the point of political subservience to the United States. Moreover, Woolf argues that withdrawing from Germany would probably weaken the chance of a Social-Democratic Germany, allowing either the right-wing Christian Democratic party or the Communist party to come to power. Given these alternatives, Woolf urges Britain to remain in Germany but to reduce its commitment. Woolf thus saw Britain's role in the postwar world as a basically neutral political force, a role appropriate to its position as a second-class power. At the same time, he felt Britain could foster the growth of socialism and democracy to counterbalance political and economic domination by either the United States or the USSR.

In *Downhill All the Way*, Woolf reviews his political activities during the years 1919 to 1939, which centered around the Fabian Society and the Labour party. At the end of World War I, Woolf believed that the Labour party was "the only political alternative to conservativism and the Tory Party" (219), and he saw the Fabian Society as acting as "an instrument for the political education of the labour movement and ultimately of the Labour party" (218). As the focus of his published political writings during this time suggests, Woolf's most significant political work grew out of his efforts as secretary for the two advisory committees of the Labour party on imperialism and international affairs. When these committees began their work, imperialism, colonialism, and war were still supported fully by the majority of Europeans, and no effective system for international government had been implemented. Nevertheless, the Advisory Committee on Imperial Affairs attempted to play an important role in British foreign policy by urging the Labour party to meet the demands in India for self-government and Dominion status (277), by providing a detailed report on conditions in Africa, and by developing a policy for governing the colonies. Similarly, the Advisory Committee on International Affairs was an important influence on Labour party policies, as it tried to develop an efficient form of international government through the League of Nations. Clearly, during the pre- and postwar years, Woolf's practical political work complemented and influenced his published studies on war, international government, and imperial affairs; thus, both political and literary work characterize his contribution to society during this time.

Chapter Four
Studies on Socialism and Cooperation, and Responses to Barbarism

Woolf's study of imperialism, war, and international government in the post-World War I years developed into a broader concern with man's ability to achieve social progress and maintain the values of civilization. When World War I challenged social optimism about the possibilities for civilization, Woolf began to see that the forces subverting peace and the values of civilization lay in a complex interaction between the social and economic structure of society and individual and communal psychology. He therefore started a lifelong examination of man's conflicting impulses toward civilization and barbarism throughout history. First, he focused on the economics and communal psychologies of capitalism and socialism in his studies of the Co-operative Movement—*Co-operation and the Future of Industry* (1919) and *Socialism and Co-operation* (1921)—evaluating to what degree capitalism and socialism each fostered the values of civilization. Then, in the late 1920s and the 1930s, the rise of fascism influenced him to examine man's rejection of civilization and turn toward barbarism in two studies, *Quack, Quack!* (1936) and *Barbarians Within and Without* (1939). Woolf clearly considered fascism to be a political ideology of barbarism, and he portrayed it as such through political and religious allegory in his only drama, *The Hotel*, written in 1939. In addition to these works, he sought a more comprehensive understanding of man's development as a social and political being. His studies *After the Deluge* (1931) and *Principia Politica* (1953), written during the pre- and post-World War II eras, represent the mature development of his political theory.

The Co-operative Movement

As discussed earlier, Woolf first analyzed capitalism and socialism as social and economic systems in 1912 when he worked with
the Hoxton "Care Committee" of the Charity Organization
Society, which provided private charity to working-class and poor
families in London. Woolf soon began to see poverty as being
caused by a capitalist economic system and a class social structure,
and he considered private charity ineffective in aiding the poor.
His social conscience developed further through work with the
Women's Co-operative Guild, part of the Co-operative Movement. A thorough study of the history, principles, and practices of
the Co-operative Movement led to Woolf's support of socialism
and to his conviction that, through the Co-operative Movement,
the education of the working class could be accomplished and the
transition from capitalism to socialism could be a possibility.

Woolf believed that communal control of production and consumption would lead to a civilized society. In his autobiography,
he commented that "the nature of social or economic organization has an immense effect upon social psychology"[1] or men's
beliefs and desires. A class system, for example, fosters alienation
of individuals by class and allows for exploitation of the majority
by a minority; in contrast, a social structure which breaks down
class hierarchies fosters respect for equality and individualism,
the essence of civilization. Thus, the ideology of a capitalist
economic system encourages belief in a privileged social group
and causes conflict and competition among classes in society,
while socialism, which develops cooperation and production for
communal use, encourages a democratic ideology based on equality of all individuals.

Woolf pursued his analysis of a democratic economic system
through a study of the Co-operative Movement entitled *Co-
operation and the Future of Industry* (1919), which describes the
Co-operative Movement and evaluates its possibilities for becoming a democratic industrial system and thereby solving many
of the economic and social problems created by other industrial
systems. The Co-operative Movement, which began in 1844 in
Lancashire, grew to 3.5 million members in 1,400 cooperative

societies. It serviced 10 million people with goods valuing £100 million through factories in England and other countries.[2] As an association of consumers, it was open to any person, with each member having one vote, and with profits being divided up according to the member's amount of purchase. Since production in the Co-operative Movement system was organized for consumption, not profit, it would eliminate "the waste of capitalist production of producing goods which nobody wants and then convincing people to buy them merely to have money making money" (38–39). Woolf links this system of consumption to the distinction between a civilized and barbarous society: "It is not production, but consumption which makes civilization differ from barbarism.... Clearly you may tell the nature of a man not by his work, but by what he consumes" (48–49). Moreover, if industry is to be democratic, it must be controlled by the community and organized for consumption; also, the people must have a democratic spirit and an interest in government and industrial organization. Woolf sees evidence of this spirit of democracy in the active role of Co-operative Movement members in discussion and decision-making, and he acknowledges the efforts of working-class men and women to educate themselves to understand and participate in the technicalities of modern industry: "Extreme poverty, lack of education, and inordinately long hours of heavy physical labour do not make it easy for the democratic spirit to operate.... The wonder is that in the face of these difficulties, the participation of the members in the work of the societies and movement has been so wide"(55–56). Woolf particularly comments on advances in self-education in the Women's Co-operative Guild, which he describes as "an educated democracy of many (30) thousand women who understand the principles of co-operative industry and strive actively to put them into practice" (121). Although they had been denied formal education, the women were able to extend their self-education in industrial matters to social reforms and civic matters, such as pension, public health, insurance, food control, and maternity benefits.

In addition to encouraging participation in decision-making and self-education, the Co-operative Movement established a higher level of pay for its members. This included a minimum

wage of 17 shillings for women workers in many trades, based on
the principle that "no woman should be employed in any work...
unless she is paid a living wage" (67). Moreover, the Co-
operators helped determine working conditions. This, for Woolf,
is of primary importance because it gives the worker a sense of
power, responsibility, and pride in his work, and is thus a means
of eliminating class warfare. Yet despite these positive features,
Woolf points out that, in order to survive, the Co-operative
Movement needs to broaden its base by absorbing members from
all classes in society. At the same time, he realized that the spirit
of democracy and communal interest is easiest to encourage
among the working classes, for, in contrast to the middle-class
man, who emphasizes privacy and is essentially individualistic,
the working-class man "has a natural tendency to be a socialist, a
democrat, and a co-operator" (99).

Earlier, in several Co-operative Movement articles and publications, Woolf had developed similar points.[3] For example, *The
Control of Industry by the People*[4] emphasizes the democratic
nature of cooperative control of production. Moreover, in assessing the role of women in industry, he comments that "women
are the great producers of the world" (14), although he acknowledges that they will always be a minority in industry since much
of their work is unpaid. Nevertheless, he states that the Co-
operative Movement offers women the best opportunity for full
participation. Also, just as he argues in *Co-operation and the
Future of Industry*, Woolf emphasizes that democratic participation in the Co-operative Movement could not be achieved without the education of its members. In *Education and the
Co-operative Movement*,[5] he stresses that, under capitalism,
workers have been denied the opportunity for education; thus,
the great challenge for the Co-operative Movement is to provide
courses on history and theory of the cooperative system, economics, industrial history, and trade unionism (8–9).

In still another pamphlet, *Co-operation and the War. I: Effects
of War on Commerce and Industry*,[6] Woolf analyzes how war
creates a loss of confidence in the credit system, which in turn
leads to a demand for gold that causes prices to rise and unem-

ployment to increase. Yet the Co-operative Movement, Woolf argues in *Co-operation and the War. II: Co-operative Action in National Crises*,[7] could cope with economic panic by regulating prices and creating accurate information about the supply of goods, and by controlling the withdrawal of capital (14). Finally, in a later publication, *After the War*,[8] Woolf argues against the British government's policy of support for a capitalist industrial system and imperialist exploitation of foreign resources, and he claims that a system of protection will raise the prices of necessities for workers. Thus, he again supports the cooperative system of production and distribution of goods as an alternative to capitalism.

Two years after he wrote *Co-operation and the Future of Industry*, Woolf explored the possible role of the Co-operative Movement in a Socialist society in his work *Socialism and Co-operation* (1921). The capitalist and the Socialist each believe that his social organization is morally right and desirable and will produce "good,"[9] but although the capitalist claims to recognize the interests of the whole community, he believes that the interests of individuals and classes should determine the organization of society. He therefore encourages competition between individuals and classes, supporting the privileges of a minority. For Woolf, the ideologies of self-interest and competition which result from capitalism "contaminate and rot the whole fabric of society" (10). In contrast to capitalism, Woolf argues, socialism organizes society for communal interests and emphasizes having individuals "accept communal interests as the motives of their social actions" (19). Even though Woolf recognizes that "our psychology remains oligarchic" (80), rooted in the concept of privilege, and is thus far from being democratic, he argues that if capitalism were to be rejected, industry could be organized around the majority group of consumers, as in cooperation, and could thus foster the growth of socialism.

Woolf further points out that, in a capitalist society, work is considered the most important aspect of a man's life, whether or not it is satisfying to the worker or productive in terms of meeting the consumption needs of the society, primarily because capitalist society does not value the object produced, but the profit which can be obtained from it. Socialism, however, would change this psychology of production so that the quality or usefulness of the object and the quality of life of the working man would be most important; as a result, production would be reduced and would no longer be the individual's main activity. Finally, in a cooperative economic system, each member would contribute equally to production and share equally in consumption. Production and distribution would be regulated by the decisions of an executive committee, elected by the community, which would calculate the goods needed for consumption, but consumers would also have a role in determining production by their desires for certain objects. Thus, a balance of power between organized consumers and organized producers would be established.

Socialism and Co-operation was written for the Independent Labour Party series. Many years later, Woolf commented in his autobiography that he had always been "a heretical socialist," and that his ideas were not acceptable to either the capitalist or the socialist. Nevertheless, he believed that no matter how disinterested the public might be in this work, his basic argument—that socialism was a means to a prosperous and civilized society—was valid.[10]

Civilization versus Barbarism

The psychology of civilization continued to be a main concern for Woolf throughout the late 1920s and the 1930s, as he moved from a study of economic systems in relation to communal psychology to an examination of the values of civilization and barbarism. In *Quack, Quack!*, written in 1936, Woolf examines the relationship between communal psychology and individual and national behavior. His main concern is to analyze the betrayal of civilized values, which he identifies as "the political reaction against reason, intelligence, and humanity and...the reversion to the primitive psychology of magic and superstition."[11] Although his focus is on twentieth-century pre–World War II society, he also traces the development of civilization and barbarism back through the history of man.

The use of reason began in primitive society and allowed man to progress beyond the level of animals, to free himself from "the mechanical tyranny of his senses" (11) and achieve some degree of control over his environment; however, primitive man believed in magic, or that nature and inanimate and animate existence were controlled by supernatural beings. As this false belief grew into a system of absolute truths, "the whole of life was dominated by the quacking of quacks" (15). The magician, witch doctor, and rain maker became powerful cultural figures, and the central leader or king was considered a god, a "divine public miracle worker" (30), upon whom the prosperity of the community depended.

In contrast to the false beliefs of primitive society, civilization emphasized the "dominance of reason, intelligence, and knowledge over instinct, habit, and superstition" (17). Yet the history of man reveals that the values of civilization are difficult to maintain; Woolf claims that "civilizations rise, but they also fall... the psychology of civilization is of comparatively recent growth, a thin crust of reason, culture, and humanity which covers and conceals the hot passions and instincts of an animal and the crude delusions of a savage" (19). The threats to civilization are multiple: the inclination to believe in magic which exists within each individual; the latent power of a number of barbarians within society who have only contempt for civilized values of art and culture and democratic equality; and the refusal of the privileged minority to share "the material fruits of civilization" with the majority (22). Twentieth-century European society provided the example of how civilization can be submerged by the forces of barbarism. At the end of the nineteenth century, society was moving toward civilization, as political and economic equality seemed possible; however, the privileged minority, which refused to give up its vested interests in a nonegalitarian social organization, fostered class war and national war. The ideal conditions for the emergence of barbarism were thus created, culminating in World War I and the economic disaster of the 1920s, which led people to look toward the political magic of a king/leader/miracle worker to solve economic chaos and national humiliation.

For Woolf, the growth of fascism out of the post–World War I chaos is "the supreme example in modern times of the reversion to savagery and the belief in political magic" (37). The Führer or Duce is in a position similar to that of the primitive king, suppressing the use of reason in politics and demanding absolute acceptance and obedience. In addition to destroying political reason, the fascist rulers appeal to primitive passions, particularly by emphasizing national unity, which Woolf describes as "the blind herd-instinct for comfort, warmth, and a common smell" (44), and by creating a psychology of hatred for those who are different. Moreover, the speeches of fascist leaders and the leader-follower relationship they established are similar to the actions of primitive god-inspired chiefs or priests. Thus, it is not surprising to Woolf that when he compares photographs of Hitler and Mussolini to those of Hawaiian war-god effigies, he finds a similar expression of superhuman sternness and "the generalized emotions of the savage" (47), which have the psychological effect of instilling fear.

The repercussions of the reversion to the barbarism typical of fascism are extensive. First, there is political repression; then, since "people cannot be savage in politics and remain at the same time civilized in their private and social lives" (78), barbarism spreads to the educational system and the media. The general public becomes ignorant of what is happening in the world and is more susceptible to superstition, blind obedience to authority, and acceptance of militarism. This deterioration into ignorance and violence can be seen in Fascist society. To give the masses a sense of worth, the Fascists developed the concept of Aryan supremacy. Woolf points out the meaninglessness of the Nazi Aryan doctrine, in which the purity of one's blood depends upon the purity of the blood of one's grandmothers and determines one's right to German citizenship, as he emphatically comments that "there is not and never has been an Aryan race...the Germans like all nations on the earth today, are racially mongrels" (88). Yet this Nazi delusion of racial superiority has great appeal to those who are trying to transcend a sense of inferiority, since it reinforces one of the most primitive emotions, the instinct for self-glorification (90). Moreover, the belief in Aryan racial superiority extends to persecution of the Jews and involves the primitive psychology of the scapegoat in which the tribe rids itself of evil by displacing evil on to an alien group, either by expelling the aliens or by sacrificing them. Here Woolf also applies Freud's theories of psychoanalysis to Nazi ideology. First, Freudian theory suggests that civilization depends on the repression of savage instincts; secondly, the concept of an inferiority complex identifies the motives behind the Nazi urge for political and international domination.

The reversion to barbarism in the twentieth century is not typical only of the Fascists and Nazis. Identifying aspects of barbarism in England, such as the reverence for royalty that involves an attempt to maintain a system of political and social inequality to keep the majority powerless, Woolf comments that, during the last thirty years, there has been an intensive effort in the media to "establish in the people a superstitious 'loyalty' towards the royal family" (33), which makes a "rational and intelligent attitude towards social problems impossible" (34). The concept of monarchy and totalitarian rule is barbaric: "divine kings, heroes, and great conquerors have always been a curse and scourge to humanity....Eventually all civilized people have either to abolish their kings or turn them into political figure heads" (31). The Englishman's reverence for royalty is complemented by a mild form of scapegoat hunting which identifies the trade unions and the working classes as the source of all social evil (103), and by a more vicious form of scapegoat hunting that focuses on Soviet Russia and the Communists. Similarly, the Communists in Russia, Woolf argues, are subject to barbarism. Reverting to magic and superstition and abandoning reason, the

Communists believe in the "political magic" of their leader and in the "efficacy of scapegoats, namely the capitalist and the bourgeoisie" (104).

Woolf's belief that political ideology is an indication of social and personal life leads him to consider the presence of barbarism in intellectual thought and culture. Asserting again that civilization depends on repression of instincts and the use of reason or skepticism to reject absolute truths, Woolf argues that intellectuals, or "the trustees of civilization," who are writers, thinkers, artists, teachers, scientists, and priests" (109), should be dedicated to objective truth. Since, however, "there is nothing inherently good or bad in classes ... the intellectual, like the politician, is a weak human being ... he is the easy prey of his own and other people's instincts and emotions" (111). Intellectual quackery in religion and philosophy involves acceptance of the false standards and values of politicians and the rejection of spiritual and intellectual standards. The nineteenth-century revolt against reason by Kant, Fichte, Carlyle, and Nietzsche, for example, was a reaction against Hume's philosophy of skepticism. Woolf claims that Carlyle's philosophy of hero-worship was a forerunner of Nietzschean and Fascist philosophy, and was well suited to exploit the passions of nationalism and imperialism. Similarly, Woolf comments that Spengler's philosophy rejects analysis and reason and puts intuition first; hence, it is "metaphysical quackery" or "the abandonment of and contempt for reason as a means to truth in non-political speculation and the substitution for it of so-called intuition, magic and mysticism" (160).

Woolf's final example of intellectual quackery is the philosophy of Henri Bergson. Because Bergson realizes the limits of intellect as a means of obtaining truth, he rejects skepticism, reason, and logic and emphasizes intuition. Concluding that Bergson's philosophy is metaphysical quackery, he asserts that the true threat to civilization is when civilized men, like Bergson, are caught up in a revolt against reason: "Civilizations are not destroyed ... by the Herr Hitlers; they are destroyed when the M. Bergsons have to be numbered among the intellectual quacks" (193). Woolf understands that "the desire for certainty is very strong in human beings" (161). This makes absolute truths appealing; thus, it takes unusual courage to say, "I do not know" or "I see no meaning" (180). Woolf argues, however, that man must use reason to examine the universe and his relationship to it; because reason will lead man to skepticism and agnosticism (162), it will prevent both the rejection of civilization and the embracing of barbarism.

Barbarians Within and Without (1939) explores problems similar to those in *Quack, Quack!* Woolf continues to be concerned with the concepts of civilization and barbarism, particularly in relationship to the democratic, Fascist, and Socialist societies of twentieth-century Western Europe. Again, his approach is historical as he traces the roots of civilization and barbarism back to early Western cultures and distinguishes two types of society, that in which "the organization is based upon authority and obedience and that in which the organization is based upon liberty, equality, and consent."[12] In the former, "the standards of social value are power, patriotism, 'leadership,' loyalty, and obedience" (63). In the latter, the social standards of value are "happiness, an equal right to political power, education, knowledge and truth" (63). The Athenian state, which was based on individual and communal freedom, represents civilization, whereas Sparta, organized on the basis of authority and obedience in order to provide control of power by a minority, represents barbarism.

Although Western societies in the past have accepted the values of civilization, Woolf argues that they have not always been successful in shaping their societies according to those values because of an essential conflict. Equality, a basic characteristic of civilization, is a social relationship between individuals which is translated into the social structure and social institutions. Throughout history, however, all civilizations have been class societies with a hierarchical class system which denies the possibility of social, political, and economic equality. Woolf comments that the upper-class minority is a privileged class and is unwilling to give up its privileges for "there is nothing to which men cling more tenaciously than the privileges of class" (68).

When class war develops in order to preserve political and economic power for the minority, it is a sign of the crisis and contradiction in Western civilization. Woolf thus maintains that if the possibility for civilization is destroyed, it is not primarily because of the barbarians like Hitler and Mussolini, whom he calls "the barbarians without," but because of the contradictions of the civilized, "the barbarians within."

Freedom, also a basic criterion of civilizations, is difficult to maintain because self-interest is a primary motive of human behavior. This leads Woolf to comment on the relationship between instincts and behavior, the aspects of individual psychology which determine man's inclination toward civilization or barbarism:

Anyone can be a barbarian; it requires a terrible effort to be or remain a civilized man. . . . The control or sublimation of instincts is always an essential part of [civilization] . . . the immediate satisfaction of the simple and primitive instincts is characteristic of those forms of society which are the antithesis of civilization and which we may call barbarism. The barbarian is, therfore, not only at our gates; he is always within the walls of our civilization, inside our minds and our hearts. . . . He offers immediate satisfaction of simple instincts, love, hatred, and anger. He offers to help us to forget our own unhappiness by making other people more unhappy. (65)

Woolf's analysis of instincts and behavior acknowledges Freud's study *Civilization and Its Discontents*, as he points out that the Fascists' manipulation of man's desire to satisfy his instincts through Hilter's psychology of persecution offered the possibility of happiness to one group of individuals by making another group unhappy, that is, by releasing instincts for hatred and anger against the Jews as they became national scapegoats.

Woolf analyzes the rise of fascism and how three factors—power, economics, and ideas—which determine social relations and social structure were important. The Nazis gained power through organizing a private army which they used against their opponents, destroying or imprisoning them and securing key government positions. This transference of power was possible because of economics. In Germany, an intensification of the class war, combined with a Socialist government and the threat of a strong Communist party gaining power, led the capitalists to support the Nazis. In addition, the economic disaster of the post–World War I reparations led to financial ruin for many German citizens, causing "economic and social shell-shock" (105) and leading them to look to the Nazis as the solution to economic chaos and loss of national pride. Thus, after acquiring political power, the economic conditions in Germany enabled Hitler to control the public and establish his ideas, or his social objectives and standards of value, for the entire society.

Woolf's comments on the Communists are also critical. Using economic equality as a criterion of a civilized society, Woolf examines the Marxist program of soviet government and argues first that socialism "solved the economic problem in the only way possible for the development and extension of western civilization. It abolished private ownership in the means of production and established communal control over economic power" (141). For this reason, socialism represents the possibility for the greatest civilization in human history. Yet Woolf then recognizes that this possibility was undermined by the government's creation of a "dictatorship, autocratic and authoritarian" (148), which rejected political democracy because it was equated with capitalist liberalism (150). Socialist society thus fails to maintain the structure and values of civilization, although its ideology, developed from the theories of Marx and Engels, has its roots in civilization.

Barbarians Within and Without reveals Woolf's understanding of contemporary political and Socialist developments. Nineteenth and early twentieth-century Western civilization seemed to be developing a system of justice and humanity despite class inequality and imperialist domination. The social, economic, and political realities of post–World War I society, however, indicated that civilization in all of Western Europe was being subverted by the forces of barbarism. As Woolf well knew through his study of history and war, war has multiple destructive effects on civilization: communal freedom is destroyed as autocratic control of power is instituted; truth and knowledge are undermined by war lies and propaganda; human beings are motivated by "the primitive instincts of hatred, fear, or self-preservation" (133); and human action is channeled into destruction and killing. Thus, at the end of his study, Woolf appropriately evokes the biblical figure of Jeremiah to lament the loss of civilization's standards of justice and humanity in the face of pre- and post-World War I life.

A World War II Drama

Woolf brought together his analysis of barbarism in *Quack, Quack!* and fascism in *Barbarians Within and Without* in his only play, *The Hotel*, written in 1939, just before the outbreak of World War II. The play is clearly an antiwar drama portraying the way a deterioration of moral values leads to international conflict. Woolf describes this work as "written in the tension of those horrible years of Hitler's domination and of the feeling that he would inevitably destroy civilization."[13] Yet Woolf's mode is allegory; he uses figures from Christian and Hebraic traditions to develop contemporary political and historical events, and the play rests on a framework of biblical figures and phrases. Clearly, the hotel is a microcosm of society which symbolizes the fallen nature of mankind. According to Peter Vajoff, the hotel proprietor who comments in language parallel to the biblical description of creation, "in the beginning," it was the Grand Hotel of Paradise (11). Now it is appropriately called the Grand Hotel of the Universe and Commerce, and an "air of extremely dilapidated and faded magnificence" (11) barely disguises its inner corruption: a supply of armaments in the cellars and boiler room. Vajoff describes the armaments in detail, revealing that they represent the latest advances in technology. Hence, scientific knowledge, usually an indication of social progress, now serves forces of destruction and moral corruption, transforming the hotel, a former paradise, into a modern Hell.

The symbolic nature of the setting is complemented by characters who embody the communal psychologies of barbarism and civilization. For example, Peter Vajoff, like the Apostle Peter, who denied Christ, rejects Christian morality and turns toward the values associated with barbarism. Insensitive to the sufferings of mankind, he regards people with scorn. Moreover, he claims he is only a businessman and is untroubled by political or moral allegiances, thus rejecting political and moral responsibility. Yet Vajoff is appropriately the center of Woolf's play. By providing each hotel guest with different services, he portrays the way modern conditions of industry and commerce are shaping the organization of society along international rather than national lines.[14]

To counterbalance Vajoff's loss of positive morality, Woolf develops Vajoff's son Christopher as a sacrificial Christ-figure. First, Christopher protests against war, as weapons for destruction offend his moral values, his belief in the importance of compassion for other people, and his reverence for life. Moreover, when his father comments that men are "bugs, nasty little black bugs" (32), Christopher paraphrases Christ's words, "But I pity them, father; they can't know what they are really doing" (33), and he further asserts his respect for all forms of life. Christopher also challenges Vajoff's values by accusing his father of aiding the very men he scorns because he is selling armaments to both sides. Vajoff, however, attempts to excuse himself by explaining that he has lost his idealism and his faith in human nature (35). At this point, Vajoff cannot see that his attitudes and actions foster the growth of power politics which threaten individual freedom and social progress.

The character of Jacoby, who represents the archetype of the Wandering Jew, reveals another response to moral values in modern society. Expelled from his homeland Breslau by the Germans, Jacoby is looking for a new homeland, not necessarily the promised land in biblical terms, but a land of internationalism where an individual's ethnic and religious heritage is not a source of alienation and prejudice.

Through Jacoby and Christopher, Vajoff develops an awareness of humanist values which constitute the psychology of civilization. First, as the hotel guests deny responsibility for Christopher's death, Vajoff realizes that, in the sacrifice of his

son, he has "paid the price" for the deterioration of moral values
in modern society to which he has contributed by dealing in
weapons for destruction without any sense of moral responsibility for his actions. Jacoby's humanism now has an important
meaning for Vajoff. Unlike the other hotel guests, Jacoby sin-
cerely identifies with Vajoff's grief. He has experienced personal
bereavement in the loss of both his son, who was beaten to death
in a concentration camp, and his wife, who has killed herself.
Jacoby admits to Vajoff that he has not found consolation for
suffering. Instead, he has discovered that what sustains him is the
determination to live, to survive adversity, and to continue to
search for an intellectual understanding of the meaning of life.
Although he understands how individuals and nations adopt
debased and destructive standards of value, and therefore judges
the hotel guests who have tried to deny their reponsibility for
Christopher's death as guilty of destroying "peace and sanity and
civilization" (90), Jacoby can still survive disillusion about mankind without becoming cynical and without despairing. Thus,
through Jacoby's influence, Vajoff recognizes ties of common
humanity, and this prompts him to decide to "shut up shop" (94).
Symbolically, Vajoff's understanding of the fatal nature of decadence in interpersonal and international relations occurs simultaneously with a loud explosion, as the armaments in the boiler
room destroy the hotel.

Parallel to Woolf's examination of the disintegration of a
positive morality in individuals in *The Hotel* is his condemnation
of vicious political systems. The characters who represent world
powers in the play are corrupt literally and symbolically. Their
greed for power, their desire for weapons of destruction, has led
them to Vajoff's hotel and its cache of armaments. Woolf portrays these political figures as repulsive, and he purposely develops them as ethnic and national stereotypes. Antonelli and
Schwarzer, for example, are unappealing caricatures of their
national and ethnic heritages. Antonelli is "a small dark lean
Italian" (17) with a cynical smile, while Schwarzer is described
stereotypically as a scowling "bald-headed, fat German with a

toothbrush moustache, a heavy jaw, and spectacles" (17). Both men engage in business with Vajoff. When Vajoff demands payment for the arms, Schwarzer is so aggressive in his threats to destroy Vajoff if he causes any complications in their plans that Antonelli has to warn him that he "can't treat old Vajoff as if he were one of his German Jews" (30), suggesting Schwarzer's belligerent anti-Semitism. While Antonelli appears to be more subtle and crafty than Schwarzer, he is equally aggressive; he may smoothe matters out at the moment, but he is vindictive and plans revenge on Vajoff for his arrogance.

Vassilevsky, a Russian Communist agent, is also presented critically in the play. Although he claims he is interested in the arms to help the Spanish workers' rebellion, Vassilevsky wants to acquire them in order to maintain a balance of international power. At the same time that he agrees with Christopher that "bombs don't make a nice world no matter who uses them" (46), like Vajoff, he feels this is an "academic" question which cannot be adjusted to the realities of power. He believes that compared to Antonelli and Schwarzer, and even to Vajoff, he has a moral right to the bombs, as "the lesser of two evils," yet this belief indicates his moral corruption and, hence, his responsibility for Christopher's death.

The political figures of *The Hotel* thus dramatize the psychology of barbarism with its acceptance of violence, cruelty, and persecution, as it appeals to the emotional and irrational side of man's nature. Barbarism is also contrasted, however, with the psychology of civilization, as represented by Christopher, which is based on justice, tolerance, and humanity, as well as an assertion of communal ties and an intellectual understanding of man's nature and place in society. Woolf's use of Christian and Hebraic figures and values to parallel contemporary references and contexts establishes levels of religious and social allegory which reveal a continuing conflict within the psychology of man: should he pursue individual freedom through power and aggressive asssertion of individuality, although that path constitutes a communal psychology of barbarism and leads to war, or should he pursue cooperation and communal goodwill, the basis of civilization, which lead to individual freedom and social progress?

The Hotel links the recurrence of war in twentieth-century "civilized" society to man's acceptance of a communal psychology of barbarism, yet Woolf affirms some possibility for peace and civilization. Through the character of Jacoby and by the transformation in Vajoff's understanding of individual freedom and social responsibility, Woolf suggests that twentieth-century man's turn toward a psychology of barbarism is perhaps only a temporary rejection of civilization, only a momentary relapse in the process of man's social progress. Although *The Hotel* is not well known, it remains an important work in Woolf's canon, providing a view of society between the two wars and, through its use of allegory, portraying man's struggle against individual and national tyranny.

Further Studies on Communal Psychology

Woolf envisaged *After the Deluge*, which he wrote in 1931, as the first of a three-volume study of "the psychology of man as a social animal."[15] Analyzing the ideas and ideals of democracy, he traces how they developed from the concept of individuality and led to new attitudes about happiness, civil liberty, political democracy, the state, and culture. Early in his study, Woolf reveals his view of history as a series of events which indicates man's progress or regression toward civilization (51). His main interest is "mankind in masses or groups" (47); thus, he considers historical events to be the outward indications of the political contents of communal psychology. Again, Woolf defines communal psychology as it encompasses all levels of society as

the beliefs, desires, aims, and actions of rulers, governments, statesmen, but behind these, moulding or at least influencing them, are beliefs, desires, aims and actions of groups of men in political parties, industrial, financial, and commercial companies, workers' organizations, philanthropic, nationalist, or patriotic associations, and behind these is... popular opinion. (30)

Woolf also comments that the political content of communal psychology is largely shaped by the structure of society and by the beliefs and desires of past generations, which he calls "the dead hand of history."

The human suffering and destruction of material goods during World War I led Woolf to examine the political ideas which motivate men toward war. Between the French Revolution in 1789 and the end of World War I in 1918, there were great changes in the social organization of civilization. In the eighteenth century, the institution of monarchy dominated the social structure of European countries and was based on acceptance of the political and social ideologies of birth and inheritance. Feudalism and the political concept of the divine right of kings, which were still in existence, were causing social, political, and economic inequality. As the difference between the privileged classes and the masses of society widened, however, the need for reform developed. Woolf comments that in a period of "communal discomfort and misery," people seek the causes of suffering, and this results in social and political action; once social reform begins, "the psychology of individuals changes and there rapidly follows a complete change in communal psychology" (129). As people sought to change the feudal social structure and to exert political power, they destroyed the communal psychology or belief that politics is determined by God. Moreover, the concept of individuality emerged and was reflected throughout social experience, in all forms of mass culture, as well as in the theories of social and economic equality and political liberty.

Woolf identifies democracy and nationalism as the two dominating political ideologies of the eighteenth century. His thorough analysis of the concept of democracy indicates that it demands a new relationship between politics and happiness, that a democratic social and economic structure would develop according to the idea of individuality, or that everyone has an equal right to happiness and civil liberty. Woolf also points out that accepting democracy means rejecting two Christian beliefs: that earthly misery has a set place in human experience, and that sin exists and causes a need for religious and social law, and thus leads to the development of the modern state and government.

The volume which was to follow *After the Deluge* was supposed to be a study of the history of democracy in the nineteenth century. Woolf intended to assess whether or not society had become democratic and how effective the political machinery for implementing democracy had been. That volume was not written until 1953. Earlier, Woolf again briefly considered the nature of democracy in an essay, "What Is Democracy?" As in *After the Deluge*, Woolf comments that the French Revolution destroyed the concept of class privilege and substituted the notion that each individual was entitled to equality, which means treating people as individuals rather than as members of different classes. Woolf points out that equality of opportunity and happiness is related to education; indeed, he argues that the survival of democracy depends on the application of equality of education. In *Co-operation and the Future of Industry* and *Socialism and Co-operation*, Woolf had praised the Women's Co-operative Guild as a progressive social organization which emphasized self-education and political involvement for its members. Similarly, in "What Is Democracy?" he claims that women's rights and the women's movement are based on the concept of equality, and thus the emancipation of women "may prove to be one of the greatest social revolutions in human history."[16] Woolf further comments that, generally, the ideal of democracy has not been applied in the area of distribution of wealth and property, since financial and industrial wealth remains in private hands. He warns that if a country does not actively strive to apply the idea of democracy in all aspects of social life, it will turn toward totalitarian rule and the denial of individual rights.

Principia Politica, written by Woolf in 1953 at age seventy-three, is described as "partly political autobiography and... mainly concerned with the fundamental political psychology of our era, with the contemporary form which the eternal struggle between liberty and authoritarianism has assumed today."[17] Woolf comments that he narrowed his focus in this volume to the modern totalitarian state, hoping to discuss modern democracy in another study. As in his earlier studies *Quack, Quack!*, *Barbarians Within and Without*, and *After the Deluge*, Woolf's analysis encompasses history, anthropology, literature, and political science. He begins his study with a focus on communal psychology, or the social and political ideas which men hold. Since he believes that history involves both men's actions and their motives for action, Woolf is interested in the way ideas develop in relation to social standards of value, and in how ideas shape history, particularly in regard to political systems.

The positive or ethical standards of value for Woolf are truth, justice, tolerance, humanity, and fraternity (51). These values are incorporated into the basic democratic ideals of liberty and equality, which were present in Greek society, the teachings of Christ, the goals of the French Revolution, the nationalist revolutions in nineteenth-century Europe, the feminist movement, and the movement for colonial liberation. Also important in relation to standards of value are the concepts of sin and punishment: "sin and the way in which human beings deal with it, and therefore with the question of punishment and standards of value are one of the keys to civilization. To be a slave to it is barbarism; to control it is civilization" (65). Woolf, moreover, credits Freud with illuminating the relationship of the subconscious to sin and punishment, and to civilized standards of value which demand that men control primeval passions and conflicts. Similarly, freedom, which Woolf considers both "the greatest value in the individual's psychology and way of life" (112) and an essential aspect of civilization, is based on control of instincts and desires. Woolf analyzes two approaches to freedom. The first, the authoritarian approach, inculcates "fear of some authority—a God, a parent, a nurse or schoolmaster ... or ... the sense of sin or guilt" (113), while the second, the libertarian approach, encourages freedom through love and reason. Asserting that affection and cooperation can be developed to replace fear, hostility, and aggression, Woolf rejects authoritarianism as a means of achieving freedom.

Woolf, however, recognizes that authoritarianism has dominated man's history. It flourishes when "contact between govern-

ment and governed... [is] immediate and direct and the orders
... [are] simple and direct" (144); however, authoritarianism has
proven to be effective only for short periods of time. As society
becomes more complex, as in the present century, authoritarian
systems are difficult to maintain. In the modern authoritarian
society, which Woolf designates as the totalitarian governments
of Nazi Germany, Fascist Italy, and Communist Russia, "the
sphere of obedience is determined by the claim of the party and
leader to be the sole repositories of certain absolute truths regarding human affairs" (152). As a result, "a religion of state" develops, and government controls all aspects of life. Woolf parallels
the Church to the totalitarian state, commenting that both rely on
an appeal to emotions. Although both fascism and communism
are authoritarian systems, Woolf points out that the origins of
fascism are the social standards of value most appropriate to "the
lowest depths, intellectually and morally, of modern urban
society" (168), while the origins of socialism and communism are
"the highest social ideals" (169)—economic and political equality. When communism evolved into an authoritarian system,
Woolf commented on his sense of disillusionment:

I know I am prejudiced against communism, which seems to me in some
ways worse than nazism and fascism. *Corruptio optimi pessima*—the
greatest evil is the good corrupted. The Hitlers and Mussolinis are just
thugs or psychopaths.... But communism has its roots in some of the
finest human political motives and social aspirations and its corruption
is repulsive.[18]

Woolf recognized that the Soviet government had increased
industrial and agricultural productivity and had achieved a high
standard of living for the masses of people through a more
equitable distribution of wealth than in capitalist societies. He
considered these important advances, yet he maintains that they
are not sufficient for establishing the social standards of value
necessary for civilization.

Woolf concludes his analysis in *Principia Politica* by commenting that the main difference between authoritarianism and civili-

zation is the individual and communal psychology of obedience (285). In the authoritarian society, obedience is imposed by forces outside the individual, and man is "forbidden to use his reason" (286). In the civilized society, obedience is centered in the individual, and it is a means of obtaining individual and communal goals. Moreover, Woolf claims that the authoritarian system is an anachronism because it fails to produce political and social stability in modern society:

History, in the shape of Hitler and Mussolini, showed us that it does not work, that, beneath the façade of strong and stable government, the rulers are ignorant, violent, and afraid; the ruled cowed, ignorant, and afraid...the result...is a dangerous disequilibrium leading to internal violence and external wars. (33)

The Soviet government had been in existence for about twenty-five years when Woolf was writing *Principia Politica*; nevertheless, he believed that "the organized ignorance and artificial insemination of stupidity" in Russia could not continue "without producing social disintegration or explosion" (304). In modern society, a partnership between governnent and governed is essential, yet it is impossible to achieve that partnership in an authoritarian system. Similarly, internal policies in a totalitarian state do not allow for contact with the world which is so necessary to a modern society that is based on international economic, political, and social relations. As a result, the authoritarian nation is in "a state of latent or dormant war" with the rest of the world, which, Woolf maintains, eventually leads to the outbreak of war. For these reasons, Woolf concludes that the totalitarian dictatorship is neither a desirable nor "a viable form of government for the 20th century" (314).

In his autobiography, Leonard Woolf commented that experiences in his life transformed him from "aesthetic animal to political animal"[19] and confirmed his belief in the important influence of social, economic, and political factors on individual and communal psychology. Social and political ideas dominate Woolf's work of the 1920s and 1930s, characterizing it as literature of political consciousness. Whether he was dealing with economic systems, as in his studies on socialism and cooperation, or with historical events and political systems throughout history, as in his studies on civilization and barbarism, or democracy and authoritarianism, he was concerned with evaluating the social standards of value which lead to a communal psychology of civilization. During the 1920s and 1930s, when economic and political events threatened both individual and social survival, Woolf's protest against the forces of barbarism in economic, social, and political life, and his emphasis on the values of civilization, constitute a strong statement of humanitarianism.

Chapter Five

Contributions to Journalism and the Hogarth Press

Woolf's career as a journalist spanned over fifty years of his life and involved such work as writing political and literary articles and reviews for journals; founding, developing, and running the Hogarth Press; and acting as literary executor of Virginia Woolf's works following her death. After he returned to England from Ceylon, Woolf began contributing articles on national and international issues to the *Co-operative News* and the *New Statesman*.[1] From this point on, he was involved with several publications simultaneously. During the years 1915 to 1919, he was associated with the journal *War and Peace*, which later became *International Review*, and he acted as editor of this publication for a year (1918–19). Later, in 1922, he was the editor of foreign affairs for another journal, *Contemporary Review*, but soon after, in 1923, he became the literary editor of the *Nation*. Although he resigned that position in 1926, he continued to serve on the editorial board of the *New Statesman & Nation* and to write book reviews for this journal for four more decades. Similarly, in 1930, he helped to found a new publication, *Political Quarterly*, holding the position of joint editor with W. A. Robson until 1959, and contributing political articles and book reviews to this journal until his death.

Woolf's numerous articles and book reviews reveal that he was comfortable writing about history, politics, and social institutions. He covers such diverse subjects as war, peace, imperialism, politicians and statesmen, crime, the judicial system, the BBC, and the Co-operative Movement. He was also equally comfortable, however, writing about all forms of literature—autobiography, biography, political biography, fiction, drama, and poetry. Many of his literary reviews discuss English, Russian, or French writers, some of whom he admired and some of whom he scorned. Nevertheless, no matter what subject he surveyed, or whether he reviewed figures from the past or those who were his contemporaries, his writing reflects an extraordinarily high standard of moral, political, and literary values. The quality and extent of this literary work suggest that Woolf played a major role in twentieth-century British journalism and publishing.

Early Political Journalism

War and Peace, The Nation Supplement, A Journal of International Politics and The League of Nations was established in 1913. Some of the contributors to this journal were G. Lowes Dickinson, Bertrand Russell, G. D. H. Cole, J. A. Hobson, and Norman Angell. By the time Leonard Woolf joined the editorial committee in 1916, he had contributed a few anonymous pieces. In addition, a signed contribution appeared in January 1917, in an issue devoted to the role of force in international government and entitled "Shall the Nations Enforce Peace?" Woolf's introduction to this issue first defines international government as a lawmaking body which represents what the community sees as right, and whose general rules and laws are made by the community. Yet since disagreement over the use of force was weakening support for international government, Woolf argues that force should be accepted because governments are using force, but he adds that force should "only be used as a collective sanction of international law and order," and he ends by commenting that there will have to be "a change of the international heart" toward force for peace to be possible (54).

Another article, "Gird Up Thy Loins," appears in the July 1919 issue of the journal. In this essay, Woolf acknowledges the post-war disappointments of the people in England and the United States who had supported the League of Nations and the Wilsonian principles, and who had gotten a peace "so opposed to the rights of self-determination, liberty, and democracy that it can only be enforced by permanent military means, a peace of military alliances, and economic exploitation" (520). Nevertheless, Woolf argues that the League can be made into an effective system of international government, and he therefore urges Americans to accept the League.

From 1918 to 1919, as editor of *International Review*,[2] Woolf was responsible for two sections, "Facts and Documents" and "An International Diary." "The World of Nations: Facts and Documents," a twenty-to-thirty page section, covers such issues as the Covenant of the League—its constitutions, and its methods of settling international disputes and of preventing war (February-March 1918)—and the revised covenant, which Woolf claims had "gained enormously in clearness and precision" (June 1918, 470); events in Germany, including the Separatist movement for a Rhine Republic (November-December 1918); the general strike and nationalization of the coal industry in England (April-May 1918); texts of treaties between different nations; and excerpts from foreign newspapers about the peace terms, the blockade of Russia, and the Bolshevik movement.

"An International Diary" covers events in Central Europe and the development of the League. For example, at the end of 1918, Woolf focuses on actions by the Allied governments against the Russian Bolsheviks which he felt would lead to war. Because the Allied countries were relying for support on "small groups of reactionaries, officials, and officers of the Tsarist Regime," Woolf urges Britain to reconsider its present policy toward Russia (November-December, 7). Moreover, Woolf believed that the blockade of central Europe was an act of stupidity and inhumanity which was causing the Russian people to starve and was preventing Russian industry from having access to raw materials. Thus, he urged all governments to take steps under international action by the League of Nations to stop the blockade, and to feed the people and start industry. Similarly, Woolf criticized the demand for German reparations because the payments were too high and because Germany could not pay for the expenses of the war while the Allies were crippling the country's industry.

Another "International Diary" article, "The Fall of Bela Kun," appearing in the July-August 1919 issue, sums up part of Woolf's early political outlook. He comments that "the reason why nearly all Governments are bad will be found in the nature of politicians... if ever, progress is made, it is made in despite of these men" (73). Similar criticism of the Allied governments dominates his article "Europe's Doom" in the same issue:

Bankrupt States, rising prices, coal famine everywhere, starvation.... A statesman contronted with such a situation would... pursue... peace, stability of government, the revictualling of every country impartially, rigid economy and retrenchment in every direction. Instead of this, the Allied policy has continually yielded to the most reactionary, imperialist, and militarist forces: the Great Powers have sought for their own temporary and imperialist interests, have bolstered up the nationalist aspirations of small groups in some small States, and have actually in Eastern Europe deliberately set one small State to attack another. (77)

These articles reveal that Woolf's "International Diary" section and his selection of documents for "The World of Nations: Facts and Documents," which centered on the issues of war and peace in the post–World War I chaos, were shaped by a political philosophy of international government as the basis for peace.

In 1922, Woolf became foreign-affairs editor of the journal *Contemporary Review*, and he was responsible for a fifteen-to-sixteen-page foreign-affairs section in each month's issue. During the year, the key national and international events discussed were the League, the reparations problem, stability in Central and Western Europe, and international relations with the Far East. In an article in February 1922, Woolf analyzes the League's success in settling conflict in the Balkans. When Albania reported that Yugoslav troops were invading from the North, the League's Ambassadors' Conference decided on the borders, and, with the acceptance of the decision by both Albania and Yugoslavia, tensions were resolved. In contrast, the Poland and Vilna question was one of the "symptoms of the instability, almost anarchy in the political fabric of Europe" (250). All the states in the League had voted unanimously that Poland should evacuate the Vilna, yet Poland had maintained its occupation. Still another problem area involved the League's control of the

Saar under provisions in the Treaty of Versailles. Germany accused the League's commission of acting to divide the Saar from Germany by giving France more control by using French troops instead of local gendarmeries, as well as making use of the franc compulsory and introducing the French language.

In the February issue, Woolf also considered the internal problems of several countries. On the question of financial stability in Russia, he analyzed what had caused the current economic distress and discussed the government's attempts to stabilize the economy. Woolf also examined political and financial instability in Belgium. After the war, Belgium was left with "a depreciated currency, an overwhelming debt, and a budget which refuses to balance." (242). In addition, serious problems were developing around demands that the Flemish people be given equal treatment. Since the Flemish Belgians were being opposed by the Walloons, who were under the influence of France, Woolf argued that internal stability of Belgium was essential for international stability. Similarly, in Hungary, opposition to the government was rising and involved support for the return of the Hapsburgs; however, Hungary's neighbors, particularly Czechoslovakia, would feel that their autonomy would be threatened by such a change. Moreover, anti-Semitism was emerging in Hungarian politics. In April, Woolf reports that the leader of the Awakening Hungarians party was quoted as saying that they will not hesitate to use physical force in the fight against the Jews, and he also reports on armed bands in Budapest "marching through the streets and attacking Jews and other persons" (512).

In May, Woolf's leading section of "Foreign Affairs" entitled "Armies and Armaments" notes that there have been some strong efforts toward disarmament. In Japan there was an attempt to limit the military, which seemed to have developed in response to public opinion. In addition, limitation of arms was attempted by the Conference of Baltic States in Warsaw. These countries also proposed a new scheme for keeping peace internationally by regulating the number of troops in the frontier zones through mutual agreement. In the November issue, Woolf reported on the League's actions on disarmament: its recommendation that military expenditures by League members not be increased; and its creation of a commission to consider the disarmament issue further.

Woolf seems to have written little political journalism after 1922 until 1930, when he helped to found *Political Quarterly*. His political articles for this new journal indicate that he was moving away from the documentary journalism, or reporting on political events as they were developing in order to inform the public, which characterized his work for *International Review* and *Contemporary Review*. Still, the *Political Quarterly* articles reveal that Woolf felt his role was to educate the general public, since he often traces the history of issues, defines terms, and refers to other books or pamphlets on the same area. One of his *Political Quarterly* articles, "The Ideal of a League Remains," discusses his lack of power as a journalist because his was a minority opinion.[3] Nevertheless, in numerous articles for more than four decades, he continued to protest social injustice and to comment on events in a pre- and postwar world.

An unusual article entitled "The Future of British Broadcasting"[4] reveals Woolf's political outlook. Woolf comments that broadcasting "may well prove to be the most revolutionary invention in human history" (172). Since it can affect men's minds, it could also work toward creating the "prerequisites of spiritual civilization [which] are knowledge and opportunities of training the mind in the understanding of intellectual problems and the appreciation of works of art" (173). Yet since Woolf also recognizes the dangers involved in the power of broadcasting to mold public opinion, he urges the BBC to present all points of view so that the public can become informed. Moreover, he hopes that the BBC's board of governors will avoid the dangerous attitudes of "safety first and Pecksniffian respectability, of vested interests, party politics, propaganda, bureaucracy and officialdom, and the dead hand of convention" (180).

Turning to Woolf's writings on international events, one of the earliest articles, "From Sarajevo to Geneva,"[5] explores the differences between pre- and post–World War I Europe: "Sarajevo was the symbol of nationalism; Geneva is the symbol of

internationalism" (187). Woolf sees nationalism and internationalism as different communal political psychologies. Internationalism, which has resulted from the industrial and scientific
revolutions and modern commerce and communications, demands a system of international organization and government.
The League in Geneva represented such a system, but Woolf
comments that "international psychology is still weak, vacillat-
ing, and uninstructed" (197) because nearly all statesmen maintain a nationalist view and because the public desire for peace is
not yet strong. By 1933, Woolf's belief in the possibility of
establishing internationalism had diminished. He wrote in
"From Geneva to the Next War"[6] that the international inclination toward war is due to the recent years' economic distress and
to nationalist ideas and policies which are gaining in favor (33).
This has been paralleled by the rise of Hitlerism, the failure of the
League in the areas of disarmament and Japanese aggression in
Manchuria, and Britain's imperialist foreign policy. Although
people have turned against the League, Woolf urges its support
and cautions that the movement toward war develops "because
ordinary men have neither the knowledge nor the will to force
their statesmen and governments to pursue objects and policies
incompatible with war" (43). Some of these points are developed
further in "Labour's Foreign Policy."[7] Woolf again comments
that the world economic chaos indicates the breakdown of civilization, as well as the weakness of a capitalist system. Yet he urges
that nationalism give way to internationalism and states that
there must be a change from capitalism to socialism. In addition,
Woolf analyzes the world situation, pointing out that Japan,
Germany, and Italy have militarist governments. Concluding his
analysis, Woolf suggests that the Labour party in Britain should
support the League and should develop a policy to deal with the
Fascist powers (517).

Several articles on the role of the League appeared during the
late 1930s. "Meditation on Abyssinia"[8] argues that the world has
accepted violence as a means of settling problems. For example,
the League is attempting to liquidate Mussolini while others are
trying to liquidate the League, and Woolf comments that this use

of force makes it difficult to stabilize international relations. Five months after the Abyssinian crisis, in "The Ideal of a League Remains,"[9] Woolf attributes the League's failure to prevent international aggression to a lack of understanding among member nations of both the term collective security and the obligations of a country as a member of the League (333). Nations, he argues, must believe in collective security as a means to strength and must abandon reliance on armaments. The British, for example, have chosen to rely on force, and Woolf writes that "like good, civilized, impotent men...they set to work to build up armaments, to make Britain so strong that not even Hitler or Mussolini will attack us. A dream which the whole of history proves to be a suicidal delusion" (345). Until people recognize this dream as a delusion, however, Woolf believes that only the ideal of the League will remain.

Writing further on the attempts of nations to rearm, Woolf comments in "Arms and Peace"[10] that to take the pacifist position and to "so watch the destruction of all liberty piecemeal in one country after another may be more than the human nature of the most pacifist democrat or socialist can stand" (34). Moreover, he believed that isolation would strengthen the Fascist powers and would still lead to the problem of national security. Similarly, the policy of alliance would be unsatisfactory, as it would require armaments and thus "would be a policy of suicide" (35). Although this article does not seem to offer the non-Fascist nations an alternative, Woolf does present one in "The Resurrection of the League."[11] He argues that the nucleus of a resurrected League could create a peace front in Europe, and he therefore urges that Great Britian and France should ally. Woolf also emphasizes that the USSR would have to be involved in this peace front, even though he knew there would be great opposition to this point.

After the first week of World War II, Woolf's article "De Profundis"[12] appeared. Here he comments that the failure of peace was the failure of international security; this in turn led to the increased growth of a war psychology that undermined the commitment to international security. Woolf also writes that nations have acted as sovereign independent states, and have concentrated their power in armaments, thereby contributing to anarchy. The alternative Woolf poses is a system of law and communal control of power, and as the article concludes, Woolf predicts that when the time for peace arrives, something like the League will be created, and a federation of states may be involved; both systems will depend on "a very advanced form of social co-operation and of communal psychology" (476) which Woolf hoped the world would adopt.

Woolf continued to contribute major editorial articles to *Political Quarterly* in the 1940s. The earliest, "Utopia and Reality,"[13] emphasizes that although the world seems to regard peace as utopian and power politics as real, power politics is untenable in modern society. Woolf writes that "generally and in the long run common interests are more real than conflicting interests" (173); moreover, power politics fails because it "ignores both the reality of facts and the reality of psychology" (179). Developments in France after Marshal Pétain took control of the government are discussed in another article, "Democracy at Bay."[14] Woolf argues that Pétain, "an octogenarian French version of Field-Marshall Hindenburg,... destroyed French democracy" (335). Believing that what happened in France could be a lesson to Britain, Woolf urges that the House of Commons maintain its responsibilities and prevent "the immobilization of parliament" (337) which occurred in France, so that Britain could face the challenge of war with strength not only on the battlefield but also in government.

A striking analysis of political dictatorship appears in the article "Hitler's Psychology."[15] Hitler, Woolf argues, is impersonal, even depersonalized, "a kind of mental sac containing megalomania, hatred, and a limited number of political ideas" (373). Unlike other fanatical politicians who reveal human emotions, Hitler seems like "a robot with a single emotion of hate and fear and he makes one afraid" (374). In Hitler's language, both his speeches and his writings, "there is not one imaginative phrase.... His mind is uneducated, empty, and inconceivably narrow" (374–75); however, he convinces people to follow his ideas by appealing to "the prejudices and self-interest of the audience" (378); also, he presents his ideas with "ruthless, insane force and persistence of ... will" (378–79), attempting to "rouse passions, obscure inconvenient truths, and induce belief in untruths" (380). Woolf's analysis ends with a striking comparison of Hitler to the social criminal: "the frigid cruelty with which he tortures individuals ... and with which he humiliates and mutilates states or nations ... reminds one of sadistic and mentally disordered murderers, like Jack the Ripper" (383). Only in a world which is no longer civilized, and in a Germany demoralized by economic collapse and fear, could Hitlerism be accepted.

As the war events progressed, Woolf focused on the development of an alliance between the United States and Britain. He examines the Roosevelt-Churchill declaration in "How to Make the Peace,"[16] writing that it is a means of establishing Anglo-American cooperation, and stressing that the USSR should become involved. Woolf, however, was most concerned with the process of achieving peace; thus, he argued that the economic reconstruction effort should be controlled through an international Economic Commission and should involve a change in the concept of state sovereignty; similarly, the political reconstruction effort should be controlled by the peace aims and internationalism. Woolf therefore also stressed the importance of an international peace system to which Germany could belong when ready to be a loyal and peaceful member (373).

Another important postwar issue is discussed in "The Future of the Small State."[17] Here Woolf argues that sovereignty of the small state is the concern of every nation since it involves economics, international economic reconstruction, self-determination, and nationalism. He suggests that frontiers be drawn to keep national minorities to a minimum, that a charter for rights for minorities be constructed, and that transfers of population be considered to avoid future tensions (218–19). Woolf also claims that national self-determination cannot exist if Great Powers control small states, but that the way to peace will be to institute international government which will limit the political and economic independence of all states, large and small (223). Thus, when he examined the proposals for the United Nations in 1945, he focused in his article "The United Nations"[18] on the distribution of powers, arguing against the Russian government's proposal that the Great Powers be given an absolute veto on any issue, because he felt it would increase the vulnerability of small states and thereby contradict the possibility and premise of collective security.

Criticism of the ruling party and leaders of the British government frequently appears in Woolf's writings. In "The Man of Munich,"[19] he analyzes Neville Chamberlain's role in the events which led to war. Woolf writes that politicians like Baldwin and Chamberlain had a "sterile conservatism [which] had drained them of all social understanding or creativeness" and made them "negative, timid, unrealistic, and unprincipled. They tried vainly to face the future by turning their backs to it" (201). Moreover, the conservatives maintained the vested interest attitude of their class, which Woolf felt led to the inaction that allowed Hitler to consolidate his power. Woolf's condemnation of Chamberlain ends with a warning that "the Chamberlain attitude and policy are not dead in this or several other countries" (205).

In contrast to his focus on political figures and analysis of events of the war years, Woolf's article "Music in Moscow"[20] discusses the position of artists in a totalitarian state and points out that writers and artists in Russia, as in Germany, have accommodated the government's demands that art be the mechanical reproduction of reality or government propaganda. Although music in Russia has had more freedom than art or literature, in 1948, the four major Russian composers—Muskovsky, Shostakovich, Prokofiev, and Khachaturian—were attacked for practicing their art in an "anti-Soviet" and antipeople way (215). In response, Woolf claims that great music has nothing to do with politics or society (215). Although capitalism has not allowed artists to have complete freedom, Woolf believed that Russian communism attempts total control of artists and is thus "completely destructive" of both artists and art; and, Woolf writes, when art is destroyed, so is society (218).

In the 1950s, Woolf wrote mostly book reviews for *Political Quarterly*; however, three major articles appeared in 1952, 1955, and 1956. In the first, "Something Out of Africa,"[21] Woolf focuses on the question of uniting Southern and Northern Rhodesia and Nyasaland in a federation. Although most Africans opposed the federation because it would bring them into contact with Southern Rhodesia's racist system and the control of white men, the whites of these territories, as well as the European powers, supported the federation. Woolf describes this situation as "the beginning of what may well be one of the greatest and most disastrous racial conflicts in human history," and he writes that behind it was "the menace of white South Africa and its insensate native policy" of apartheid (325). The article also points out that South Africa fears any African movement for independence, for as Woolf claims, "liberty is the most infectious of all political diseases, except perhaps equality" (326). Finally, Woolf predicts that "sooner or later the Africans will oppose force with force and organized racial dominance with organized racial resistance" (320).

In his second article, "What is History?",[22] Woolf examines the contemporary historian's craft through an extended review of Arnold Toynbee's *A Study of History* and Isaiah Berlin's *Historical Inevitability*. Toynbee approaches history "as a religious, philosophical, or metaphysical mystery," rather than as "a record of human society in terms of cause and effect" (223). Although Woolf understands that many individuals find it "too painful to accept the inhuman universe" which science and reason reveal, and thus they have turned to religion, he cannot accept this view of history.

The third article, "Espionage, Security, and Liberty,"[23] centers on the emergence of several cases of international espionage involving the Soviet Union, and the question of national security. Woolf argues that the organization of the Russian espionage system is "extremely dangerous to states against which it operates" (155) because it surpasses conventional military surveillance practiced by all countries, and that this Communist spy system "undermines and corrupts public life" (161). Woolf therefore urges that a system of screening public servants with access to government secrets be developed, but he also argues that governments should restrain themselves and not emphasize secrecy and security too much, since that could lead to greater espionage involvement (162).

During the 1940s, 1950s, and 1960s, Woolf's book reviews for *Political Quarterly* continued to reveal his standards of values in politics. In his autobiography, he frequently commented negatively about the trade of journalism and the style of journalistic writing. When reviewing *The Life of Joseph Chamberlain, Vol. IV, 1901–1903* by Julian Amery,[24] he first focuses on style, writing that J. L. Garvin, editor of the *Observer*, who wrote the first three volumes of Chamberlain's biography, "suffered badly from the occupational disease of his trade—a hardening of the brain centre which produces thought and a loosening of the centre which produces and controls words": hence Garvin's "brilliant verbosity" but "inability for hard and concise thinking" (396). Moreover, in his review of *The Observer and J. L. Garvin, 1908–1914* by Alfred M. Gollin,[25] Woolf claims that Garvin was always on the "wrong side," that is, "the side which fights blindly...against every proposal or policy which alone might secure necessary social changes, a peaceful and prosperous development of human society" (394), because he identified with the interests of the ruling classes and favored nationalism. Woolf similarly reveals his high standards for political life in another review of a biography of Lord Clifford Allen.[26] Describing Allen as "a cold man" with "a terrible amount of high-mindedness" who was also "a confirmed masochist," Woolf argues that the British public can accept this type of personality since they "adore high-minded masochists and political Pecksniffs." Woolf also points out that the public can be satisfied only so long with the mediocrity of a politician like Allen; "sooner or later...people begin to feel bored or uneasy," and then they see through the façade of respectability and political responsibility (97).

Several other reviews are critical of political figures.[27] For example, about Harold Macmillan's writing in *Winds of Change* and *The Middle Way*,[28] Woolf first states that he has a "flat, dull and pedestrian" style, characterized by "the drone of the cliché, the inevitable adjective, and the mechanical metaphor"; no one,

Woolf claims, "ought to write like this" (96). Yet Woolf also relates these comments about style to politics, as he criticizes Macmillan for "something disturbing equivocal" in his political attitudes; while "nothing untrue is said...the truth itself is blurred and out of focus" (97). As a result, Macmillan never faces historical and political issues. Similarly, in his reviews of *The Autobiography of Bertrand Russell* Woolf is critical of Russell's politics.[29] He clearly admires Russell's stance as a "pugnacious pacifist," which was Russell's response to social injustice. Further praising Russell, Woolf comments that "the number and range of his books are extraordinary...all these are illuminated by his wit, the brilliance of his mind, and his astringent individuality" (315). Although Woolf finds Russell's autobiography fascinating, he comments on Russell's weaknesses, particularly that he is subject to "intellectual petulance or arrogance" (315) and "emotionalism [which] often affects his reason and his judgement," and leads to a "violence of his prejudices" and "a warping of his judgement" (316). When reviewing Volume 2 of Russell's autobiography,[30] Woolf analyzes Russell's political impotence, attributing it to the fundamentally negative attitude he had because he disliked men and their ideas and actions. In a letter, Russell had written: "I hate...the pacifists who keep saying human nature is essentially good, in spite of all the daily proofs to the contrary. I hate the planet and the human race—I am ashamed to belong to such a species" (345). Such hatred, Woolf points out, is "politically disastrous," as political attitudes must be based on reason, not emotion (345). Russell, Woolf argues, allowed his emotions to lead him to make irresponsible statements, and as a result, emotion outweighed his genius and reason.

Considering his frequent and devastating criticism of writers and politicians, Woolf's unqualified praise for some writers and their work is striking. For example, in his review of *The Russian Peasant* by Sir John Maynard,[31] Woolf comments that Maynard "has a meditative mind, a historical imagination, judgement disciplined by culture, and the ability to write English. His book ...is fascinating to read" (205). He also admired Gerald Brennan's account of the background of the Spanish Civil War, *The Spanish Labyrinth,*[32] calling it "a remarkable book, which deserves careful study" (289), and writing that it has a "combination of knowledge, intelligence, and impartiality" and that it reveals a "speculative, ruminating mind" without which history becomes a "bare record of events interspersed with superficial generosity" (290). Similarly, Woolf expressed warm appreciation for Beatrice Webb's autobiographical work *Our Partnership,*[33] claiming that there is great interest in the "immense intelligence and honesty" of her diaries,[34] which contain her "penetrating analysis of characters" (343).

Literary Reviewing

In contrast to his journalism work for *Political Quarterly,* which consisted almost completely of political articles and book reviews on social and political figures and issues, much of Woolf's writing for the *Nation,* which later became the *New Statesman & Nation,* was on literature. In fact, his literary journalism began when, as literary editor, he produced "The World of Books" page in the 5 May 1923 (Volume 33) issue. This front page of the weekly book-review section reveals Woolf's literary, historical, and political interests, as he discusses works of fiction, autobiography, biography, history, politics, and social commentary. Throughout the years, a number of articles were devoted to the problems and quality of journalistic writing. For example, in "The Journalessayist,"[35] he wrote that in the past, the essay could be "fluid, discursive, meditative," whereas in the present, the main problem for the journal essayist is space—"how to produce something complete in itself" that does not exceed three columns. To Woolf, most journalistic writing lacks style. He later comments in "The Romance of a Drowned Parrot"[36] that the "curse of journalistic criticism is that it tends to a sloppy or confused use of standards," and he argues further in "The Most Dangerous of Trades"[37] that journalists think in units of about 2,500 words, and this leads to "disconnectedness and even inconclusiveness." Still another negative comment about journalism appears in "From Falstaff to Micawber":[38] "The curse of journalism is . . . the belief that to be serious, learned, analytic is to be dull and boring, and that the greatest sin which can be committed in print is not to be entertaining." Woolf felt that if the standard of journalism with its emphasis on entertainment should dominate literary criticism, it would be disastrous. Yet in a later article, "The Ideals of Journalism,"[39] he argues that over the past twenty-five years, the quality of journals had improved: "They are not only more alive, but more intelligently written, and written, too, for more intelligent readers." Woolf also rallies to the side of reviewers, defending them from accusations that their work is "dictated by personal feelings or . . . [is] incompetent." Claiming that he has "hardly ever detected a case of wilful dishonesty," Woolf emphasizes that the reviewer performs a useful role in informing the public about contemporary literature.

Just as Woolf's comments on journalism suggest an important role for reviewers, his comments on the book trade argue that this industry plays an important role in society. In "Publishers and Old Books,"[40] he writes that "the education (in the widest sense) of the people must depend upon it," and he comments further, in "The Making of Books,"[41] that the producing and selling of books can have "important effects upon the intellectual and aesthetic life of a nation." He also argues, however, that there are "very serious evils in the present system of making and selling books," namely overproduction and high prices: first, "the market is flooded with . . . books which have no kind of point or value" so that books of merit can be outnumbered and overshadowed by those of poor quality; second, because of the high price of books, many serious works do not sell well, since not many readers can afford to buy them.

On the subject of book reviewing, Woolf writes that literary critics are generally "incorrigibly conservative," expecting literature to conform to form and content that they already know. Nevertheless, as a reviewer, he was receptive to innovation and was particularly interested in contemporary literature. In "The New Art of Biography,"[42] he assesses the state of literature:

We live in an age in which ... the literary Constitution is not very strong
or healthy.... Poetry has become catalogic and unintelligible; the essay
has been killed by the article; the novel, where it is not machine-made
for the circulating library, is perilously near dissolution; only Mr. Shaw
stands between the play and complete extinction; while, as for history
and scientific or learned books, it seems to be accepted that a marriage
between literature and learning is not eugenic and that the common
reader will not read a serious book nor the expert a well-written one.

As Woolf wrote in another article, "The Bolshies on Parnas-
sus,"[43] these changes in modern literature raise important questions. For example: Why can one age accept tradition while
another cannot? Why have writers today had to reject past
forms? and Why is there "tremendous obscurity" in most modern
poetry and fiction? He responds to some of these questions with
comments on the modern novel and biography. In "The Novel of
To-Day,"[44] Woolf writes that critics often attribute the weaknesses in modern fiction to lack of form, lack of sympathy for
people, or lack of philosophy. Woolf, however, believes that
modern novels are weak because there is no unity, no central idea
which holds the work together and which is "akin to belief." In
contrast to the novel, biography is flourishing because, as he
discusses in "The Science and Art of Biography,"[45] readers in the
modern period have an unusual interest in biography. To Woolf,
the aesthetic of this genre poses the problem of "the relation
between biography as a science and biography as an art." Biographers are partly scientists as they seek to tell the truth, and as a
result, the need to comment on reality imposes a framework of
history and facts; however, another framework, that of art, is also
demanded. The biographer, for example, must be able to create
the psychology of an individual, for, according to Woolf, the
psychological aspect of biography constitutes the ultimate challenge of the modern biographer.

Woolf also discusses contemporary aesthetic theories in the
plastic arts. In "Mr. Roger Fry,"[46] he admits that while most art
criticism and aesthetic theory seems a "vague and dreary mud-
dle," Roger Fry's work makes art criticism an "exciting adven-

ture." Woolf finds Fry's anthology of essays entitled *Transforma-tions* to be his best work. The range of subjects in these essays is amazing, and Fry's "remarkable qualities...sensibility...intelli-gence, imaginative ability, fantasticality and philosophic curios-ity" are evident, as is his ability to "make you see what he sees and feel what he feels." Moreover, Fry's essays on aesthetic theory, and particularly his view that illustrations can act as comple-ments to a literary text as if they were "a running commentary, like marginal notes written by a reader," are praised by Woolf, who also considers Fry's essay "Culture and Snobbism" a percep-tive discussion of the "unfortunate plight of the true artist con-fronted by the cultured, the snobs, and the Philistines." Finally, Woolf comments on how Fry's essay "Some Questions in Esthet-ics" broadens his previous aesthetic views so that they emphasize that the plastic aspects in a picture are not the only means of creating aesthetic emotion. This point was especially important to Woolf who believed that the artist could produce aesthetic emotion through psychological relations—the way a plastic form in a picture communicates a concept—and that in this way, graphic art could be allied to other arts such as literature and music. Equally important was that this emphasis on psychologi-cal relations would now allow Fry to accept representation as having value in painting.

Woolf develops the question of the artistic value of representa-tional painting in "Man and ——?"[47] which discusses John Sar-gent's work. To Woolf, Sargent is more than a pure representa-tionalist because he tries to give "a vision of attributes which are not usual—of human character, for instance." Furthermore, although interested in visual details, Sargent did not portray the material world by itself, but in relation to beauty and human character. Woolf admits that Sargent may not be a great artist, perhaps because he was "a man without passion" and perhaps because his concept of beauty and of human nature is shallow, yet he still values Sargent's attempt to go beyond mere representa-tion.

The aesthetic problem of the relationship between matter and form in literature is explored in a discussion of the novels of

Henry James in "Phantasmagoric Life."[48] Woolf sees James as "detribalized," experiencing the "personal tragedy of...spiritual suspension in a no-man's land...between two countries, two continents, two civilisations." Because of this and because he was a romantic, James was never able to see Europe realistically; thus, his search for realism led to failure. James then abandoned the "novel as history approach" and created his own form based on a "phantasmagoric life of personal relations and psychological subtleties," which Woolf considers remarkable for its beauty, but characterized by a sense of uneasiness and insubstantiality.

Woolf reveals his personal taste in literature in several articles. As he states in "Lord Northcliffe Round the World,"[49] one criterion for his interest in a book is the way a writer "brought the flavour of his character into the book." On autobiography, he comments in another review, "Charming Memories":[50] "I go to autobiography for something different from great literature, or even good writing...I must have the illusion that the autobiographer is talking to me." As for "great" writing, he defines its qualities in many articles. For example, about Jane Carlyle's letters, he wrote in "Mrs. Carlyle"[51] that they reveal the art of a fine letter-writer and novelist: the ability to analyze and create characterization, to record conversations, and to create "the atmosphere of a scene or of a character through a conversation." Similarly, E. M. Forster's novel *A Passage to India* is praised in "Arch Beyond Arch"[52] as "superbly written," with humor, "command of dialogue," and impressive characters, and with an interweaving of several themes which comment perceptively on human nature and experience. Later, turning to Peacock in his article entitled "Peacock,"[53] Woolf claims he is "a great writer because he has a perfect style; it is perfectly adapted to what he wants to say." Humor, brilliance, clearness, and simplicity characterize Peacock's works, and Woolf credits him with being "one of the first novelists to create an intelligent woman who was both charming and alive." Woolf further defines a great book, in "The Last Conrad,"[54] as having both a main idea and the structure necessary to control and express that idea. Yet he is also most appreciative of fine style, and in "Laurence Sterne"[55] he describes

Sterne as "one of the greatest writers of English prose...a pure artist," who is unrivaled in the style of writing which is based on a sentence structure which Woolf calls "trailers," in which the "sentence flows on, turning and twisting and doubling with the writer's thought, the words bubbling up into images and fancies, falling again into smooth and subtle rhythms." To Woolf, the "extraordinary beauty and subtlety of these trailing sentences" provide the perfect mode of expression for Sterne's wit, humor, and imagination.

In 1927, Woolf collected and published a number of his book reviews for the *Nation* in *Essays on Literature, History, Politics, Etc.*[56] This volume presents Woolf's views of writers and politicians past and present and reveals that Woolf is concerned not only with an individual's works but also with his character and with his relationship to his time. These criteria can be seen in all the literary essays, but particularly in "Ben Jonson," where Woolf indicates his affection for Jonson. Describing Jonson's character as "hewn out of rough rock, intense vitality, immense robustness" (16), Woolf claims that although Jonson has been neglected, he is one of the greatest English writers (14), as well as "the first English critic, a first-rate prose writer, an original thinker, and a great character" (16). Moreover, Woolf clearly believed that a critic and reader of literature—whether fiction or nonfiction—should explore the personality of the writer; thus, in his essay "Herbert Spencer," he describes Spencer as a man of strong emotions and "indomitable individuality" (25), and he comments that "great individuality of character springs not from the reasoning part of the mind, but from the emotional"(34).

In contrast to Jonson's energy and greatness as a writer and Spencer's individuality, Woolf focuses on Hazlitt's limitations, claiming that he "went as near to achieving greatness as any man who has missed it" (21). Although Hazlitt's "passion for personal and political liberty" (23) represented a very advanced position for his age, he was unable to transcend personal limitations to make his social and political views universal (24). Similarly, the main character trait affecting Hazlitt's writing was that he was ill-natured and thus "never able either to transcend or to universalize his bitterness" (21) into the impersonal passion which Woolf claims is essential for greatness (22). Woolf also finds Hazlitt failing to achieve an admirable style of writing; despite humor and imagination, Hazlitt's sentences are like "brilliant jets of fire" (22) which soon irritate the reader. In contrast, the style Woolf admires is best exemplified by William Cobbett's writing, a style Woolf describes as "plain, absolutely unaffected, vigorous and supple, beautiful" (26). Cobbett's writing also strikes Woolf as typically English, for his sentences have "something of the atmosphere of the English country and the English climate, as well as of the English language and the English character" (27). Nevertheless, with Cobbett, as with Hazlitt, Woolf finds that a need to attack others constitutes a major flaw in personality and artistry. This criticism again affirms Woolf's point that a writer must transcend the personal to the impersonal.

When Woolf was a Cambridge undergraduate, Samuel Butler was considered an important writer because he criticized conventional manners and thinking. Writing about Butler years after his Cambridge days, Woolf still believes that Butler should have an important place in the history of English society as "a great iconoclast"; however, he modifies his earlier unqualified admiration and points out that although he values Butler's "peculiar humor, his dialectic, his precise eccentricities, a certain dryness of mind"(46), he also realizes that Butler's works make one shift from "enjoyment to boredom . . . from admiration to contempt" (44). Moreover, he recognizes that a lack of emotion or passion will limit both Butler's popularity as a writer and his ability to write great literature (48), for even his best works "lack the warmth or glow which seems inseparable from great literature" (48). Thus, in this essay, Woolf again seems to stress that a literary critic must be able to go beyond personal likes and dislikes when assessing a writer's works.

In an essay on Conrad, Woolf's comments are also a mixture of praise and blame. He praises Conrad as a self-conscious stylist, even though contemporary critics object to anyone emphasizing a writer's style because they insist on the importance of meaning. Yet when Woolf turns his attention to content in Conrad, he

attributes Conrad's weakness as a writer to his handling of
content, claiming that Conrad had no message; "politics and
social questions did not appear in his books" (59). Woolf also
writes that Conrad had a "few simple ideas" which he emphasized in each work, and that this limited range of concerns makes
readers unsympathetic. Furthermore, he claims Conrad's works
are "melodramatic" because he eliminates "everything which
makes life itself and the people in it so subtle, unexpected,
confused, and sordid" (64). Woolf, however, concedes that there
are works by Conrad in which the characters are psychologically
complex, and thus the reality of the characters involves the reader
and makes the work a success, for, Woolf concludes, if books lack
that psychological dimension, they are "splendid shells, magnificent façades, admirable forms, but there is no life in them" (70).
This analysis of Conrad's strengths and weaknesses leads Woolf
to a definition of a great book: "there must be a central, living idea
which all through the writing of a book must be giving off radiant
emanations...and the author must also have in his mind the
image of a form or shell which can take and hold and mould and
restrain this idea" (70).

One of the most striking essays on literature in this volume,
"The Modern Nightingale," comments on contemporary poetry.
Woolf writes that poetry, which is more "naked and direct" than
prose (91), is a better indication of the intellectual and spiritual
qualities of an age. In the modern age, which Woolf terms "an age
of doubt and disillusionment" (91), poets have either been writing poetry in traditional form, which "answers to nothing...a-
live in the living world" (92), or have been attempting to find
new poetic forms. Woolf does not believe that a poet has to use
traditional forms (92); indeed, he believes the progress of literature demands deviations from conventions, and that this is particularly true for poetry, since traditional forms of poetry are not
suited to the contemporary mind and experience. If poets are
having difficulty developing new forms, Woolf suggests that
there should be a moratorium on writing poetry for about fifteen
years (95), which might prevent contemporary poets from
mechanically adopting older modes of poetic expression. To

Woolf, T. S. Eliot is the contemporary poet who has rejected old forms and developed a new mode of poetry. Unlike the poet in the Victorian period who was seen as a nightingale singing a sweet tune, Eliot's poet now makes his nightingale sing " 'Jug, jug' to dirty ears," thus capturing the spirit of the modern age (101). Woolf argues that readers should not be dismayed if they do not understand Eliot's poetry completely, as long as they can understand his technique: "First, he works persistently through allusions.... Secondly, he attempts to communicate rather subtle emotions by the crude and violent juxtaposition of discordant scenes, thoughts, emotions" (192). Before ending, however, Woolf turns to Eliot's weakness, commenting that he is too insistent on the same concerns, and cautioning that by emphasizing emptiness, Eliot may be creating too sterile a form for poetry.

Woolf focuses on another aspect of contemporary literature in his essay "The First Person Singular." Writing that he notices a repeated use of the word "I" in Alec Waugh's book *Myself When Young: Confessions*, he states that "the ego in print is a very tricky and erratic thing" (108). Autobiography is the genre which lends itself to the use of the first-person singular, and Woolf thus cites Benjamin Franklin's autobiography as the type of work which benefits from displaying one's ego. Then, Woolf ends with a further note of caution to the modern writer that the egotistical book is suspect, for it can "be either the most charming or the most infuriating form of literature" (112); in addition, the writer runs the risk that "his ego which appears to be infinitely important to himself will appear to be infinitely unimportant to everyone else" (113).

Woolf's final literary essay, "Winged and Unwinged Words," reviews *Public Speaking and Debate* by Holyoake, written in 1895. Woolf defines oratory as an art in which the audience is not important, whereas public speaking aims to persuade the audience. Woolf believes that "public speaking or skilled persuasion has killed oratory or the art of speaking" (117). Although Holyoake's main point about public speaking is that it persuades the audience by an appeal to reason, Woolf argues that this is a delusion; the public speaker must appeal to passion (118), as did

Gladstone, whose art of persuasion was his ability to sway the audience by establishing strong emotional contact.

Woolf's concluding essay, "The Gentleness of Nature," which is less a review than a meditation about nature and man's attempt to tame the natural world, reveals another side of Woolf's literary talents. In this essay, the sight of a plover close to death is striking to Woolf because, in the West, man has "succeeded so amazingly in taming Nature that she hides entirely from us her ruthless ferocity, her dark and gloomy ways" (250). In the East, however, Nature controls man's life. Woolf describes his experiences in the jungle areas of Ceylon during the onset of rinderpest disease among buffalo, which resulted in mass death for all the animals. As a sign of how "the grim cruelty of Nature had full sway" (253), animals fed off diseased animals and died, and the only watering hole within twenty miles became too polluted for elephants to drink from it. This essay is a striking contrast to the others in this volume. Here Woolf's tone is lyrical and meditative, though intense, while in some of the other essays, he is often cynical and sarcastic, relying on twists and turns of intellect to exert critical judgment and to impress his reader. In the literary reviews, he seems to be in awe of no man, criticizing the powers and limitations of mankind; in this last essay, he is clearly in awe of the powers of nature and animal life, those forces which are larger than man.

In the 1940s, Woolf's reviews for the *New Statesman & Nation* continued to reveal how his journalism work complemented his interest in literature. He writes again on the role of the publisher and on publishing as a business. In "Books in General,"[57] Woolf argues that in the last thirty years, publishing has become a mass-production industry subject to "all the symptoms of monopoly capitalism," and thus oriented to making profits from "the large-scale degradation of the public taste" (285). In search of profits, publishers try to press "best-sellers" on the public through advertising and, in turn, they pressure authors to write books which will appeal to a mass audience. Woolf opposes this process because it is "insidiously destructive of art" (285). The relationship between economics and literature is again the subject of another, although very different, essay, "The Economic Determination of Jane Austen."[58] Here Woolf emphasizes that every novelist is affected by the economic system of his time, because "economics determined both his mind and his environment" (39). Austen's "social and psychological environment was...of the eighteenth century country gentleman," which was unaffected by the industrial revolution and growth of capitalism (40). In addition, since her family ascended to a titled class, her view of money, property, work, and the professions is typical of a landed aristocracy or gentry. Finally, her social standards, which are "entirely those of money and snobbery," reflect the emerging influence of the capitalistic bourgeoisie (41).

The role of the writer as social critic and satirist is examined in reviews of George Bernard Shaw's works. As a young man, Woolf had been influenced by Voltaire; his own writing often involves social criticism, expressing scorn or satire of men's social and individual weaknesses. Thus, his appreciation of Shaw as a social satirist is not surprising.[59] Woolf praises Shaw's "superb gift of wit and humor" (376), and he argues that Shaw's writing functions in the Victorian era as Voltaire's did in the eighteenth century—to attack and destroy cruelty, hypocrisy, and outdated notions. Although he acclaims Shaw as a great writer and a great man, as well as one of the most amusing of men (376), Woolf is also critical of Shaw's thinking. While Shaw "can destroy evil things by his superb gift of comedy...he has little or nothing to put in its place...he cannot be serious because he cannot be passionate" (376). Shaw's religious and political works, therefore, fail, and he is unable to create fully developed characters. Woolf argues this point further in another review, "G. B. S.,"[60] commenting that Shaw used nonsense to destroy "false and cruel gods"; however, Woolf warns that "you cannot convert the world to sense by talking nonsense; you may destroy one false God... but the world will immediately begin to worship another....It is only by talking bleak, bare sense and converting the world to it that you can make the world sensible" (188).

Throughout his literary essays, Woolf refers to the opinions of "highbrows." One can assume that he means intellectuals, artists, writers, and critics, but it is possible to understand this term further by looking at a Hogarth Press publication, *Hunting the Highbrow* (1927).[61] With humor and satire, Woolf considers a serious topic—the position of the intellectual or artist in society—and he also reveals more of his views about literature, literary criticism, and art. At the beginning of *Hunting the Highbrow*, Woolf writes that "the highbrow is an extremely unpopular person" who is pursued by the press and the general public (5), yet he identifies himself as on the side of the highbrows, and criticizes those who attack highbrows for thinking that their artistic taste is superior. In a parody of the language and approach of the scientific naturalist, Woolf divides highbrows into different categories. Aesthetic highbrows, for example, usually have more sophisticated taste than their peers; thus, they are disliked because they do not admire what the general public likes. Woolf asserts, however, that popularity is not the test of artistic merit; indeed, he writes: "most great literature is not easy to read or understand; it is often extremely boring; it is very rarely entertaining or amusing" (29).

In contrast to the aesthetic highbrow, the intellectual highbrow can be threatening to many men because he challenges conventional notions and prejudices and reveals how "thinking is painful and distasteful to us" (41). Here Woolf inserts a sharply critical comment on the educational system, stating that it teaches "children and young people that to think is a dreary and laborious process" (42), and he attacks other institutions, such as the press, the political and legal systems, and the ideologies of religion and patriotism, for implying that the intellect is "suspect and unpopular" (43). In contrast, Woolf argues that intellectual work is "extraordinarily pleasant" (43), but more importantly, he points out that the intellectual comes to play a significant role in society when conditions of the masses become intolerable and social revolt is imminent. Nevertheless, he recognizes that the intellectual's power is limited because it is difficult to change the traditions of prejudice, passion, and unreason which people follow; for this reason, intellectuals can have a place in society only if human psychology will accept reason as a means of determining communal affairs. If man can become a "rational political and social animal," then the intellectual highbrow will be respected by society.

Hunting the Highbrow is clearly a serious essay, but one cannot help appreciating how Woolf has welded together the serious and the comic. Humor is inevitable as one reads Woolf's ridiculous Latin names for the categories of highbrow: "altifrons altifrontissimus, altifrons aestheticus, pseudaltifrons intellectualis, and pseudaltifrons aestheticus." Particularly amusing is his description of this last species of highbrow as "lurking in the undergrowth of Cambridge, Oxford, Chelsea, Bloomsbury" and as being "a cross between...the bore and the snob" (39). He develops this humor even further by commenting that these creatures have little faith in their own aesthetic judgments; thus, they exalt "the latest thing either in antiquity or modernity" (40).

In still another work, *A Calendar of Consolation,*[62] Woolf reveals his familiarity with literature and his standards of literary taste. This unusual, little-known work of his is well described by its subtitle: "For each day of the year a profound, original, and often suprising quotation." The Bible, Shakespeare, and many English, French, and Russian writers are represented, and the quotations seem to sum up many of Woolf's perspectives on life. For example, as Woolf frequently challenged social, political, moral, and intellectual conventions, it is not surprising to find several quotations in the same vein. Woolf quotes Swift: "A nice man is a man of nasty ideas" (3); Pope: "I never knew any man in my life who could not bear another's misfortunes perfectly like a Christian" (3); Dryden: "Repentance is but want of power to sin" (48); and Shakespeare: "Though I am not naturally honest, I am so sometimes by chance" (16). In addition to attacking conventional social and moral concepts, Woolf's criticism of man's lack of civilized values was an important part of his life's work. This concern is reflected in his quotations from Jeremy Taylor: "Our hearts are hard and inflexible to the softer whispers of mercy and compassion, having no love for anything but strange flesh and heaps of money and popular noises, for misery and folly" (7); and Disraeli: "You are now, my dear son, a member of what is called

the great world; society formed on anti-social principles" (29); or
Hazlitt on women: "Women care nothing about poets, or philosophers, or politicians.... No true woman ever regarded anything but her lover's person and address" (77); and Spenser: "No
greater shame to man than inhumanities" (64). Man's inhumanity and lack of positive moral values may have led Woolf frequently to despair, that mood being reflected in his choice of
Shakespeare's lines: "How weary, stale, flat, and unprofitable/
Seem to me all the uses of this world!" (15). Yet Woolf was always
able to transcend despair to assert positive values, through his
literary and political work; for this reason, Virginia Woolf's lines
about death at the end of her novel *The Waves* seem to reflect his
attitude toward overcoming despair, disappointment, and loss:
"Death is the enemy.... Against you I will fling myself, unvan-
quished and unyielding, O Death" (15).

Woolf's horror of fascism and nazism and his attempts to
point out how they were debased political systems which destroyed respect for learning and culture may have led him to
emphasize Hitler's blatant antiintellectualism by quoting from
Hitler's *Table Talk*: "I never read a novel. That kind of reading
annoys me" (25). In general, Woolf did not admire politicians
and would have well agreed with Walter Savage Landor's comment: "There is no state in Europe where the least wise have not
governed the most wise" (30). Also, Woolf seems to have wanted
to reveal the lack of foresight and good judgment in politicians
when he quoted Sydney Smith: "I profess myself, Sir, an honest
and upright member of the British Parliament, and ... an enemy
to all change and all innovation" (46). Similarly, Woolf believed
that religion, medicine, and philosophy could be subject to
quackery, or a false system of values; hence he quotes Horace
Walpole: "Long ago I said that the Devil's three names Satan,
Lucifer, and Beezelbub, were given to him in his three capacities
as President of Priests, Lawyers, and Physicians" (59).

Woolf's study of history and his personal experiences in
twentieth-century society led him to believe that human nature
had not improved and society had not progressed. A quotation
from Macaulay expresses this outlook: "Succeeding generations

change the fashion of their morals, with the fashion of their hats and their coaches; take some other kind of wickedness under their patronage, and wonder at the depravity of their ancestors" (28). Moreover, as a person who rejected conventional religious belief, Woolf could identify with a comment by Samuel Butler: "To put one's trust in God is only a longer way of saying that one will chance it" (43); and as an admirer of Freud, Woolf quotes: "One feels inclined to say that the intention that man should be 'happy' is not included in the plan of 'Creation'"(86). Happiness, to Woolf, is something man has to strive to achieve through a just social and economic structure, and through personal relationships which emphasize mercy, compassion, and equality. Woolf believed that man could establish a civilized society and achieve happiness through these values. His lifelong dedication to bettering society through his literary and political work, which stressed rationalism as a means of understanding social, economic, and political realities, and individual and communal consciousness, is summed up well in a quotation from Aristotle's *Ethics*: "The only complete happiness for a man consists in contemplation or the activity of the intellect, provided that it last for the whole of a man's life, for incompleteness is irreconcilable with happiness" (116).

Later Political Journalism

After Woolf resigned his position as literary editor of the *Nation* in 1926, he continued to write book reviews for this journal in the late 1920s and, after it merged with the *New Statesman* in 1931, for over four more decades. That Woolf took the art of writing seriously is clear from each review he wrote; however, in "Words and Things,"[63] he presents an interesting analysis of the social responsibility of language. He first defines semantics as the relationship between the use of words and thoughts and beliefs. In his theory of communal psychology, Woolf had argued that thoughts and beliefs are based on social and economic factors; he supports that view here, but also argues that often "words and things are inextricably confused or ... exist by themselves—detached from both things and meaning" (778). As a result, we sometimes pursue ideals even though we do not know the meaning of the words which express those ideals, and even though those ideals, or words, lead us to destructive acts. Like the misuse of language, illogical thinking was something Woolf abhored. In "Back to Mumbo-Jumbo," a review of *Man and Master* by Gerald Heard,[64] Woolf criticizes the use of generalizations, false analogies, and obscurity in literature, history, or science because they are qualities in thinking which are typical of "the priest, medicine-man, Fuehrer, prophet, astrologer, saint" (28). Heard makes "sweeping historical and psychological statements" (28) without presenting proof, and he exalts the unconscious and rejects reason; moreover, he urges a return to consciousness through a rigid class system which would allow the elite class to practice a "higher psychology" based on "vision" or unconsciousness (28). To Woolf, this view can be summed up as "mumbo-jumbo."

In the 1930s, many of Woolf's articles were on historical and political topics. In "Russia and the Russians,"[65] for example, Woolf comments perceptively on the role of a historian. First, he claims that historians are generally shortsighted as they judge events by a contemporary time-scale (24), and then he defines the task of the historian as amassing a range of information. Yet for Woolf, the ultimate challenge for the historian is to synthesize details and provide a point of view. This criterion allowed Woolf to recognize the unique contribution of H. G. Wells to history. In "Mr. Wells's Works and Days,"[66] he reviews Wells's *The Work, Wealth and Happiness of Mankind*. Wells's thinking is not a scholarly analysis of political, economic, and historical problems; instead, it is imaginative and gives a "panoramic picture" of his subject. Although most of the book is descriptive, Wells also explores "the psychology of the capitalist system; he analyzes the personal motives and the social effects of men... [and] the ideology of classes in society." Moreover, Wells never loses sight of his overall subject or design; thus, Woolf writes that Well's work "has the supreme merit of making his reader think" (266).

Some of Woolf's most interesting comments are on the art of political biography. He was particularly critical of what he called "the Times obituary" or "the Albert Memorial" approach to biography which dominated the Victorian period. In this approach, the subject is praised, indeed even "whitewashed" into a saint; as a result, a subject who is really "a second-rate politician, an imbecile-king or tenth-rate general" often appears to be a man who was misunderstood.[67] Woolf, however, believed that one cannot write impartially (i.e., blindly) about political figures because they affect the lives of everyone. Thus, in his review "Lord Asquith,"[68] he focuses on Asquith's influence on "the bitter and painful" history and politics of his time (485). Although Asquith was a likable man, Woolf claims that he lacked "creative imagination and [the] will to action" (485); consequently, he was unable to control events or to put "into practice some great political principle or social ideal" (486).

According to Woolf, the political biographer either analyzes the political environment, including history and its relation to individual psychology and political policy, or he concentrates on a psychological portrayal of the individual behind the position of statesman and behind the politics.[69] Yet Woolf also emphasizes in his review "Gotterdammerung"[70] that in a political biography, both an objective evaluation of the subject's contribution to historical events and enough material from which to develop an understanding of the man behind the statesman are necessary. Political biographers often fail to fulfill either of these requirements. For example, reviewing a biography of Balfour, Woolf points out how Balfour's political failings are not evaluated. Claiming that Balfour never understood the important issues of his time and that he was "false to the primary principle of parliamentary democracy" (784), Woolf attributes these failings to Balfour's Conservative party ideology which rejected any aspect of democracy that would threaten class privilege. Similarly, Woolf finds that political biographers often fail to analyze the psychology of their subjects. In "Robespierre,"[71] a review of J. M. Thompson's biography, Woolf praises Thompson's thorough

historical data but comments that the real challenge of Robespierre's biographer, which is to understand his psychology, is not
met. Thus, his praise for political biography goes to a study of
Bakunin, which incorporates psychological analysis of the subject, as well as analysis of historical events and political ideas.[72]

Woolf's interest in international affairs is also evident in his
reviews. He discusses the League of Nations and its role as a
system of collective security in both war and peace efforts in "The
Defeat of Pacifism," his review of *Collective Security* by H. M.
Swanwick.[73] The only way nations can prevent war and, thus, that
the human race can save itself from extinction, Woolf claims, is to
establish an international system of collective security. Unlike
Swanwick, who represents the pacifist view that the League
failed to establish a collective security system because of the
sanctions clause in the Covenant allowing for the use of force,
Woolf believes that international force must be subject to international control: first, members must be obligated not to use
force; then, should this obligation be broken, assistance must be
provided to those nations that are victims of aggression.

Another area of international affairs that Woolf was interested
in was imperialism. In his review "British in India,"[74] Woolf
comments that the story of British rule in India is "peculiarly
depressing" and reveals 250 years of "human greed, corruption,
and savagery" (997). This history is usually distorted into propaganda of hatred, pitting one nation against the other. Woolf
credits Edward Thompson and G. T. Garrat, the authors of *The
Rise and Fulfilment of British Rule in India*, with being unbiased;
although they are antiimperialist, they are also aware of the
positive motives behind imperialism—those of empire building
and of improving conditions in the native country. Nevertheless,
their work primarily reveals to Woolf "the astonishing capacity
of patriotism for finding food for self-glorification" in "the
revolting record" of British rule in India (998).

Woolf frequently compared past historical events to contem-
porary events. In "The Great Divide,"[75] a review of Armand
Charpentier's work *The Dreyfus Case,* Woolf comments that in
Europe in the 1930s, "thousands of people have recently suffered

or are suffering the fate of Dreyfus" (778). The Dreyfus case represented "that great divide between modern civilization and modern barbarism" (779), the first time judicial morality was challenged by antidemocratic forces, and that "patriotism, nationalism, anti-semitism, and militarism" were allowed to distort truth (779). Dreyfus's vindication was a victory for civilization, but as Woolf points out, it was only a temporary victory, for barbarism has surfaced again in twentieth-century Europe in the form of fascism and nazism.

In the 1940s, Woolf believed that democracy was under siege, because of internal forces linked to capitalism and imperialism and because of the external threat of war due to the growth of fascism and nazism. Woolf deals with these antidemocratic social forces in several essays. As early as his days at Cambridge, Woolf argued that intellectuals should be part of politics, and he now presents this point in "The Politician and the Intellectual."[76] The intellectual has not been popular in British society and has not played a role in British politics because of the Britishers' distrust of thought and the intellect. Although Woolf claims that the left "has always been less afraid of intellect and reason than the Tories" (56), changes in modern society reveal "that nations perish if they cannot alter their traditions and methods to meet changed conditions" (57). Woolf holds up Greek society as a model of a civilization which incorporated its intellectuals into political life, and he warns that today's conditions demand national and international planning which is "severely intellectual"; consequently, "statesmen, economic and political administrators must all be intellectuals" (57). Moreover, "Principia Sociologica," Woolf's review of *Man and Society in an Age of Reconstruction* by Karl Mannheim, suggests some changes in social structure and social thought.[77] Woolf agrees with Mannheim's view that "the separation of politics, economics, and psychology is for the sociologist no longer possible" (807), and he supports Mannheim's emphasis on the idea that changes in society make the nineteenth-century ideologies of liberal and individualist freedom, embodied economically in laissez-faire capitalism, impossible.

Education, Woolf believed, would also have to change after the war. In his autobiography, he writes very critically about his experiences in public schools. Similarly, this view is expressed in his review of T. C. Worsley's study *Barbarians and Philistines: Democracy and the Public Schools*.[78] Woolf finds Worsely's book to be both a "devastating analysis" of public schools and the school system, and a proposal for the educational system of the future. After the war, Woolf argues, Britishers will have to "undertake the even harder battle of conquering ourselves...if our school system is not remodelled...even though we have beaten Hitler, we shall again have lost the war for democracy" (164). Worsley's analysis reveals that the aristocratic class, which is barbarian, and the middle class, which is philistine, have shaped the school system so it has combined barbarism "with a thick covering of bourgeois respectability and Christianity" (164). Moreover, a close connection between the school system's authoritarianism and the nation's imperialism exists, for as Woolf points out, the "sahib" of the pre-1900 world is the prototype of the Nazi, Fascist, or Communist of the twentieth century (164).

Another sign of social decay during the war years was the growth of suburbs. Woolf was particularly dismayed by the destruction of the Sussex countryside by real-estate development. In a review of Lewis Mumford's *The Culture of Cities*,[79] Woolf describes this urban spread as "a malignant disease at the heart of our civilisation... [which like] the characteristic of death... reduces the dead...to sameness" (253). Mumford's perspective on the relationships of cities and architecture to culture is developed with admirable historical knowledge, and imagination and passionate interest. The city, argue Mumford and Woolf, "is a visible organ of social values and social purpose" (253). The shapeless metropolis is a sign of "civil and social chaos" (253) caused by the capitalist system and its emphasis on property and profit (254); its alternative would be "decentralization and the planned region" achievable through communal control of property and power. Woolf's ending comment further links the condition of a country's social environment to its political future: "For civilisation which is just private property and profit is the civili-sation...of the slum in peace and of the shambles when the aeroplanes drop their bombs upon the slum in war" (254).

Turning to political issues, in "The Future of Imperialism,"[80] Woolf links war to imperialist expansion. Although Britain is fighting a war to destroy Hitler, it is also fighting to preserve its empire. This attempt to create an economically self-sufficient empire conflicts with the international world trade system neces-sary for international peace, and since "economic facts impel us towards international organisation...the parochial politics of nationalism" cannot survive. Only "the fathomless stupidity of the human race," Woolf writes, prevents planning and control-ling such an international system of trade (77). Woolf also focuses on political parties and policies which seemed unable to prevent the social and moral decay of twentieth-century Europe and the inclination toward war. Although Woolf was consistently critical of the Conservative party in everything he wrote, his many years of work for the Labour party did not prevent him from recognizing the ways the Labour party had failed to be a truly progressive force in British politics. In "English Social-ism,"[81] a review of G. D. H. Cole's study *British Working Class Politics, 1832-1914*, Woolf argues that the Labour party was hindered from a Socialist development because of the trade-unionist orientation of its constitutents and because of its tie to liberal ideology. The typical trade unionist, whose original affilia-tion was the Liberal party, is anti-Socialist because trade union-ism is linked to the capitalist system (304). Thus, the only possibility for change in the Labour party's orientation would be to educate the members in socialism.

Another major area of interest in Woolf's writing was interna-tional morality. He comments that the standard of international morality is lower than the standard of individual morality in civilized countries, because international morality mainly reflects the morality of the class which shapes foreign policy, and, accord-ing to Woolf, the standards of that class are "notoriously low" (176).[82] Pursuing the subject of foreign policy further in his essay "Statesmen and Diplomatists,"[83] he discusses two political fig-

ures, Castlereagh and Canning. Woolf credits Castlereagh with
working against a punitive peace after the War of 1815, but he
maintains that, like most statesmen, Castlereagh did not possess
any political or historical foresight. Moreover, something "inhu-
manly cold" about Castlereagh prevented him from being
responsive to the people (176). In constrast, Woolf praises Canning as "one of the most human and warm-blooded of statesmen"
(176), a man of vision, who "in his methods with regard to the
Press and public opinion... was the first modern" (178). Other
statesmen, however, do not merit much of Woolf's praise. He
seems to have little respect for a diplomat like Metternich, who
regards life, people, and nations as part of the art of diplomacy,
and whose "horizon was the green baize of the diplomatic table"
(180). Similarly, Woolf judges Disraeli to be a "man of genius but
too erratic and inconsistent to be a great statesman" (182), a man
who liked to play a leading role and to manipulate others according to his plans.

Turning to the modern period, Woolf views politicians, particularly those in power at the time of World War I, as helpless
figures who did not have control over events but were controlled
by them. In his essay "Please, Sir, it was the other Fellow,"[84]
Woolf points out that the attempt by diplomats after World War
I to avoid responsibility for the war indicates that they must have
contempt for the ordinary people to imagine that the public will
accept these false apologias (204). According to Woolf, such
statesmen should not be allowed to have political power, since he
believes that they have neither regretted their policies nor
learned from their mistakes (210). Returning to the issue of the
relationship between those in power and the public, Woolf
explores the gap between the average person and the statesman
in "Politics in Spain,"[85] contrasting the peasant in Spain who
lives close to the land without any concern about politics with the
politicians of Madrid who intend to make Spain an imperialist
power. To fulfill this goal, Spain is attempting to control two
areas of Africa, Morocco and Rio de Oro, and as a result, the
Spanish peasant is "taken for months or years from his fields to
be slaughtered in the one or interned in a fort in the other" (217).

Woolf's final comment, that "although there are no politics in Spain, there are politics in Madrid" (217), concludes his essay with a note of criticism and condemnation.

Finally, Woolf comments on the role of politicians in the war years. About Hitler, he writes in his article "Hitler Speaks"[86] that he is a man of "terrific will power" with a Machiavellian view and the "remarkable instinct of seeing the means most appropriate for achieving his object" (208). Woolf also describes Hitler's speeches as "a monotonous snarl of hatred" (208), and he denounces Hitler's world-view of anti-Semitism and racial purity as a "tale or myth of the super-village idiot" (209). In another review a few years later,[87] Woolf wrote that Hitler's rise to power indicated how the "world conqueror or the successful gangster... is... likely to be like Hitler a moron" (588), and that a phenomenon of history creates the circumstances for a social situation in which "violent, brutal, stupid and ruthless men" can seize power (588). Similar to this analysis of Hitler is Woolf's discussion of Stalin in "The Stalin Mystery."[88] Stalin first appears to Woolf as a "man of inflexible intention, iron will, and superhuman foresight" (46). In reality, however, he is a "stupid man, with little power of understanding... a political situation or of framing a long-term policy" (46), a man whose thinking is "bumbling and platitudinous... his reason often intellectually childish" (46). Woolf further recognizes that Stalin achieved power by controlling both appointments in the party and in the Central Control Commission, which was responsible for purges. Although Stalin's consolidation of power is awesome and seems impregnable, Woolf warns that his authoritarianism will not last.

Woolf further assesses the role of politicians in leading society to war in "The Nemesis of Being Too Late."[89] Arguing that statesmen do not prevent war because of their "occupational disease... the habit of acting too late" (5), he comments that the prewar crises of 1907-1914 and 1933-1939 parallel the arms race crisis and imminence of war in the late 1950s. Woolf addresses the question of what Britain's role, and particularly the Labour party's policy, should be at this time. Britain must reject the United States policy of an arms race and must urge countries to negotiate about disarmament. If the United States does not comply within six months, Britain should require withdrawal of all United States military and equipment. Moreover, disarmament of nuclear weapons should be followed by disarmament of conventional weapons and an end to the manufacture of nuclear weapons. Finally, Woolf believed that the United Nations could play an important role in world disarmament, and he comments in another review, "Not So Utopian,"[90] that world disarmament may sound "terribly Utopian... but perhaps there is no alternative to annihilation but Utopia" (670). Woolf also again discussed the role of world government in a review of *A History of the League of Nations* by F. P. Walters.[91] An account of the League's efforts and the reasons that it failed can be important to understanding succeeding forms of international government. Woolf states here that "as machinery the League was good enough to prevent war and lay the foundation of international government"; thus, it failed because governments did not desire peace. In the 1950s, history seemed to be repeating itself as governments made the effective functioning of the United Nations impossible. In reaction to this situation, Woolf comments that "the amoeba, the worm and the slug are said to learn by experience, but not that political animal, man" (377).

Book Publishing: The Hogarth Press

To evaluate Woolf's contribution to book publishing through his role in the development of the Hogarth Press, we can turn to his autobiography and to John Lehmann's book *Thrown to the Woolves*. In *Beginning Again*,[92] Woolf discusses how the press grew out of an interest in learning how to print, which he and Virginia shared, and out of the idea that the manual work involved in printing would be relaxing for Virginia. They were surprised to find out that they could not enroll in a school of printing because it was limited to trade-union apprentices. As a result, they decided to teach themselves, and having bought a handpress and the necessary materials, they set up the equipment in the dining room of Hogarth House. Their first publication,

Two Stories (1917), was produced in an edition of 150 copies, each bound by hand by the Woolfs in unusually colored Japanese paper (236). Along with this first publication, they started a subscriber system which continued until 1923, when the press grew to the point where it sold mainly to booksellers. For the second press publication, Katherine Mansfield's long short story "Prelude," the Woolfs used a printing machine at a jobbing printing business. At this time, the Woolfs also decided to send out review copies to the *Times Literary Supplement*, and this resulted in a flood of orders, suddenly changing the nature of the small-scale, home press they had begun.

In *Beginning Again*, Woolf lists the books published by the press for 1917 to 1920, as well as their net profit (253), and in *Downhill*,[93] those published in 1924 to 1939, as well as the Woolfs' income from the press during those years (142). Woolf wrote in *Downhill* that the development of the press "was bound up with the development of Virginia as a writer and with her literary or creative psychology" (64). Indeed, he and Virginia realized how satisfying it was to be able to publish their own works. Yet the Woolfs used the press to encourage the careers of many writers. Among the most important writers of poetry they published was T. S. Eliot. For example, the Woolfs published *Poems*, which included "Sweeney among the Nightingales," "Mr. Eliot's Sunday Morning Service," and "Whispers of Immortality," in 1919, and "The Waste Land" in 1923. About the latter work, Woolf commented that it "had greater influence upon English poetry, indeed upon English literature, than any other in the 20th century" (243). Through T. S. Eliot, the Woolfs had the chance to read the manuscript of James Joyce's *Ulysses*. Woolf describes in *Beginning Again* how Harriet Weaver of the *Egoist*, which had published Eliot's "Prufrock," brought them the *Ulysses* manuscript, which Woolf considered to be "a remarkable piece of dynamite" (246) and which Virginia recognized as "an attempt to push the bounds of expression further on" (247). The Woolfs were ready to publish it, but when they could not find a printer who would print it for fear of prosecution, they returned it to Miss Weaver.

Another important effort of the press with which both Woolf and Virginia were involved was translations of Russian literature. Through Katherine Mansfield they had met S. S. Koteliansky, who was interested in translating Russian writers. Woolf explains how they would turn Koteliansky's draft of a Russian text into English (*BA*, 247). Their first effort was a translation of Gorky's *Reminiscences of Leo Nicolayevitch Tolstoi* in 1920; Woolf commented in *Downhill*: "I do not think that I have ever got more aesthetic pleasure from anything than from doing that translation. It is one of the most remarkable biographical pieces ever written" (67). The book sold 1,700 copies within the first year and was still selling forty years later (*BA*, 248). Woolf regarded this work as a turning point for the press, for it soon became "professional, respectable and commercial" (*Downhill*, 68), and they had to employ workers and to send their work to be printed by R. & R. Clark, Ltd., of Edinburgh. Nevertheless, they continued to put their personal efforts into production of the books. Woolf describes in *Downhill* how he and Virginia worked with Koteliansky on the translation of three Russian books—Dostoevski's *Stavrogin's Confession, The Autobiography of Countess Sophie Tolstoi,* and Ivan Bunin's *The Gentleman from San Francisco*—which they bound in colored papers over boards (74). Although at a later stage this handbinding could not be done, and the books were sent to a commercial bookbinder, the autobiography reveals that Woolf took pride in the quality of each Hogarth Press publication; Woolf writes in *Downhill* that "looking at them today any bookseller would admit that they are extremely well-produced books and that their jackets are admirable" (76).

In 1922, the Woolfs were debating whether or not to give up the press because it was beginning to demand too much of their time. They had two offers which they turned down, and their decision to stay independent allowed them to control both the business and editorial policies of the press. Often, Woolf comments in *Downhill*, the success of the Hogarth Press was the result of both the conscious decision which he steadily upheld not "to publish anything unless we thought it worth publishing," and his business philosophy that expansion would have caused bank-ruptcy by creating too many overheads which would pressure them to publish anything in order to increase sales (255). Also, Woolf prided himself on being a first-class businessman (77), and he kept all of the accounts for the press following his own unorthodox manner of accounting (78).

Even though the press remained small, Woolf comments with pride that it was still able to handle a best-seller such as Vita Sackville-West's novel *The Edwardians*, which sold almost 30,000 copies in the first six months (158). Woolf was also particularly proud of the press's record of never running out of bound copies of any book, and of thus always being able to supply orders. He attributed this to a particularly careful system of checking and decision-making as to when to reprint and rebind every book.

Another large undertaking the press was able to handle successfully was the publication in four volumes, each over three hundred pages, of the English translation of Freud's collected papers. These volumes sold well in the United States and Britain. As a result of this project, the Woolfs signed an agreement with the Institute of Psycho-Analysis to publish the International Psycho-Analytical Library, and over the next forty years they published seventy volumes for the library. Later in 1953, the press undertook publication of the standard edition of the complete psychological works of Freud. Despite many publishing problems about foreign copyrights, this ambitious venture was successful.

The area in which Woolf was likely to have had the strongest role was the press's publications on politics, economics, history, and sociology. In these fields, Woolf identified the books he felt were most important: *The End of Laissez-Faire* and *The Economic Consequences of Mr. Churchill* by Maynard Keynes, Norman Leys's books on imperialism in Africa, and *White Capital and Coloured Labour* by Lord Olivier. The press also published a number of books on war, international government, and the League of Nations. Woolf further encouraged political publications in the *Hogarth Essays* series of pamphlets, which was begun in 1924, and the *Day to Day* pamphlet series, begun in 1930. Although these pamphlet series were hardly money-making ventures, Woolf undertook four other series: *Hogarth Lectures on Literature, Hogarth Sixpenny Pamphlets, Hogarth Living Poets,* and *Hogarth Letters.*

A list of Hogarth Press books also reveals an outstanding selection of poetry publications. The Woolfs were concerned about losing touch with the younger generation of poets and writers, and they hoped that these artists would be drawn to the press by John Lehmann, who began his work for the Woolfs in 1931. In 1932, Hogarth published *New Signatures, Volume 24* in the Hogarth Living Poet Series; this volume included poets such as Richard Eberhart, William Empson, Julian Bell, John Lehmann, W. H. Auden, C. Day Lewis, Stephen Spender, and William Plomer. This was not the first of such important poetry publications, for the press had published two anthologies, *Cambridge Poetry, 1929* and *Cambridge Poetry, 1930*, as well as works by C. Day Lewis and William Plomer, before this time.

In the last volume of his autobiography, *The Journey Not the Arrival Matters*,[94] Woolf completes his picture of the development of the Hogarth Press. In 1938, John Lehmann had become a partner as a result of Virginia's having sold out her 50 percent interest. Woolf had begun to feel that the daily work involved with running the press was absorbing too much of his time, particularly since he wanted to devote time to writing, so he welcomed Lehmann as a partner. Yet the partnership was never smooth—something both Woolf and Lehmann have admitted, although each has a different view of what the problems were. Woolf identifies *New Writing* as Lehmann's initial contribution to the press after becoming a partner. They managed to bring out three volumes of *New Writing* before the war began, and once paper rationing was a reality, they decided to decrease the size of *New Writing* in order to continue to publish it through 1942. Woolf felt the content of these volumes was "remarkable and valuable," and that "the status of contributors and the standard of their contributions were extraordinarily high" (105). Yet after their joint commitment to *New Writing*, Woolf and Lehmann began to differ about the direction of the press. Woolf explains in *Journey* that the press managed to keep operating during the war years by devoting the greatest amount of paper to reprinting the books which sold steadily; this included the works of Virginia, Vita Sackville-West, Freud, and Rilke (107). He was not inclined, as was Lehmann, to expand by adding new authors. As he had felt during the early years of the press, Woolf still believed that expansion would finally ruin the press. Lehmann disagreed and tried to introduce new authors, but by the end of the war he resigned, and Woolf let the publishing company of Chatto & Windus, Ltd., buy out Lehmann's share. Under the new association, Woolf was able to retain his editorial control over what would be published, and Chatto & Windus would handle production, sales, distribution, and accounting (112). The press thus remained primarily small and independent, publishing about twenty books a year. Woolf felt that he and Virginia had started the press, that it was a "personal product," and that it would remain so until his death, when he believed that it would die out, since there had been no personal successor (123). Finally, Woolf maintained that the success of the press was due to the unusually talented writers that he and Virginia—and John Lehmann— attracted, and to his business skills and antiexpansion policies which helped him to avoid disaster in the form of either "the Scylla of the take-over or the Charybdis of bankruptcy" (126).

John Lehmann's account of the Hogarth Press in *Thrown to the Woolves*[95] reveals further aspects of its development and Woolf's role. For example, Lehmann discusses how he introduced Stephen Spender, whom he met through his sister Rosamond, and W. H. Auden and Christopher Isherwood to the press. Also, Lehmann himself was published by the press, contributing a volume of poems in 1934, *The Noise of History,* which recorded his reactions to events in Germany and Austria during Hitler's rise to power. While in Europe, Lehmann developed his idea for an international magazine on literature and political issues, which was to be called *New Writing* and which would publish the 1930s English poets and important writers from the Continent such as Silone, Giono, Oleysha, Pasternak, Brecht, and Lorca (55).

At the same time, he also hoped the press would become the British publisher of major young American and Continental writers. For example, he writes that he urged Woolf to accept Saul Bellow's manuscript of *Dangling Man* in August 1944, since Bellow did not have a British publisher, but Woolf rejected the idea. Similarly, he proposed publishing Jean-Paul Sartre's fiction and drama, but again Woolf was negative, and the press lost both opportunities. This pattern of author-policy disagreement influenced Lehmann to give up his partnership share in the press. He writes in *Thrown to the Woolves* that he believes the press could have expanded more successfully than it did if it had kept its authors and its employees, primarily by giving them better conditions (154). Lehmann also comments that certain business practices of Woolf's were inefficient, particularly the promotion and traveling arrangements. Finally, he points to Woolf's conservative attitude toward money, reflected in the low salaries for staff, and to his inefficient bookkeeping practices and mishandling of Virginia's foreign copyrights (130–31) as a few examples of the management problems Lehmann was aware of during his years as partner of the Hogarth Press. Nevertheless, these criticisms not withstanding, the Hogarth Press, largely through Leonard Woolf's influence and direction, undoubtedly has played, and even continues to play, an important role in British publishing.

Woolf as Literary Executor

Still another area of Leonard Woolf's literary work which should be considered is his role as literary executor of Virginia Woolf's work. At the time of her death, there were many manuscripts left unfinished, as well as many volumes of her diary, and an unusually large amount of correspondence. Woolf first devoted his attention to her last novel, *Between the Acts,* correcting the spelling and providing instructions to the printer. In the editor's note to this work, he wrote that Virginia "would not, I believe, have made any large material alterations in it, though she would probably have made a good many small corrections or revisions before passing the final proofs."[96] This is an unusual comment, however, since, as Woolf well knew, Virginia revised her work many times; moreover, she had only recently completed *Between the Acts* and had left six different typescripts of another work she was writing at that time, an essay on Mrs. Thrale. Moreover, Woolf was responsible for editing and publishing a number of volumes of Virginia's essays, and it is possible that in publishing these works he may have had to choose between different versions of an essay. Thus, a careful study of the manuscripts of the posthumous publications of Virginia's work might indicate whether or not Woolf's choice of material, editorial corrections, and instructions to the printer affected Virginia's content and style.[97]

Woolf did exert his personal judgment about which sections of Virginia's diary should be printed as editor of *A Writer's Diary*.[98] Since his death, the complete diary and her letters have been published. Other unpublished works have also been collected, and one wonders if Woolf knew of the existence of these manuscripts and had a choice about whether or not they should be published. For instance, John Lehmann writes in *Thrown to the Woolves* that the manuscript of *Friendship's Gallery,* a very early unpublished work of Virginia's, was brought to his attention in 1959. Although it had been offered for sale to Woolf earlier, he had not bought it. When Lehmann wrote to Woolf about it, Woolf commented that it had been written as "a kind of private joke, and not very good. I would not agree to its publication unless someone could convince me that my first impression was wrong.... But I was probably wrong not to buy it as I am against publishing" (151). Lehmann thought differently about the value of the manuscript and again wrote to Woolf, this time suggesting that *London Magazine*, which he was editing at the time, publish the first two chapters, which, he wrote, "seem to me to have a delightful and characteristically Virginian atmosphere of playful high spirits. The Japanese story (?) is a bit of a bore, but I would be very glad to publish the first chapter, or the first two chapters separately, as a fragment of Virginia's earliest known work" (151). Since Woolf was still set against publication, the manuscript remained unpublished.[99]

In conclusion, it would be difficult to evaluate which aspect of Woolf's journalism and publishing work is the most important. The literary reviews are perhaps the least-known part of his work; however, they constitute a body of literary criticism which allowed Woolf to perform two roles: that of the book reviewer and that of the critic. In the former role, he tried to inform the public about contemporary literature; in the latter, he tried to create aesthetic and social standards for writers past and present in almost all genres. Moreover, he set high standards for all aspects of literature—for the publishers and the sellers of books as well as for the writers. Finally, in his literary aesthetic, he stressed that a writer is influenced by the social, economic, and political factors of his time, and that, as a result, art is a social product as well as a personal product; however, he also argued that writers must transcend the limitations of personal temperament and prejudice, and of social and literary conventions, to achieve the impersonal and the universal in literature. These critical perspectives on literature probably influenced his handling of manuscripts for the Hogarth Press and his editing of Virginia's books. In addition, the political reviews and articles complement his full-length political studies which were published throughout his life, as well as the work he did as secretary of the Labour party advisory committees on international affairs and imperial affairs. Finally, each area—the literary and political reviews and articles, the direction of the Hogarth Press, and the editing of Virginia's works—reveals his awareness of the importance of literature to man and society, and his dedication to a high standard of values in journalism and publishing.

Chapter Six
Perspectives on the Past:
The Autobiography

Woolf as Autobiographer

The five volumes of Leonard Woolf's autobiography, written in retrospect during the last years of his life,[1] reveal Woolf's personality, experiences, and values. The early years, 1880 to 1912, present the search for roots in his Jewish background and in his childhood and home life; his intellectual development at St. Paul's and Cambridge; his initial judicial, administrative, and business training as a civil servant in Ceylon; his development as a writer of fiction and journalism; his marriage; and the beginning of his political work and career as a publisher. The middle years, 1912 to 1945, are dominated by marital life, political work, and preoccupation with World Wars I and II. Finally, the late years, 1945 to 1969, are devoted to political theory, political work, travel, and the reflection and evaluation which came with the writing of the autobiography.

In the foreword to *Growing,* Woolf comments on the problems of writing an autobiography. First, writing in retrospect creates the "distortion of truth [which] comes frequently from the difficulty of remembering accurately the sequence of events," and yet he believed that the autobiographer is under "an obligation not to conceal" the truth about himself (148). As for the scope of an autobiography, Woolf states that it should present a picture of "one's own personality and of . . . the society and age in which one lived" (148). Then, in *Downhill,* he wrote that material factors, such as finances, houses, and environment, influence one's life, and therefore had to be discussed if "one is writing a truthful autobiography" (141). Finally, in *Beginning Again,* he broadens his focus to another dimension when he describes his autobiography as "a true account of my life in relation to ... the work I have done, and to people, whether intimates, acquaintances, or public persons" (23).

Woolf also argued in *Journey* that an autobiography—or at least his autobiography—could not have a strict chronology; thus, digressions would be essential: "For the autobiographer to force his life and his memories of it into a strictly chronological straight line is to distort its shape and take and falsify his memories. If one is to try to record one's life truthfully, one must aim at getting into the record something of the disorderly discontinuity which makes it so absurd, unpredictable, bearable" (69). As this comment suggests, Woolf does not maintain a strict chronology of events in the autobiography. Indeed, the most important events are interrupted by long descriptions of friends and acquaintances, or by facts and figures about the Woolfs' income or the finances of the Hogarth Press. Moreover, as Woolf was particularly sensitive to environment and believed that it affected one's personality and life-style, much of the autobiography presents his responses to the parts of the countryside in Ceylon and England where he lived, and of the European Continent where he traveled. Similarly, Woolf writes at length about the houses he inhabited, commenting in *Beginning Again* that "in my experience what cuts the deepest channels in our lives are the different houses in which we live" (62).

The autobiography is especially interesting for revealing how Woolf viewed himself. For example, in *Beginning Again*, Woolf describes himself as having been "born an introspective intellectual" (16), while in *Journey* he comments quite differently that he was successful as a man of business (124). Woolf often divided his life by occupation—schoolboy, university student, civil servant, writer, editor, and publisher. In *Downhill*, he comments that "one should change one's occupation every seven years" (127), and he followed that rule in his own life. Also, he seemed to thrive on undertaking diverse activities, and as Virginia commented, he would work on several areas simultaneously,[2] thereby encompassing both a wide range of interests—history, foreign policy, war and international government, communal psychology, and the Co-operative Movement—and his ability to work in almost all literary forms—journalism, fiction, drama, literary criticism, and autobiography. This diversity of interests was complemented by his attraction to both the city and the country. London was the focus of intellectual and political work and friendships, but Woolf was also fascinated by "an element of earthy strength and individuality" (*Beginning Again,* 63) in the villagers of Sussex, even though he realized that village life "was a terribly hard life and an uncivilized society, both physically and spiritually...full of...village women worn out by childbearing and domestic slavery, [and] men of considerable brutality" (67). Also, although he understood that it "took ten to fifteen years before the villagers regarded one as other than a stranger" (68), and although he was a Londoner much of his life, Woolf became involved in Rodmell community work. During World War II, he was part of the fire service and had to patrol the village at night and to help man a pump during fires caused by bombing (*Journey,* 34); later, during peacetime, he was involved with communal work for over twenty years as clerk to the Parish Council, manager of the Rodmell Primary School, and president of the Rodmell Horticultural Society (151). The two geographical poles of London life and Sussex country life complemented opposing needs in Woolf's temperament: the intellectual stimulation of literature and politics; and the emotional satisfaction of both leading a simple life close to nature, and being part of a community.

The Early Years

In *Sowing: An Autobiography of the Years 1880 to 1904,* Woolf focuses on his roots and earliest influences: family history, religion, and education. Commenting that "the main outlines of one's character are moulded in infancy and do not change between the ages of three and eighty-three" (22), he states that his childhood self contained essentially "the same little core of character as exists in me today" (23). Although Woolf points out that his national roots were in English culture and his intellectual roots were in Greek civilization, he acknowledges the influence of Jewish culture and religion. Identifying with "Semitic ancestors... already prisoners of war, displaced persons, refugees, having begun that unending pilgrimage as the world's official fugitives and scapegoats" (13), he traces his personal family history back to his grandfather. Benjamin Woolf, an inhabitant of Bloomsbury and a successful tailor, is described as having a look of "stern rabbinical orthodoxy" (15); he also maintained a rigid adherence to Jewish culture, which was revealed through a provision in his will that none of his property would pass to his children if they married outside the Jewish faith. Yet Leonard Woolf explains that he transcended both orthodox religious belief and ethnic isolation, and he attributes this to the modified cultural and religious environment of his parents' home. Woolf's father was "a believing, but not an orthodox Jew... not much concerned with sin" (21), and although his children were given a strong moral training, they were not overwhelmed by the psychology of guilt which dominates orthodox Judaism. As a result, Woolf developed an even more liberal and liberated attitude toward religion than the rest of his family. After his fourteenth birthday, he announced that he no longer believed in God and would not go to synagogue. At that time, and in retrospect, this rejection of religion seemed natural rather than catastrophic, as Woolf felt no desire or necessity to worship "Gods, kings, queens, and princes" (44). Woolf's rejection of religion was also based on his ability to accept instability and the impermanence of happiness; in turn, his religious skepticism and lack of belief in an afterlife convinced him of the impossibility of absolute truth. Woolf claims that this attitude of skeptical tolerance is essential for civilization (86), a point he developed more fully in his studies on civilization and barbarism.

Family life before the death of Woolf's father seemed to represent the conventional, bourgeois, patriarchal Victorian household, as typified by a hard-working father and a mother completely devoted to husband, children, and home. Woolf notes the matriarchy of the weekdays and the patriarchy of Sundays, with Sunday lunch being "a weekly apotheosis of the family"

(29). Although in later years through his perspective as a Socialist he was able to condemn the bourgeois family because of its economic basis and its exploitation of economic, sexual, and racial classes, he still regarded it as a preserve of "high psychological and aesthetic values," and he commented that family relations "were, on the whole, in my remembrance, extraordinarily human and humane" (36). The middle-class social and psychological security generated by the solid financial position of the Woolf household was, however, shattered by Woolf's father's death and the economic catastrophe that followed. Woolf describes the family as being "extremely poor" for the next eleven years, but he recognized that their poverty gave them a sense of materialist realism, and they managed to survive well through hard work.

In addition to racial and family background, Woolf explores the influence or existence of communal consciousness in the development of his personality. The recurrence of certain images and psychological states suggests to him a "primeval pessimism" (38) which is peculiar to man. Woolf identifies his first experience of the "cosmic melancholia... [which] is hidden in every human heart" (39) as happening in the back garden of the family home in Lexham Gardens where he observed dozens of spider webs. The image of the spider-haunted garden was to suggest terror and futility in life, and was to contrast with the protective, comfortable environment of the nursery, with its fire, representing "the Platonic idea... of security and peace and civilization" (55). A second experience of fear and unhappiness occurred at age eight and was provoked by the sudden appearance of a thundercloud blocking out the sun. This seemed to Woolf symbolic of "that sense of profound, passive, cosmic despair, the melancholy of a human being, eager for happiness and beauty, powerless in face of a hostile universe." (42).

Education was another major influence in the early years. Woolf records his surprise that his early education was very poor even though his parents valued books and knowledge. Nevertheless, he gained an informal education in the outside world, "lessons in the sociology of classes" (57), and he describes in vivid terms the social violence he observed as the lower classes expressed their anger. Woolf was profoundly affected by the extremes of social behavior caused by the squalor and poverty of London slum life, which, he believed, reduced people to animal behavior (55–57). Formal education, however, began at St. Paul's Preparatory School. Woolf's memories of this institution are hardly pleasant, and he comments that he is amazed "that the human brain could survive the desiccation, erosion, mouldiness, frustration" of the educational system (59) as exemplified by St. Paul's. After two terms, Woolf was educated by tutor at home, but later on was sent to an expensive school in Brighton, where soccer and cricket were more important and were taught with more enthusiasm than all the other lessons. Woolf recognized at this early stage in his education that the boys were not taught to become responsible members of society since they were not taught contemporary events or how to apply their learning to daily life (67). Moreover, anyone who showed an interest in learning, or revealed that he was intelligent, was considered "entirely despicable" (65). Woolf therefore soon learned to develop a facade or shell to conceal his inner self, which was sensitive and intellectual, but he also realized that this outer self could "grow inward so that what began as a protection and screen of the naked soul becomes itself the soul. This is part of that gradual loss of individuality which happens to nearly everyone" (72). Woolf's years at St. Paul's encompassed the passage from boyhood to manhood, which he also describes as the time when "the irresistible steam-roller of society... [was] flattening us all out in the image of manliness or gentlemanliness which our parents or lords and masters considered appropriate" (79–80). In the midst of this process, the transition to puberty and the emergence of strong sexual feeling occurred. Woolf comments that although the older boys in private school explained copulation and birth, no adult ever discussed the subject of sex with him, and he was tormented "by the nagging of sexual curiosity and desire" (82). Years later, he condemned this approach to sexual education as leading to an unhealthy mental and physical state (82).

In contrast to his unhappy and dissatisfying experiences during his early education, Trinity College at Cambridge, which Woolf entered in 1899, provided an exciting and satisfying period of intellectual study. It was also during this period that Woolf's first close friendships developed. With Saxon Sydney-Turner, Lytton Strachey, Thoby Stephen, and Clive Bell, Woolf joined the Apostles, a secret society, which was described as dedicated to "the pursuit of truth with absolute devotion and unreserve by a group of intimate friends, who were perfectly frank with each other" (129–30). The Apostles were particularly influenced by G. E. Moore, whom Woolf considered to be a great man, whose mind was "an extraordinarily powerful instrument; it was Socratic, analytic" (132), and who had both a passion for truth and the ability to distinguish what was important in life. Woolf believed that the main influence of Moore and his major work, *Principia Ethica,* was that he rejected religion and intricate philosophical systems, and provided a system of determining what was right and wrong. To Woolf, this philosophy implied a high degree of social and moral responsibility, for it was concerned with the consequences of a life of action. Thus, early in his Cambridge days, Woolf believed that intellectuals ought to take part in practical politics.

Woolf describes the early twentieth century as an era of revolt against the social system and moral codes of bourgeois Victorianism which were stifling Englishmen. A sense of personal and social liberation had developed, fostered among Woolf and his fellow Cambridge intellectuals by the drama of Shaw and Ibsen and the novels of Samuel Butler and Thomas Hardy, who represented an attack against hypocrisy and convention. Similarly, Woolf describes how the poetry of Swinburne impressed these young men with its lyricism and passion. The most significant historical event of this time, the Dreyfus case, represented an important challenge by intellectuals to the social institutions of Church, Army, and State, and the vindication of Dreyfus seemed to be a turning point in European civilization, suggesting "that the world might become permanently civilized" (163). Woolf comments that this spirit of optimism was not unrealistic in such a period of revolt against the past.

At the end of five years at Cambridge, Woolf had to determine a course for his future. He had come to Cambridge intending to be a barrister like his father, but he soon decided he would go into the civil service. Since he did not do well in his exams, he was not able to enter the Home Civil Service as he had expected, and therefore chose the Colonial Service, with a position in Ceylon. He ended his Cambridge years with a sense of intellectual stimulation and emotional satisfaction. Looking back over the formative years of his life and evaluating his ties to family, race, and school, he comments that his loyalties involved a mixture of love and hate: "The first wounds to one's heart, soul, and mind are caused in and by the family.... Most people are both proud and ashamed of their families, and nearly all Jews are both proud and ashamed of being Jews" (196). In contrast, Cambridge represented a stage of complete commitment and contentment which was to mark the end of his youth and the beginning of a turning point in his manhood as he left for Ceylon.

A remarkable aspect of *Sowing* is the detailed and vivid portraits Woolf creates of people who influenced him and of his Cambridge friends. These portraits reveal both Woolf's generosity—his ability to find the best in each individual—and his critical honesty. The earliest portrait of unusual depth and visual interest is of Woolf's early tutor, a Mr. Floyd, whom he describes as a typical English eccentric. Woolf's humor is evident in his choice of adjectives and in his sense of Floyd's personality and physical incongruities. Floyd is described as a long-legged man with "an absurd goatee...a large, wide-awake black hat...[and] a curious look in his eyes of abstraction and ferocity" (60); also, Woolf credits Floyd with a genuine passion for books, a feeling that they had something pleasurable in them and were not merely instruments of educational torture. Like his portrait of Floyd, Woolf gives each of his Cambridge friends a fully developed description. Saxon Sydney-Turner, Woolf's first acquaintance at Cambridge, is characterized as being "immensely intelligent and subtle, but [having] little creativeness" (103).

Woolf felt that his friend's physical appearance—short and thin, with a pale face and straw-colored hair—and his ability "to glide rather than walk...noiselessly" (105) paralleled a mental ghost-like nature. Moreover, Saxon "rarely committed himself to any positive opinion" (107), and Woolf expressed his concern about Saxon's psychological state, his attempt to withdraw from life and people "by spinning around himself an elaborate and ingenious series of cocoons" (115–16). Woolf's portrait of Saxon is presented with the delicacy and distance his character inspired. In contrast, Lytton Strachey is portrayed almost as a caricature: a man with a long, thin, ungainly body, which seemed at times to be tied up in knots; and with a Strachean voice of unusual rhythmic accents and an odd tone which would often, unexpectedly, go up into almost a squeak. Yet Woolf's affection is evident as he credits Strachey with being "one of the most amusing conversationalists" (121) with "snake-like witticisms" (143) which were the outward projections of "the passions of the artist and of the man who is passionately attached to standards of intellectual integrity" (121) and who is also intolerant of stupidity and philistinism.

Woolf's portrait of Thoby Stephen is a striking contrast to the emphasis on intellectual traits with Saxon or Lytton. Thoby impressed Woolf with his physical magnificence and with what Woolf called his "monolithic common-sense" (123), and he combined "sweetness of nature and affection with rugged intelligence and a complete lack of sentimentality" (124). This almost lyrical and unqualified appreciation which Woolf had for Stephen differs from his mixed evaluation of another friend, Maynard Keynes. Keynes, an original thinker, was brilliant in theory and practice, but Woolf concedes that Keynes had "some streaks of intellectual wilfullness and arrogance which often led him into surprisingly wrong and perverse judgments" (145). As with Lytton, Woolf acknowledges that Keynes was a lovable character to his friends, but that to strangers he could often be impatient and rude.

Perhaps more striking than his descriptions of his Cambridge friends are his portraits of the Stephen family. Woolf describes

Virginia and Vanessa Stephen as "formidable and alarming."
Their beauty was overwhelming, but Woolf was aware of another
aspect of their nature; behind their demure behavior was a "look
of a great intelligence, hypercritical, sarcastic, satirical" (184).
Woolf also expresses an almost unqualified admiration for Leslie
Stephen, whom he describes as a "beautiful Victorian old [gentle-
man] of exquisite gentility and physical and mental distinction,"
who was "immensely distinguished" (181) by his work, and who
could look beyond the awkwardness and naiveté of the young
Cambridge undergraduates to appreciate their intelligence.
Woolf had met Stephen only three years before his death, but
years later when writing *Sowing,* although aware of the criticism
of Stephen by his children, and especially of the critical portrayal
of him by Virginia in the character of Mr. Ramsay in *To The
Lighthouse,* Woolf still maintained that Leslie Stephen was a
more admirable figure than his children could admit (182).

In *Sowing,* Woolf frequently compares life in England to life in
Ceylon; thus, one senses how opposite the two environments
were, and that the transition from the British upper-middle-class
life-style of Cambridge or the Strachey and Stephen households
to the jungles of Ceylon was hardly smooth. *Growing: An Autobiography of the Years 1904 to 1911* chronicles Woolf's experiences in Ceylon. Leaving England at age twenty-four seemed to
be a second birth to Woolf, opening his eyes to the social and
cultural influences that affect individual personality and interpersonal relationships. While at Cambridge, Woolf was not
involved much with political issues or the practice of politics. He
describes himself as arriving in Ceylon as "a very innocent,
unconscious imperialist." Yet as one of "the white rulers of
Britain's Asiatic Empire" (25), Woolf was soon to observe imperialism from the inside and become aware of its nature and
problems, and his experiences were to turn him into an
antiimperialist.

When Woolf found himself among other Englishmen on the
ship to Ceylon, he comments that he became aware of an "elaborate system of castes and classes" and how it generates "an
uncomfortable atmosphere of suspicion and reserve" (12). A

similar rigid class hierarchy with its tensions existed in Ceylon because civil servants had a higher social position, as well as higher salaries and greater power, than the other classes of the British—the army officers, planters, and businessmen. Woolf comments that he was able to fit into the class society both on the ship and in Ceylon by adopting a facade to conceal his intelligence and what he refers to as his mental, moral, and physical cowardice (37). He also adjusted to the routines of civil service life, those of office work during the day and a ritual tennis game in the evening. The exclusively white society maintained by the British created an "imperialist isolation" which, Woolf claims, fostered the psychology and behavior of the displaced person. He further comments that he felt as if he were playing a role on the stage, and he describes the other British civil servants similarly in a letter to Lytton Strachey: "All the English out here are continually saying things which, if you saw them in a novel, you would say 'people don't say those sort of thing.' They are always sentimentally soliloquising with an astounding pomposity" (47).

At first, Woolf felt estranged from the Ceylonese, whose social psychology involved mysticism, "cunning and stupidity... something of the litheness and bearing of jungle animals," and "a profound melancholy and fatalism" (54). Soon, however, he began to find the Ceylonese temperament and approach to life fascinating, and he became intimately aware of the class and caste system in Ceylon through transactions with the people involving "the most trivial, or the most important business, listening to their requests, their lies, their fears, their sorrows, their difficulties, and their disasters" (52). Another aspect of Woolf's involvement in Ceylonese life was his love of the countryside. Woolf marveled at the "austere beauty... the silence, the emptiness, the melancholia, and so the purging of the passions by complete solitude" (27) as he traveled through the countryside, sensing the slow rhythm of life typical of a nonindustrial civilization.

As for the work in Ceylon, it was both challenging and frustrating. The most interesting aspect was its variety, which included government administration, law and order, agriculture, construction, health, and education. Woolf believed it was important to tour the province, "acquainting himself with the characters and work of his headmen and the conditions of the people, considering possibilities of improvement and development, enquiring into requests and complaints, and settling the interminable disputes and feuds of village life" (56). These challenges, however, could be offset by dismay over the conditions of life and the difficulties of the work. Woolf honestly reveals both his depression and his struggle for psychological survival by quoting from a letter he wrote to Lytton Strachey: "I don't see how it is possible for you to imagine what actually I am doing.... The worst of it is its futile fullness: one is simply overwhelmed in the swamps of petty little things.... Its sordidity is almost superb.... It is impossible to feel that it is real.... It is absolutely incredible how futile life can be: and if one doesn't become engrossed in its futility, I don't see that there is anything to stop one going mad" (61). Thus, Woolf recognized that in order to hold on to reality, he had to concentrate on his work.

Part of Woolf's duties in Jaffna involved acting occasionally as superintendent of police, and this work revealed to him the difficulties of dealing with crime. Although he believed that law and order were essential, "because without law and order, strictly enforced, life for everyone must become poor, nasty, brutish, and short" (79), Woolf became sympathetic toward the criminal, for he recognized that the forces of justice were often corrupt. Moreover, he never felt at ease in the role of judge, and he described his mixed emotions in *Sowing,* where he recalled that just as he would be ready to sentence a Ceylonese villager guilty of a crime, his hands would begin trembling, perhaps because of some "unconscious consciousness that the judge was no less guilty than the bewildered man in the dock" (99). Also, even though he considered himself to be a lenient judge, he was constantly on guard against "the occupational disease of judges [which] is cruelty, sadistic self-righteousness" (*Growing,* 90). These experiences in Ceylon led Woolf to view capital punishment as "disgusting and disgustingly inefficient," as well as useless as a deterrent to crime. He perceptively observed that it created a "mystique of horror which . . . tends to induce pathological or weak-minded people to commit the crimes for which men have recently been executed," an effect similar to that of the sensational or popular newspaper on social behavior (168). Finally, like his views on capital punishment, Woolf was negative about the prison system, considering it "more barbarous and iniquitous even than the law" (169).

Woolf's next appointment took him to Kandy, located in the "soft, warm, damp, luscious luxuriance of the tropics" (132), and he writes both that Kandy "was to a large extent Europeanized" and that "it did a good deal to complete my education as an anti-imperialist" (133). As in Jaffna, the club was the center of British social life; to Woolf, it was also "a symbol and centre of British imperialism" with its "terribly masculine and public school atmosphere" (135). While in Kandy, Woolf participated further in the trappings of imperialism when he arranged a reception for the Empress Eugenie of France. Although he was startled by the pretentious formalities involved with the empress's life, he could respect the rituals in the feudal society of the villages of Kandy, which he considered to have "a satisfying depth, harmony, beauty" (158). Woolf comments further on similar contradictory feelings about his position as a white imperialist:

I certainly, all through my time in Ceylon, enjoyed my position and the flattery of being the great man and the father of the people. That was why, as time went on, I became more and more ambivalent, politically schizophrenic, an anti-imperialist who enjoyed the fleshpots of imperialism, loved the subject peoples and their way of life, and knew from the inside how evil the system was beneath the surface for ordinary men and women. (158–59)

Still another area of conflicting feelings was his attitude toward being a successful civil servant. He recognized that ambition and a desire for approval were part of his character, but at the same time, he despised success. Thus, he sought to gain promotions in the civil service, even though he doubted he would make a permanent career out of it, and even though he was certain that he did not want to be a successful imperialist (180).

Woolf's last assignment was to be assistant government agent in Hambantota District from 1908 to 1911. By this time, Woolf felt that he was losing touch with Cambridge life and friends and becoming more involved with Ceylon life. In Hambantota, he was completely isolated from Europeans and therefore had some relief from the stifling social life he had to endure in Jaffna and Kandy. Woolf was devoted to his work, and because he "fell in love with the country, the people, and the way of life" (180), he immersed himself in understanding the people. He also took his administrative responsibilities seriously and tried to become the most efficient administrator, "to make the Hambantota District the best administered in the island" (181). To fulfill this aim, he improved the methods of taking census, collecting salt, and controlling rinderpest disease. Despite his successes as administrator, Woolf was not idealistic; he realized that his sincere efforts to improve the lives of the people were often not appreciated by the natives and sometimes even met with communal hostility. This, he believed, was symbolic of imperialism, which he described as "the absurdity of a people of one civilization and mode of life trying to impose its rule upon an entirely different civilization and mode of life" (193). He also sensed a great gap between himself and the villagers, since they had little understanding of his intentions and his respect for them. Like George Orwell, in his well-known essay "Shooting an Elephant," Woolf realized that violence against him was always a possibility; the people "would have thrown stones at me or shot me in the back... had they dared" (193–94).

Throughout *Growing,* Woolf describes the jungle animals with fascination and reverence. In the Hambantota section, there is a particularly striking description of a night Woolf spent at a water hole observing the sounds and life of the jungle:

As the night goes on the silence of the jungle grows deeper ... but every now and again it is broken by a soft, sibilant shiver of all the leaves of all the trees.... This colossal whisper dies away as suddenly as it floats up out of the trees—complete silence to be broken again by strange snufflings and shufflings of some invisible creature nearby, the rattling of a porcupine's quills, the sudden snarl far off of a thwarted leopard, the bell-like call of a deer, or the tortured howling of jackals. (197)

Finding himself face to face with a leopard, he became "fascinated by his ferocious eyes and his magnificent beauty" (196). Similarly, a jackal leaping into the air seemed "part of a completely silent, slightly mad, sinister world" (196). The jungle impressed Woolf with its solitude and silence, and as "a world of great beauty, ugliness and danger" (211), and this experience remained in his memory for many years.

Another key experience for Woolf while in Hambantota was the Kataragama Pilgrimage, which attracted pilgrims from southern India as well as from all over Ceylon. Woolf found the pilgrimage to be a fascinating mixture of "pathos and absurdity, of love and cruelty" (229). The horrible physical conditions— intolerable heat and the troublesome mosquitoes and eyeflies— did not overshadow his respect for and interest in the people's belief or their motives for making the pilgrimage. To him, "the pilgrimage was an authentic, spontaneous explosion of the hopes and aspirations of ordinary men and women who had lived hard and bewildered lives" (231). As a European administrator, however, Woolf sought to improve physical conditions for the pilgrims by urging the government to provide temporary housing and the minimum sanitation necessary. When he returned to Ceylon in 1960, the physical conditions were far superior to those in 1910, but Woolf was disappointed to observe that Katagarama, like other places of European pilgrimage, now represented "the commercialized exploitation of credulity" (232), since each religious practice was tied to money.

Growing presents many incidents which reveal Ceylon customs and indicate that Woolf got intimate glimpses into the lives of the Ceylonese, which he then renders to the readers of this volume of his autobiography. Also, along with *Diaries in Ceylon,* which describe in greater detail Woolf's administrative duties,

Growing provides insights into the nature of British administrators and British administration. As for Woolf, when he sailed from Colombo back to England in May 1911, he probably sensed that this represented the end of his life in Ceylon. He had a year's leave from the service, yet he realized that because he disapproved of imperialism, he would not be able to pursue his civil service career further. The end of *Growing* thus appropriately records his correspondence with the Civil Service Office, which culminated in his resignation from the service,[3] and formally marked his reentry into life in England.

The Middle Years

Beginning Again: An Autobiography of the Years 1911 to 1918 opens with Woolf's return to England. After seven years in the East, Woolf, not surprisingly, felt out of place in England, and he writes about experiencing the same sense of the unreality of life and of being a stranger acting a part which he had felt in Ceylon. Yet he was ready to "plunge straight back into the life of Cambridge" (18), and to rediscover the part of him which was still a Cambridge intellectual. He soon joined the group of young people meeting socially at the Stephen home in Gordon Square, which later became known as the Bloomsbury Group.

As in the two previous volumes of the autobiography, character descriptions are a striking part of *Beginning Again*. Early in the volume, Woolf presents unusual portraits of Vanessa and Virginia Stephen. He describes Vanessa as "frightening and formidable, for she was blended of three goddesses with slightly more of Athena and Artemis in her and her face than of Aphrodite" (27). Although Vanessa had an unusual tranquility, Woolf sensed a nervous tension behind that calm, which he felt was similar to the strain of mental instability in Virginia (27). As for Virginia, Woolf describes her "almost ethereal beauty," but he also notes that "her anxiety and pain made the beauty itself painful" (28). More important, however, is Woolf's comment that "Virginia is the only person I have known intimately who had the quality one had to call genius," which Woolf defines as the ability to go beyond ordinary mental processes to creative, imaginative discussion (31), and he likened this creative genius to the "raptus" or inspiration experienced by other great artists (32).

In Bloomsbury in 1911, Woolf sensed changes in the artistic and social climate, which led to greater freedom of thought and intimacy of expression, particularly between the sexes. At this time, Woolf immersed himself in the Russian ballet, finding it more exciting than anything he had seen on stage. Opera, too, was very popular, particularly Wagner, but Woolf found Wagner distasteful, as he believed his work to be "both cause and effect" of the German philosophy of life which "ended in the apogee and apotheosis of human bestiality and degradation, Hitler and the Nazis" (50). The freer social climate was complemented by a political and social optimism, a belief that "human beings might really be on the brink of being civilized" (36), and that the concept of white supremacy, which was basic to militarism, imperialism, and anti-Semitism, was being challenged. To Woolf, life in Sweden just three years before World War I represented "civilized stability and security...prosperity and communal happiness" (46). The war of 1914, however, destroyed this seemingly recently semicivilized society, and altered the nature of the world so that Woolf felt organized communal violence and a sense of doom had become a way of life (43).

Changes in Woolf's life during his first year back in England were extreme: he fell in love with Virginia Stephen; realized that he would not return to the civil service; and began his career as a writer. When Woolf first proposed to Virginia Stephen in January 1912, she refused him. He nevertheless decided to resign from the civil service and, determined to live off his £600 in savings, he continued to work on his first novel, *The Village in the Jungle*. Three months later, Virginia agreed to marry him, and after several months of meeting her relatives and friends, the marriage took place on 10 August 1912. Soon afterward, Woolf became aware of the constant threat of nervous or mental breakdown under which Virginia lived. Since Virginia's mental health influenced so much of their life, Woolf devotes a long section of

Beginning Again to it. He first believed that Virginia suffered from neurasthenia, but that if her life were carefully controlled to include enough rest and food, particularly as soon as symptoms of excitement appeared, she could avoid major breakdowns in which she either talked incoherently, had delusions and heard voices, or refused to talk or eat or even to believe she was ill (76–77). When Virginia experienced a breakdown, Woolf felt "there was a moment when she passed from what can be rightly called sanity to insanity" (78), and that even when she was well, she had some of the behavior and symptoms of her periods of insanity. Moreover, he comments that Virginia's mental instability and insanity were connected to her genius, and that the nervous strain of her creativity and imagination could endanger her mental stability. Woolf explains how this susceptibility to breakdown under stress led him to suspect that childbearing would be too dangerous to Virginia's mental health. Although her doctor, Sir George Savage, did not agree, Woolf distrusted his opinion; he consulted two other specialists, Maurice Craig and T. B. Hyslop, and when they advised that she should not have children, they followed this course.

The section on Virginia's mental health reveals that Woolf's autobiography is as much a comment on Virginia's life as on his own. Indeed, Woolf provides important details about her work which are generally not available elsewhere. For example, he comments on the royalty arrangements and number of copies sold for her first novel, *The Voyage Out,* and indicates the growth of her popularity as a writer by giving the sales figures for some of her later works. Woolf also presents similar facts and figures for his own first novel, *The Village in the Jungle,* commenting that writers rarely reveal these figures, but that they are interesting because they indicate not ony the impact of a writer's work on the public but also the economics of a writer's life. Although he claims not to have worried about economic insecurity and states that Virginia was "usually quite sensible about money" (93), the low income from their writing forced Woolf to stop writing novels and turn to journalism. Despite good reviews and sales of his first novel, his second novel, *The Wise Virgins,* published in

1914, had brought in only £20. Commenting about this book that "the war killed it dead" (91), Woolf does not indulge in disappointment or regret, but begins his new careers in journalism and practical political work.

Beginning Again thus also chronicles the way Woolf's political work started, and how working with the Co-operative Movement led Woolf to become involved with the Fabian Society and Beatrice and Sidney Webb. Woolf's views differed from those of the Webbs in many areas—notably political, religious, and social issues—yet he writes that he respected their social work, and that he admired their deep mutual affection and devotion. Through the Webbs, Woolf also became more involved with journalism, particularly in writing for the *New Statesman*. Clifford Sharp, the editor of the *New Statesman*, was a difficult, highly critical man, who believed "in keeping his contributors up to the mark by a liberal use of cold water" (130). Through his work for Sharp, Woolf came to realize that journalism could be "a highly dangerous profession" because it leads to "a kind of fatty degeneration of the mind" (131–32) caused by the need to be writing constantly. Journalists, also, are subject to "the hallucination that they control and exercise great power. The hallucination of power corrupts as efficiently as power" (132). Woolf further believed that journalistic writing destroys creative impulses and allows the writer to escape responsibility. Desmond MacCarthy seemed to Woolf to be an example of a journalist who failed to become the writer he could have been because he allowed the temporal commitments to journalistic writing to absorb his energies, and because he fell victim to the irresponsibility journalism fosters due to the belief that the responsiblity for one's work lies with the editor, not one's self.

Beginning Again also records how the years 1914 to 1918 were dominated by Virginia's illness. As Virginia was finishing *The Voyage Out,* Woolf could observe that mental and nervous strain was causing her to experience insomnia and headaches, and as she continued to be sleepless and worried, Woolf feared a suicide attempt. Virginia did attempt suicide by taking a large dose of sleeping tablets from a box which Leonard accidentally left unlocked. Woolf writes that he did not blame himself for this oversight, because he felt that it was nearly impossible to maintain the complete surveillance over Virginia which was necessary to prevent her from a desperate act. Woolf also discussed how he did not feel guilty about the poor medical advice he obtained, since he had consulted five specialists considered to be at the head of their profession. With hindsight and as a result of carefully observing Virginia's symptoms and actions, Woolf felt the doctors' diagnosis of neurasthenia was inaccurate, and he believed that Virginia suffered from manic-depressive insanity (161) which Woolf analyzed as violent exaggerations of the swings of emotion that we experience in everyday life (160–62). In addition to having to provide constant surveillance, Woolf had to attempt to get Virginia to eat, a tedious process which he describes: "Every meal took an hour or two; I had to sit by her side . . . and every now and again ask her very quietly to eat. . . . Every five minutes or so she might automatically eat a spoonful" (163). It is thus not surprising that Woolf summed up the long months of Virginia's illness during 1914 and 1915 as "years which we simply lost out of our lives, for we lived them in the atmosphere of castastrophe or impending catastrophe" (166).

Despite the crisis at home during this time, Woolf did some productive work which included journalistic reviewing and the completion of his study *Co-operation and the Future of Industry.* He had obtained a medical exemption from the army because of Virginia's mental health and thus was able to devote his antiwar energies to his study for the Fabian Society on the prevention of war, *International Government.* Woolf comments that because of this work, he soon became an authority on the subject of the prevention of war and the necessity for international government, and thus he was pleased that his work influenced the British government committee's proposals for the League of Nations and the Versailles Conference (189).

1917 was an important year for the Woolfs as it marked the beginning of the Hogarth Press which was started as a hobby, mostly to provide diversion for Virginia during intense periods of writing. Woolf records how they bought the rudimentary supplies and equipment for 19.5s.5d. Their first publication, *Two Stories,* was a thirty-two-page pamphlet containing "The Mark on the Wall" by Virginia and Woolf's story "Three Jews" with four woodcuts by Dora Carrington. It sold for 1s.6d. and initiated the Woolfs' long career as publishers of such important writers as Katherine Mansfield, T. S. Eliot, E. M. Forster and Freud, as well as the Woolfs themselves. According to Woolf, the Hogarth Press was not supposed to become a large, commercial business; he and Virginia wanted it to be a half-time occupation, so that they could concentrate on publishing books the commercial presses would not touch. Woolf therefore continued to refuse to expand the press, as he believed that only by keeping it small could it survive financially and be the independent press it was meant to be.

The end of World War I marks the end of *Beginning Again* and the beginning of *Downhill All the Way: An Autobiography of the Years 1919 to 1939.* As Woolf's title suggests, these years were dominated by a growing pessimism because of the historical and political events which developed from the postwar chaos and the rise of fascism and nazism. Particularly appalled by the "doctrinal or racial cannibalism" (22) during these years, which turned the Spanish, the Italians, the Germans, the Africans in the Congo, and the Russians against their own countrymen, Woolf believed that no one could escape the impact of such savagery on daily life. Moreover, he felt that each person should be considered accountable for his action—or lack of action—to counteract the growth of barbarism between the two world wars (40). He thus discusses how his own political work during this period centered around the Labour party and the Fabian Society. In addition, he evaluates Virginia's political consciousness and work. Although he comments first that "Virginia was the least political animal that has ever lived," he realized that she was particularly sensitive to the social and political atmosphere. He also recognized that *A Room of One's Own* and *Three Guineas* were political works, and that Virginia had been involved at the grassroots level in Labour party politics and the Co-operative Guild. In this respect, she was definitely not "the invalid lady of Bloomsbury" many people

often claimed she was (27). Later in *Downhill,* Woolf supports
this observation further as he argues against the charge that
Virginia was too cultured: "Her novels, and still more her literary
criticism, show that she had not a trace of the aesthete or hyper-
cultured... although she was a cultured woman, the roots of her
personality and her art were not in culture and... she had a streak
of the common-sense, down to earth, granitic quality of mind and
soul" (80–81).

When focusing on the events of personal life during these
years, Woolf concentrates, as in *Beginning Again,* on Virginia's
illnesses. Yet he also gives an understanding of Virginia as a
writer which cannot be gained from other sources. There is a
marvelous description of Virginia's work habits—that she was
"an untidy writer, indeed an untidy liver, an accumulator
of... 'filth packets'" (52). Woolf comments that she reached "the
final stage of organized disorganization and discomfort" at their
home in Tavistock Square, as she sat writing among "the pyram-
ids and mountains of parcels, books, and brown paper" (53). But
he was also a much more serious observer of Virginia's craft. For
example, he "could tell by the depth of the flush on her face
whether she had been writing fiction or criticism" (54) because
he could observe the different intensities of emotion her writing
demanded (53–57). Moreover, Woolf's respect for Virginia's
genius is always evident. He credits her with having the "intellectual and spiritual toughness" (57) to be able to pursue the
demanding revisions of her work and to face the "icy judgement
of the reviewers and the public" (56). Also, throughout *Downhill,* as in *Beginning Again,* Woolf quotes frequently from Virginia's diary. He believed that Virginia used the diary to record her
process of literary creation, and since "she was almost always at
her work even when she was not working" (149), the diary
reveals her life as an artist: "the exquisite pleasure and pains, the
splendours and miseries, of artistic creation, the relation of the
creator both to his creation and his creatures and also to his critics
and to his public" (148). He was well able to appreciate her
complete commitment to her art, since they both never "took a
day's holiday unless we were too ill to work or unless we went

away on a regular...holiday" (156). As Woolf commented to John Lehmann, Virginia maintained a vigorous work schedule,[4] and despite her periods of illness, she published seventeen books between the age of thirty and her death.

Much of *Downhill* deals with Woolf's political activities and journalism. Woolf considered himself both an "unredeemed and unrepentant intellectual" and "a heretical socialist" (85). As a result, he often found himself outside the mainstream of Labour party politics, especially as espoused by the leaders of the party during the years 1919 to 1931—James Ramsay MacDonald, Arthur Henderson, and Philip Snowden—whom Woolf considered to be conservative. His socialism had grown out of his study of the Co-operative Movement, which had convinced him that a system of consumers' socialism, or community control of the industrial system, could cause a revolution in both the economic system and the social psychology which would produce a more civilized society. This was the position he tried to uphold. In addition, during these years, he was writing for the *Nation*, under H. W. Massingham, who was editor. Woolf describes Massingham as a "pillar of both liberalism and Liberalism" (92), a first-class editor, who was "extremely high-minded...a gentle man...on the side of culture" (94). For over seven years, Woolf wrote literary and political reviews for the *Nation*, and he comments that this work was satisfying because it complemented his work with the Hogarth Press. Writers who came to him via Hogarth could be given some help and income by reviewing work, while those who showed talent at reviewing could be encouraged to write a full-length manuscript.

With the same meticulous attention to details that he reveals in *Beginning Again*, Woolf records Virginia's income as a writer over the years and presents similar information about the Hogarth Press in *Downhill*. Although the press publications met with a cold reception from booksellers because of the unconventional content and appearance of the books, the press soon expanded to the point where it became "professional, respectable, and commercial" (68). Once this expansion took place, all Virginia's books could be published, and *Jacob's Room* thus became the press's first major work. Another result of expansion was that many enterprising young men and women came to work at the press. Commenting on his relationship with these workers and associates, Woolf acknowledges honestly that he was not an easy person to work with: "My experience in the Ceylon Civil Service proved that I get on much better with subordinates than with equals or superiors in business. In practical affairs I am in many ways a perfectionist—a character for which in the abstract, or when I see it in other people, I have no great admiration. I have a kind of itch or passion for finding the 'right' way of doing things, and by 'right' I mean the quickest and most accurate and simplest way. In 1923 I was still young enough to be hot tempered and allergic to fools" (78–79). As comments by those who worked for Woolf at the press reveal, this self-criticism was not unduly harsh.

Some of Woolf's most interesting comments about the Hogarth Press reveal his views of literature and writers. For example, he states that "a serious writer of genius" could produce a work which could become a best-seller, but that best-sellers are usually written by "second-class writers whose psychological brew contains a touch of naivety, a touch of sentimentality, the story-telling gift, and a sympathy with the day-dreams of ordinary people" (158–59). About the interaction between the publisher and the writer, Woolf comments that both are torn between interest in profits and interest in the art form. In the course of his relationship with writers as publisher of the Hogarth Press, Woolf states that Vita Sackville-West was the ideal author—never critical if things went wrong, and appreciative of the publisher's efforts if things went right (159). Praise also goes to James Strachey, who, with his wife, Alix, edited and translated the complete works of Freud which the press published; Woolf comments that Strachey's work is a "monument to his extraordinary combination of psychoanalytical knowledge, brilliance, and accuracy as a writer and translator" (168).

In addition to his focus on literature and political work, Woolf emphasizes social life and travel. Virginia loved society, particularly parties, and Woolf writes that she seemed to use "the kaleidoscope of human beings and of conversations as material for her writing" (98). Woolf himself disdained the salon society party where the main objective was to meet some very distinguished people, and he preferred an intimate group of friends which would allow for intellectual conversation; still, like Virginia, he was an observer of society and thus realized that the way people met and entertained one another was an indication of "what a particular period was like, the nature of its society and classes" (103). In *Beginning Again*, Woolf records that as Virginia's health improved, they began to socialize more. He describes social events at Garsington, the home of Ottoline and Philip Morrell, where well-known figures in politics and literature were invited. At this time, the Woolfs met Katherine Mansfield and Middleton Murry, whom Woolf described as seeming to belong to "the literary underworld." About Murry he wrote: "I never liked Murry; there was a strong Pecksniffian vein in him which irritated and revolted me" (203); but he found Mansfield "extraordinarily amusing" and believed that Murry "corrupted and destroyed Katherine both as a person and a writer" by imposing his "sticky sentimentality" on her sense of realism, humor, and cynicism (204). Moreover, Woolf understood that the relationship between Virginia and Katherine was complex, that Virginia valued Katherine as a serious woman writer yet felt in competition with her.

In *Downhill*, Woolf provides more interesting comments about the society world and intimate friends. About T. S. Eliot, Woolf remarked: "in conversation it was his brain that was disappointing, so much more rigid and less powerful than I had expected ... and with so little play of mind" (108). Woolf further notes Eliot's sense of priggishness and pompousness which seemed to stem from his being inhibited and formal with everyone. Eliot, however, admired Virginia as a critic, and as the Hogarth Press published many of his works, a more relaxed and intimate friendship developed between him and the Woolfs. Similar to Woolf's feelings of being temperamentally at odds with Eliot were his feelings about Vita Sackville-West, whom he describes as "handsome, dashing, aristocratic, lordly, almost arrogant" (111–12), and who was "only really comfortable in a castle," while Woolf thrived on informality (112). As with Eliot, Woolf's appreciation of Vita as a writer gradually fostered a close friendship.

Aside from friends, travel became important during the years after World War I. Woolf writes about the exhilaration of owning a secondhand Singer car in 1927 and taking off on trips through the countryside. Virginia particularly loved "touring" on the Continent, and Woolf describes their travels through the French countryside to the Mediterranean fishing village of Cassis to stay with Vanessa and Clive Bell and Duncan Grant. There is also a description of a very different trip, when the Woolfs traveled through Germany to Italy in 1935 after Hitler's rise to power. Although the Foreign Office advised Jews not to travel in Germany, Woolf proceeded with the trip, armed with a courtesy letter from the German Embassy, only to find that his pet marmoset, Mitz, who used to sit curled up on his shoulder, proved to be the perfect entrée to German curiosity and friendliness. Despite this peculiarly fortunate turn to their trip, Woolf's comments about Germany at that time reveal his sensitivity to the crude and savage political emotions which created a sinister and menacing atmosphere throughout the country.

The imminence of World War II led Woolf to assess his political work in the years after World War I. He focused on two areas: prevention of war and the development of international government; and the dissolution of imperialism in Asia and Africa. Although he comments that he had "never believed that progress is inevitable or that man is politically rational" (197), he worked for social progress and, in a political and rational mode, for the causes of peace and freedom, believing that the use of reason was essential for discovering and counteracting the causes of war. His long study of communal psychology dominated the years between the wars and the post–World War II years until 1953, and it resulted in three books—*After the Deluge*, Vols. 1 (1931) and 2 (1939), and *Principia Politica* (1953). At the time he wrote *Downhill*, he still felt that these works could help historians, philosophers, psychologists, and politicians to understand the relationship between communal beliefs and desires of people and their communal actions, particularly those beliefs and desires which lead people into war. Nevertheless, he evaluates these works with his usual honesty, writing that they were "to all intents and purposes...a complete failure" (196) for they had all received "unfavourable press, and *Principia Politica* was received with derision by the Oxford professional historians." Woolf admits that his disappointment was "deep, though not very prolonged" (204). Unlike Virginia, who felt that the fate of her works was part of her fate and who believed that her mortality and immortality depended on the mortality or immortality of her work, Woolf was indifferent about and independent from the fate of his work, and he attributes this feeling to his belief that death was ultimately personal annihilation.

Among Woolf's political accomplishments during this period were his efforts to start the journal *Political Quarterly* in 1930, and his role as editor of that journal for many years. This work was more satisfying than his work for other journals, because he "was extremely interested in the ideas with which it dealt and was working with people pursuing the same objects" (209). Woolf also enjoyed participating on the national Whitley Council for the Civil Service, which began in 1938 and involved sitting in on arbitration cases in economic disputes and labor issues. Woolf was able to indulge in his fascination with the judicial process which had developed while in Ceylon; moreover, through the tribunal, he became aware of many different occupations and their conditions. The majority of Woolf's political work, however, was in the Fabian Society and the Labour party, particularly as secretary of the Labour party's two advisory committees on imperialism and colonialism, and on international events. These two committees provided the leaders of the Labour party with reports and recommendations on issues such as the movement for self-government in India and the nature of government economic exploitation in the British African empire. Woolf writes that he felt that the British government's policy in India was a "vicious circle of repression and sedition" (226), and that the British government's response to India's growing demands for self-government came twenty years too late. Woolf was similarly impressed by the need for a change in the government's policy in Africa. He believed that the advisory committee's pamphlet *The Empire in Africa: Labour's Policy* presented important educational information about the history and methods of British rule in Africa, as well as a good policy for promoting self-government.

Woolf also comments on the work of the international affairs committee which was against the Treaty of Versailles's approach to Germany's post–World War II responsibilities, because it would lead directly to German militarism. Moreover, from 1920 to 1935, the committee urged an international policy based on the League of Nations; however, by 1935, the rise of Hitler's power and his withdrawal from the League forced Woolf and the committee to adopt a new policy and urge Britain, France, and the USSR to unite. This position represented preparation for war and was opposed by those who were dedicated pacifists.

Downhill All the Way ends with Woolf's comments about entering "the twilight" of his life. There were personal losses through the deaths in the 1930s of such close friends as Lytton Strachey, Dora Carrington, and Roger Fry. Also, the death of Vanessa's son Julian, who was killed while driving an ambulance in the Spanish Civil War, was considered by Woolf to be "a sign and symptom of the 1930s" (253). Finally, the speeches of Hitler, dominating the radio waves, were to Woolf "the savage and insane ravings of a vindictive underdog who suddenly saw himself to be all powerful" and who made the second World War inevitable (254). For a man like Leonard Woolf, who had committed himself in his political work and writing to the prevention of war and to the cause of national freedom, this period combined personal loss with political despair.

The Late Years

The last volume of the autobiography, *The Journey Not the Arrival Matters: An Autobiography of the Years 1939 to 1969,* was written when Woolf was eighty-nine years old and was published posthumously. As throughout *Downhill*, his focus at the beginning of *Journey* is on the outbreak of World War II. Woolf compares the mood at the time to the "negative emptiness and desolation of personal and cosmic boredom" one feels when waiting "endlessly for the next catastrophe" (9–10). That German brutality had led the Woolfs to obtain enough poison to commit suicide indicated the extent of horror and imminent despair experienced by Europeans. By August 1940, the war was affecting Sussex country life as planes flew over Monk's House. Woolf records joining the local fire service and fighting fires set off by a German bomber. He also records hearing the sirens and planes bombing London. During the London bombings, the Woolfs' house in Mecklenburgh Square in which the Hogarth Press was lodged was destroyed by a bomb and a land mine. The press was relocated to premises of the Garden City Press in Letchworth, and its business was conducted from there.

At this time, Woolf had completed writing *Barbarians at the Gate*, which analyzes the differences between civilization and barbarism, but the Left Book Club editors were hesitant to publish it as it was because of Woolf's severe criticism of the Communists. Woolf, however, refused to "obscure what . . . was the truth about authoritarianism in the Russia of Stalin" (12–13), and the book was published in its original form. Throughout his life, Woolf was horrified by human cruelty, and he perceptively analyzes the psychology of cruelty, commenting that "the man who massacres can only do this if he regards his victims not as individuals like himself but as non-human pawns or anonymous ciphers" (22). His own respect for the individuality of others made any scene or act of humiliation, let alone physical injury, painful. Thus, the persecution of Dreyfus, which at the turn of the century made a particularly strong impression on him, was recalled some years later by the massacre of the Armenians, and again in the 1930s and 1940s by the annihilation of Russian peasants by Stalin. As Woolf writes, early in his life, he had adopted his father's belief that the perfect rule of conduct for a man's life had been laid down by the prophet Micah in the words "do justly and love mercy" (26), and he used this motto as a standard against which to evaluate events of the war years.

As in earlier volumes of the autobiography, Woolf focuses on Virginia's work and mental health during this time. She was writing *Roger Fry*, which she found very difficult, because, as Woolf realized, she was writing against her natural inclination, which was to let vision rather than facts dominate; thus, he could well understand how writing in that way had exhausted her. After reading the Fry biography, he felt that the "two parts of the book did not artistically fit together and she allowed the facts to control her too compulsively so that the book was slightly broken-backed and never came alive as a whole" (41–42). Yet Woolf felt that during the months of 1940, Virginia seemed calmer and happier than usual. They were cut off from life in London, left to themselves without servants, in a daily routine which Woolf describes as "the pleasant monotony of living" (70). Although Virginia's diary entries from this time stress calm and contentment, they also reveal a nervous tension or sense of imminent excitement or disruption, which Woolf believed to be caused by her efforts to revise her new novel, *Between the Acts*. When she suddenly seemed to be on the verge of a breakdown, Woolf consulted a doctor and friend, Octavia Wilberforce. Sensing that Virginia was at the point of suicide, Woolf describes how he had to decide whether or not to urge her to accept being ill so that she could begin a routine of extra rest and food to get better. Since he did not take this step, he had to accept responsibility for the wrong decision (92), and thus for not preventing Virginia's suicide by drowning on 28 March 1941. The calm recital of the events leading to the suicide, as well as of the act itself, seems to suggest a lack of passion on Woolf's part; however, he comments that "the long-drawn-out horrors of the previous weeks had produced in me a kind of inert anesthesia. It was as if I had been so battered and beaten that I was like some hunted animal" (95). Moreover, Woolf records how death never seemed to be far from Virginia's mind; indeed, in her fiction, she participated vicariously in the deaths of characters which often were projections of her personality and of her personal experience. Unlike Virginia, Woolf was unable to worry about death, and he attributes this attitude to the Jewish tradition of skeptical fatalism, or the belief that "the wise man does not worry about the inevitable" (73). This strong focus on temporal reality saved him from despair and from withdrawing from political and literary work after Virginia's death.

As the years progressed, Woolf continued to take an active interest in various kinds of work: he was a member of the Civil Service Arbitration Tribunal, the literary editor of a journal, a businessman and publisher, and political chairman or secretary. He explains how all these activities provided opportunities for learning about human psychology. For example, participating in the judicial process could "give one an insight into the mind, motives, and methods of the human animal" (133); working as a chairman or secretary of a political body could allow one to observe "the psychological antics of five, ten or fifteen men sitting around a table, each with his own selfish or unselfish axe to grind" (152); and being a literary editor could bring one into contact with experts in their fields. He understood how easily one's vision could become narrowed by one's work, and he writes that "all occupations or professions, like individuals, create around themselves a kind of magnetic field" which leads to an "occupational hallucination of self-deception," giving an "enormous, sacred importance" to everything connected with oneself and one's work (143). Woolf comments that he felt himself subject to this magnetic field of illusionary self-importance and power as an editor and, perhaps, as part owner-publisher of the Hogarth Press.

Journey reviews the development of Woolf's life of political commitment: Ceylon—leading to antiimperialism; East-End social work and the Co-operative Movement—leading to anti-capitalism and socialism, and work with the Fabian Society and the Labour party; and the 1914 war—leading to expertise on causes and prevention of war, and the importance of international government. Woolf evaluates the effects of his work and commitment in these areas. Although he had the qualities necessary for the political work he did, specifically "a clear mind, capable of quickly understanding both theoretical and practical problems, and the ability to make difficult decisions and act on them" (158), he felt he had achieved practically nothing and that the world would have been the same without his efforts. Yet when Woolf evaluates his work more specifically, he is not quite as negative. *International Government* did affect the government committees which produced proposals for the League of Nations, and the Labour party advisory committees did produce information and important recommendations on imperial and international affairs, which helped to educate the Labour MPs who were working class and trade unionist. Unfortunately, the Conservative and Labour leaders of the time were not in favor of a collective security system or a peaceful breaking up of the empire. Woolf judges these leaders in his comment: "No one can deny that the policies actually pursued have produced in the last thirty years more horrors, misery, and barbarism than occurred in any other thirty years of recorded history" (166). This is indeed a strong criticism from someone who, during eighty-eight years of life, had seen injustice, cruelty, intolerance, and tyranny in all forms: the Dreyfus Case, the Armenian Massacre, Tsarist Russia, World War I, Stalin's Russia, Hitler's Germany, Mussolini's Italy, Mao's China, the Vietnam War, and the hostilities between Arab and Israeli, Indian and Pakistani, and white and black in the United States, South Africa, and Rhodesia.

Woolf obviously believed, as his life's work indicates and as he comments, that political work was an attempt to influence the historical and political events of his time, "to make the difference between a good life and a bad, between civilization and barbarism" (171). He explains his commitment to action further: "in the eye of God or rather of the universe, nothing human is of the slightest importance; but in one's own personal life, in terms of humanity and human history and human society, certain things are of immense importance: human relations, happiness, truth, beauty or art, justice and mercy" (172). Here Woolf combines the philosophies which influenced him through all stages of his life—Jewish fatalism and religious skepticism, Jewish biblical tradition through the words of Micah, Greek philosophy, and the philosophy of G.E. Moore which permeated Cambridge, the Apostles, and the Bloomsbury Group.

Woolf's life as a writer may appear to have developed mostly from his commitment to political work; thus, it is a little surprising to find him commenting on the pleasures of writing, or that writing provided physical as well as a mental satisfaction:

I like to feel the process of composition in my brain, to feel the mind working, the thoughts arranging themselves in words, the words appearing on the virgin white paper...one of the most unfailing pleasures is to sit down in the morning and write. (183–84)

In addition to writing, another continuing pleasure was travel. In his later years, he made major trips to Israel and Ceylon. He records how, in the 1920s, he had been against Zionism because he felt the presence of a "racial, religious or cultured minority always leads to hatred, violence, and political and social disaster" (185). Yet his trip to Israel in 1957 was exhilarating. Woolf was especially taken with "the immense energy, friendliness, and intelligence" of the Israelis (187) and the feeling of "comradeship, solidarity, good-will" which they had developed as they were faced with a common danger of being surrounded by hostile Arab states (187). In contrast, his return to Ceylon in 1960 was motivated by his curiosity to see how the administration of Ceylon as a free state compared with British rule of Ceylon. He was surprised to find warmth and respect for the British methods of government, and was pleased to be treated as a VIP and to learn that the Ceylon government was going to publish the official government diaries he kept as the assistant government agent in Hambantota.

Woolf ends *Journey* with his views of old age; he comments with rather dry humor that "in Britain, one enjoys great prestige merely from not dying" (210). This prestige, which Woolf termed "senolatry," is a "valuable asset, because it provides the basis for good relationships with other people" (210). He further comments that in old age, "the storms and stresses of life, the

ambitions and competition are over. The futile and necessary and
false responsibilities have fallen from one's shoulders and one's
conscience" (210). Finishing his autobiography, hardly a futile or
false responsibility, must have given him a sense of satisfaction
and completion, though the title of this final volume seems to
express best Woolf's philosophy about life and about death—that
the goals and process of life are more important than the end.

In conclusion, Woolf's autobiography provides a broad perspective on personal and social life. He set out to write the story
of his life with a double aim: "first, to show it and his little ego in
relation to the time and place in which he lived his life, to the
process of historical events, even to the absurd metaphysics of the
universe; secondly to describe ... his relation ... to persons and to
himself, his record in the trivial, difficult, fascinating art of living
from day to day, hour to hour, minute to minute" (*Downhill*, 40).
Woolf seems to have fulfilled his goal of relating personal experience to social and historical factors and to philosophical perspectives. In the area of relationships with people, however, one
senses a less than comprehensive account. For example, Woolf
makes little mention of Vanessa Bell, Virginia's sister, even
though Virginia's relationship to Vanessa was very close, and the
Bell and Woolf households visited frequently. Woolf also barely
mentions several other key friends of Virginia's, particularly
Violet Dickinson, Vita Sackville-West, and Ethel Smyth, women
who because of their involvement in Virginia's life must have
been important to Woolf's life as well. Finally, perhaps most
important, is the sense that there is an incomplete picture of
Woolf's relationship to Virginia. Woolf seems to be most
reserved about his feelings for Virginia. He expresses admiration
for her genius and support of both her literary and political work,
and he details the careful attention to the state of her physical and
mental health which dominated their lives together. While all of
these factors suggest love and devotion, Woolf never explores his
emotions. One wonders, for example, what he felt about Virginia's cynical comments about his Jewish background, and her way
of speaking in a stereotypical anti-Semitic way about Jews, particularly Leonard's mother and family. One also wonders about

his reactions to her emotional or physical involvements with women: Vanessa, Violet Dickinson, Vita Sackville-West, and Ethel Smyth.

Similarly, another unclear aspect of the autobiography involves the way that Woolf often comments in an objective, even dispassionate manner about Virginia. In *Downhill*, for example, one is shocked by a certain lack of emotion when Woolf mentions Virginia's suicide in a matter-of-fact tone at the end of one paragraph and then begins the next with facts and figures about their income. Another section which is striking for its emotional coldness—even given the emotional distance created by time— appears in *Beginning Again*, when Woolf interrupts his account of one of Virginia's mental breakdowns with a long description of the countryside in the area where they went for a rest cure. Later in *Journey*, when he discusses Virginia's final depression and suicide, it is again surprising that he interrupts his account of this crucial event with long descriptions of Elizabeth Robbins and Octavia Wilberforce. Finally, although Woolf does comment that Virginia's death was like a "blow both upon the head and the heart" (*Journey*, 127) for which he tried to compensate by hard work, it is surprising that the events of the twenty-eight years he lived after her death seem to have been almost free of memories of her. Of course, Woolf may have exerted rational control over what was probably the most highly intimate and emotional area of his life, and this may account for his emotional restraint, even reticence; nevertheless, one still feels that these are missing pieces of the autobiography.

Chapter Seven

Conclusion

Considering Leonard Woolf's varied interests and diversity of work, one might expect it would be difficult to find unity and continuity, but not so. Throughout his life and work, three concepts form a thread: communal psychology, civilization, and barbarism. Although Woolf first introduced these terms in the 1930s, primarily in such studies as *After the Deluge, Quack, Quack!, Barbarians Within and Without*, and *Principia Politica*, they are the concepts which shape all his works, as they analyze the interaction between individual and group consciousness on the one hand, and social, economic, and political institutions on the other.

For example, in *The Village in the Jungle*, Woolf's first novel and first major publication, he explores the relationship between the villagers' beliefs and a caste system of economic and social inequalities, portraying how hunger, fear, and destruction dominate village life, as well as life in the jungle. *The Wise Virgins*, Woolf's second novel and study of English social life during the pre–World War I period, and his short stories—*Stories from the East* and "Three Jews"—also explore the relationship between communal psychology and social standards of value, revealing how class and ethnic prejudice creates alienation and destroys the possibility of individual fulfillment. Later, in Woolf's studies of the Co-operative Movement, presented as *Co-operation and the Future of Industry* and *Socialism and Co-operation*, he analyzes a communal system of production and distribution of goods and services, focusing on the connection between economics and ideology. At this time, socialism came to represent to Woolf both a system of efficient production and distribution of resources and an ideology that stresses the democratic ideal of equality, which is the basis of a civilized society.

In the post–World War I years, Woolf's analysis of war, international government, and imperialism again emphasized the important effects of social and economic structure on national and international ideologies and actions. War develops, Woolf argues, when belief in and guarantees of individual liberty are undermined, and when social standards of values do not allow for the self-determination of nations. The major studies of this period—*International Government, Empire and Commerce in Africa*, and *Imperialism and Civilization*—analyze how relationships between nations are determined by concepts of international morality, which are the standards of value held by a nation as part of its communal psychology. In addition, Woolf points out that an international network of economic relationships is an important influence on fostering the ideologies of imperialism. Woolf's studies revealed that imperialism was not economically beneficial to either nation involved in the imperialist relationship. Moreover, the moral and cultural deterioration in both countries caused by imperialism suggested to Woolf that imperialism could not foster the standards of value essential to a civilized society. He thus urged the end of imperialist domination in his studies on war and imperialism, as well as when he was a candidate for Parliament in 1922, and throughout his years of work with the Labour party advisory committees on international and imperial affairs.

Woolf was deeply disturbed by the violence and destruction of World War I, and he feared the recurrence of such barbarism in the 1920s and 1930s. Again, he was not content to blame the imminence of war only on those in power. Instead, in *Quack, Quack!* and *Barbarians Within and Without*, he analyzed the communal psychologies of civilization and barbarism, pointing out how a class system and the ideologies of unreason, intolerance, and authoritarianism undermine the possibility of man's achieving the bases of civilization—reason, freedom, and individual liberty. Similarly, *Principia Politica*, Woolf's last study of communal psychology, traces the relationship of man and society to the ideologies of civilization and barbarism throughout history, particularly comparing the political systems of democracy and authoritarianism. Finally, Woolf's play, *The Hotel,* dramatizes how a breakdown of moral values occurs when an emphasis on money and power replaces human compassion and morality. The ending of *The Hotel,* however, suggests the possibility of moral regeneration, and thus represents Woolf's humanist belief in man's ability, through rationalism, mercy, justice, and internationalism, to adopt positive moral values despite the negative influences, indeed the barbarism, of economic and social structures such as capitalism, militarism, authoritarianism, and nationalism, on individual and communal psychology.

Over the years, Woolf's journalism complemented his political and literary work. He began writing documentary journalism for *International Review* and *Contemporary Review,* which reported on current national and international events, while later, for *Political Quarterly,* he discussed political issues in a more theoretical way. At the same time, his book reviews for the *Nation* in the 1920s presented his opinions on literature, as well as on journalists and publishers. Then, his literary and political reviews for the *New Statesman & Nation* and *Political Quarterly* from 1930 on continued to reveal his standards for writers and public figures past and present. Finally, in the last years of his life, Woolf's major literary work was his autobiography. In this work, he emphasized his analysis of ideology, social structure, and individual action by focusing on social structure and historical events as key factors in the growth of his own political consciousness and his commitment to practical politics and to literature.

Woolf's contemporaries were often generous in their praise of his political works and the autobiography. His reviewers most frequently respected his honesty and rationalism about personal and social relationships, and his ability to write simply and clearly. Kingsley Martin, for example, praised *After the Deluge* as "full of original and penetrating observation about the nature of society and the behaviour of human beings."[1] He also commented that Woolf is "a writer who is never for a minute dull" (145). Similar praise was given by H. N. Brailsford, who stated that *Quack, Quack!* was "brilliantly written and closely thought out from beginning to end."[2] Some years later, Barbara Wootton wrote about *Principia Politica* that "in both content and style this is an extremely original book," and that the argument "will always bear the stamp of a humane and civilized mind."[3] Wootton also admired Woolf's talent for writing realistically about political issues in clear language. There were, however, also some criticisms of these works. Martin wrote that Woolf might have extended his analysis in *After the Deluge* back to the sixteenth century to consider the idea of sovereignty and the national state, as well as the development of science, and Wootton questioned whether his claims in *Principia Politica* about the lives of ordinary men and women in Russia over the last five hundred years, as well as his admiration for the Greeks, would hold up.

On the autobiography, reviewers again stressed Woolf's honesty and desire to seek the truth and his ability to create portraits of the people he knew. V. S. Pritchett wrote in a review of *Growing* that Woolf "was...alive to what was going on around him. He had shrewd humour."[4] He also commented about *Beginning Again* that Woolf rejected "the social assumptions of his class and [put] his conscience into action."[5] Moreover, for Pritchett, Woolf's "portraits strike one as being new and truthful," and he pointed out that the portrait of Virginia is "truthfully and tenderly done" (726). For Noel Annan, *Beginning Again* revealed that Woolf's talent "lay in the comprehension of politics and [in] his expression [which] was a singular blend of truthfulness, passion and goodness,"[6] while Kingsley Martin remarked about *Downhill* that "Woolf had a clearer mind and more courage than most of his contemporaries."[7]

Political Quarterly reviews of Woolf's autobiography were particularly positive. Shelton C. Fernando, reviewing *Growing*, wrote that Woolf "was one of the ablest and most conscientious men to enter the Civil Service."[8] He then acknowledges that Woolf was a man of "domineering personality...who ruled his Province like an autocrat, though a benevolent autocrat," yet he also sees Woolf as a man who was "lonely and lovable despite his sternness, fond of bird and beast and man...intensely human, and ultimately bearing no malice even towards an avowed enemy." Fernando also indicates that Woolf was "a critic of everything he found wrong" (219) and never hesitated to apply his high standard of values to everyone, and to every action and event he witnessed. Similarly, Noel Annan reviewed several volumes of the autobiography, commenting about Woolf's role as "a shrewd, tough businessman"[9] in his discussion of *Downhill*, and arguing that this toughness allowed Woolf to persist with "the hard, slogging, unrewarding work" for the Labour party and the Fabian Society (447). Annan, moreover, considered Woolf to be not only progressive in political thought but also able to apply the necessary "toughness to work in collaboration with political machines for progressive policies" (448). About *Journey*, Annan wrote that Woolf played an important role in British society through his efforts to change British social thought, even though the ideas Woolf supported in the 1920s were not accepted until the 1960s.[10] Annan also focused on Woolf's ability to "make the jump from the theoretical to the practical" (37), and he argued that among Woolf's Bloomsbury friends and fellow writers and artists, his "middle-stamp Socialism was the most articulate political response" (39). Finally, Annan recognized that Woolf's political articles have been neglected, and he suggested that they be anthologized.

Although reviewers and many of Woolf's readers might agree with Noel Annan's comment that "Woolf has none of the arts of the writer: there is never a telling phrase or a simile that lights up the scene,"[11] they might also agree with Barbara Wootton that Woolf's analysis of himself and society was "astonishingly readable."[12] Similarly, readers probably would respect Woolf's strong sense of moral values which led V. S. Pritchett to describe him as "one of the several shrewd rationalist saints of our time,"[13] and to write that "the Jewish feeling for justice and mercy, enlarged by the half-Jewish Montaigne's hatred of cruelty and the supreme value (Woolf) put on the 'I' of man and animals, gave sinew to Woolf's scepticism and fatalism."[14] Nevertheless, the limitations of Woolf's thought and work must also be noted. Duncan Wilson, in his political biography of Woolf, claims that the influence of Cambridge and particularly G. E. Moore restricted Woolf's thinking by establishing "a reverence for close logical argument, for shocking simplicities and for systems (too often closed systems) of thought."[15] Wilson also states that although Woolf read widely, he hardly ever read materials which would challenge or extend the assumptions of his political and philosophical positions (245); as a result, Wilson argues, Woolf was "less of a systematic philosopher than he wished at times to appear" (246), and his works are thus more effective in presenting perceptive insights into social, economic, political, and literary situations than in providing a broad perspective.

As the above comments suggest, Woolf's works indicate that he was a derivative thinker, drawing on Jewish religious values, Greek philosophy, Renaissance humanism, nineteenth-century rationalism, and twentieth-century perspectives based in anthropology, Marxism, psychoanalysis, and the philosophies of G. E. Moore and Cambridge. Similarly, Woolf wrote for many audiences: for the working-class men and women of the Co-operative Movement, for the trade-unionist officials of the Labour party, and for the sophisticated literary and political readers of the journals in which his articles and book reviews appeared. These different audiences account for the varying styles of writing which characterize his work, ranging from a simple, didactic, even repetitive style to a more complex, intellectual style. Variations in tone are also noticeable, for although he writes often with both admiration and compassion as he comments on human nature and surveys man's history, he is also capable of indignation and scorn, as well as cynicism and sarcasm, when he reveals man's weaknesses.

In terms of Woolf's influence, his political works seem to have had the greatest influence on his contemporaries, and even today they provide perceptive insights into the continuing problems involved with war and peace and imperialism.[16] In contrast, his contribution to literature has rarely been considered. This may be because his literary reviews are generally unknown, and his influence on twentieth-century literature through the Hogarth Press and as editor of Virginia Woolf's works is difficult to determine. In addition, his short fiction and first novel—*The*

Village in the Jungle—present material which is foreign to Western readers, and his second novel, *The Wise Virgins*, has been largely unavailable until recently. Yet perhaps a more important factor limiting his influence is his strong belief in rationalism, which frequently led him to underestimate the complexities of art and politics, and how literature, culture, and politics are influenced by the complexities of human psychology. Thus, when he attempted to provide a literary aesthetic or a theoretical framework for resolving social, economic, and political problems, he often overlooked details and therefore was too general, even impractical. Perhaps, then, what remains most striking about Woolf's work and thought is the values he stood for: justice, mercy, equality (personal, national, and international), education, peace, cooperation, and internationalism. These values suggest that he frequently expressed a minority point of view which placed him in conflict with society's emphasis on injustice, tyranny, class privilege, materialism and antiintellectualism, violence, war, nationalism, and militarism.

Woolf has often been described variously as a penniless Jew, Cambridge intellectual, civil servant, Fabian Socialist, Labour party member, journalist, editor, publisher, writer, and man of practical politics. Virginia commented about Leonard just prior to their marriage that "he wants to keep outside Government and do things on his own account... and means to write as well as be practical."[17] Independence, literary work, and practical politics do best characterize his life. Woolf fused the intellectual, theoretical, and practical aspects of his background and temperament into the vision which influenced all his literary and political work. For Woolf, politics is not what takes place in Parliament, and not what constitutes national or international policies; instead, it is a way of seeing the world—particularly social, economic, and political institutions—in relationship to individual and communal consciousness. Thus, Woolf believed that the practical political man, as well as the artist, deals with social standards of value, recognizing that they are shaped by material factors and ideologies, and that they in turn create new material conditions and communal concepts. Consequently, the political thinker and the artist, Woolf argued, must face these concerns and struggle to institute and maintain the highest ethical values in individual life, social and political life, and in art. As a man of practical politics and as a writer, this was Leonard Woolf's lifelong interest and goal—and his achievement.

Notes and References

Chapter One

1. The following quotation seems to sum up many people's impressions: "Leonard Woolf? An ungainly writer and social reformer active in anti-colonial causes, an early supporter of the League of Nations—who thinks of him as anything other than Virginia Woolf's husband?" Cynthia Ozick, "The Loose, Drifting Material of Life," *New York Times Book Review*, 2 October 1977, p. 7.

2. George Spater and Ian Parsons, *A Marriage of True Minds: An Intimate Portrait of Leonard and Virginia Woolf* (New York, 1977), p. 55. Note particularly that when Strachey wrote to Woolf that he was considering marrying Virginia, Woolf wrote back that he would return home if Virginia would accept him.

3. Woolf claims that the war was responsible for lack of interest in *The Wise Virgins*; however, there were enough negative reactions among family, especially his mother, about the way he portrays family members in the novel, and possible negative reactions by Virginia about her portrayal in the novel, to suggest that Leonard Woolf may have suppressed circulation of the book.

4. Virginia Woolf, *The Letters of Virginia Woolf, Volume V: 1932-1935*, ed. Nigel Nicolson and Joanne Trautmann (New York, 1979), p. 388.

5. Leonard writes about this in his autobiography, and Virginia refers to it in her letters. See also Quentin Bell, *Virginia Woolf: A Biography* (New York, 1972), Chronology, 2:251. Bell records for June 17–20, 1939: "Adrian Stephen provides them [the Woolfs] with a lethal dose of morphia."

6. Virginia Woolf, *Moments of Being*, ed. Jeanne Schulkind (New York: Harcourt Brace Jovanovich, 1976), p. 166. Leonard's nervous tremor, inherited from his father, is discussed in his autobiography. See *Sowing: An Autobiography of the Years 1880 to 1904* (New York, 1960), pp. 90-102. See also Richard Kennedy, *A Boy at the Hogarth Press* (London, 1972), p. 6, for a comment on Leonard's trembling hands and head, which "gave the impression, not of infirmity, but of the vibration of a powerful intellectual machine." Also, Cynthia Ozick, "Mrs. Virginia Woolf," *Commentary* 56 (1973): 33–44, comments that

Leonard's "intelligence was reined in by a seriousness that makes him the most responsible and conscious figure among all Bloomsburyites. His seriousness was profound" (35).

7. Leonard Woolf, *Beginning Again: An Autobiography of the Years 1911 to 1918* (New York, 1963), pp. 75, 91.

8. Leon Edel, *Bloomsbury: A House of Lions* (Philadelphia and New York, 1979), p. 24.

9. Virginia Woolf, *The Letters of Virginia Woolf, Volume I: 1888-1912*, ed. Nigel Nicolson and Joanne Trautmann (New York, 1975), pp. 500, 501.

10. Virginia Woolf, *The Letters of Virginia Woolf, Volume IV: 1929-1931*, ed. Nigel Nicolson and Joanne Trautmann (New York, 1978), pp. 195-96.

11. Spater and Parsons, *A Marriage of True Minds*, p. 155.

12. Ibid., pp. 156-58. See also Chapter 6 of this study. In addition, Richard Kennedy writes that when he made some mistakes while working for the press, Leonard revealed his high standards by commenting to Kennedy that he was "the most frightful idiot he [Woolf] has ever had the privilege of meeting in a long career of suffering fools" (85). Kennedy also remarks that Leonard "believes that anyone can do anything they really want to" (36).

13. Virginia Woolf, *The Letters of Virginia Woolf, Volume V*, p. 59.

14. Virginia Woolf, *The Diary of Virginia Woolf, Volume One, 1915-1919*, ed. Anne Olivier Bell (New York, 1977), pp. 69, 77.

15. Virginia Woolf, *The Letters of Virginia Woolf, Volume II: 1912-1922*, ed. Nigel Nicolson and Joanne Trautmann (New York, 1976), p. 23. Virginia writes: "I don't follow these economic questions very easily, but Leonard seems to be able to read and write and talk to enthusiasts without turning a hair."

16. Virginia Woolf, *The Diary of Virginia Woolf, Volume One*, pp. 22-23.

17. Virginia Woolf, *The Diary of Virginia Woolf, Volume Two, 1920-1924*, ed. Anne Olivier Bell (New York, 1978), pp. 152, 212.

18. Ibid., p. 66.

19. Virginia Woolf, *The Letters of Virginia Woolf, Volume III: 1923-1928*, ed. Nigel Nicolson and Joanne Trautmann (New York, 1977), p. 35.

20. Virginia Woolf, *The Diary of Virginia Woolf, Volume Two*, p. 20. Portrayals of politicians in her short stories and novels are consistently negative.

21. Cynthia Ozick refers to Leonard as Virginia's "nurse" ("Mrs. Virginia Woolf," 34) and analyzes his devotion: "He was dedicated partly because he was earnestly efficient at everything, and also because he loved his wife, and also because he was a realist who could reconcile himself to unlooked-for disaster" (37). She further comments that Virginia's "madness fed his genius for responsibility; it became for him a corridor of access to her genius. The spirit of Bloomsbury was not Leonard's, his temperament was against it—Bloomsbury could have done without him. So could a sane Virginia" (39). For differing opinions, see Elaine Showalter, *A Literature of Their Own: British Women Novelists from Brontë to Lessing* (Princeton, N.J., 1977), pp. 263–98. Showalter views the Woolfs' marriage relationship as destructive; she sees Leonard as a contributor to Virginia's failure to confront her sexuality and achieve identity as a woman. Similarly, Roger Poole, *The Unknown Virginia Woolf* (Cambridge, 1978), argues that the Leonard-Virginia relationship was incompatible and destructive. He claims that Virginia realized the impossibility of communication with Leonard, but decided not to confront him about it.

22. Bell, *Virginia Woolf*, 1:181. Also, Leonard's short story "A Tale Told by Moonlight" portrays the failure of love when the woman is inferior. The same conflict and possibility of failure are embodied in the Harry-Gwen relationship in *The Wise Virgins*. Woolf may have chosen the name Gwen to portray in fiction the relationship which he might have developed with a young woman of the same name whom he met in Ceylon (See *Growing*, 102).

23. Ibid., p. 184.

24. Virginia Woolf, *The Letters of Virginia Woolf, Volume II*, p. 132.

25. Ibid., p. 31.

26. Ibid., p. 34.

27. Ibid., p. 192.

28. Bell, *Virginia Woolf*, 2:226. Virginia's note stresses that she is ending her life because she feels she will have another period of mental illness and cannot face it. She also stresses that she does not wish to burden Leonard: "I know that I am spoiling your life, that without me you could work" (226). This does not seem to be only a magnanimous parting gesture, for Virginia had discussed suicide with Beatrice Webb, commenting that her attempt at suicide in 1913 was prompted by "the best of motives as I thought—not to be a burden on my husband" (See *Letters*, 5:305). Roger Poole, however, claims that Virginia wrote this letter in terms that Leonard could understand. Their relationship had

never allowed for intimacy and communication; thus, at the time of Virginia's death, "they part, profoundly devoted to each other, in complete misunderstanding" (*Unknown Virginia Woolf*, 257). Also, Cynthia Ozick ("Mrs. Virginia Woolf," 41) comments that Virginia's suicide note did not express her feelings; it was "like almost every other suicide note, horribly banal, not a writer's letter at all."

29. Virginia Woolf, *The Letters of Virginia Woolf, Volume IV*, p. 17. See also pp. 206, 210.

30. Ibid., p. 88.

31. Ibid., p. 413.

32. Ibid., p. 216. Later, Virginia was to admit that Leonard's approach to recovery from her illness was right (266).

33. Ibid., p. 151. See also p. 180, where Virginia writes, "And then I married, and then my brains went up in a shower of fireworks."

34. Virginia Woolf, *The Letters of Virginia Woolf, Volume II*, p. 83. For Virginia, who revised her work many times, this must have seemed amazing. Leonard himself comments in a letter to a Mr. Jacob Schwartz of Brighton, 15 November 1969 (Berg Collection, New York Public Library), that he has no manuscripts since he typed directly onto the typewriter.

35. Ibid., p. 23.

36. Ibid., p. 514. Virginia writes very frequently about Leonard's gardening work.

37. Leonard Woolf, *Growing: An Autobiography of the Years 1904 to 1911* (New York, 1961), pp. 100-102.

38. Leonard Woolf, *Downhill All the Way: An Autobiography of the Years 1919 to 1939* (London, 1968), pp. 186-88.

39. Leonard Woolf, *Growing*, p. 38.

40. Leonard Woolf, *Downhill*, pp. 188-94.

41. Leonard Woolf, *Essays on Literature, History, Politics, Etc.* (London, 1927), pp. 250-56.

42. Leonard Woolf, *Sowing*, pp. 198-202. See also *Growing*, 195ff, 212ff.

43. Leonard Woolf, *Downhill*, p. 42.

44. Ibid., p. 43. See pp. 43-44 for positive comments about Israel.

45. Leonard Woolf, *Sowing*, p. 80. See also his *A Calendar of Consolation* (New York, 1967), p. 109, for the quotation from Montaigne.

46. Leonard Woolf, *Fear and Politics: A Debate at the Zoo* (London, 1925), p. 5. All further references will be from this edition and will be cited in the text.

47. Woolf comments on his basic support of the principles of social-ism, as well as on his disappointment about the way it developed in Russia, in his autobiography.

48. For Woolf's study of history also focusing on the French Revolu-tion, see *After the Deluge, Volumes I and II* and *Principia Politica.*

49. See the opening pages of Woolf's *Beginning Again*, where he quotes from Rilke's poem "Der Panther."

50. Leonard Woolf, *Downhill*, p. 254.

51. Leonard Woolf, *The Journey Not the Arrival Matters: An Auto-biography of the Years 1939 to 1969* (New York, 1969), p. 158.

52. Peter Clarke, "A Peculiar Kind of Socialist," *Times Literary Supplement*, 29 September 1978, p. 1072.

53. Noel Annan, "Leonard Woolf," in *The Bloomsbury Group*, ed. S. P. Rosenbaum (Toronto, 1975), p. 188.

54. Leonard Woolf, "Leslie Stephen," *Political Quarterly* 23 (1952): 196.

Chapter Two

1. Spater and Parsons, *A Marriage of True Minds*, p. 4.

2. Ibid., p. 3.

3. Ibid., p. 43.

4. Leonard Woolf, *The Journey Not the Arrival Matters*, p. 200. All further references to this edition will be cited in the text.

5. Leonard Woolf, *Growing*, p. 109. All further references to this edition will be cited in the text.

6. Leonard Woolf, *Diaries in Ceylon* (London, 1963),p. x. All further references to this edition will be cited in the text.

7. Ibid., p. lxxvi.

8. Leonard Woolf, *The Journey*, p. 206.

9. Leonard Woolf, *Diaries in Ceylon*, p. xlviii.

10. Leonard Woolf, *The Village in the Jungle* (London, 1961), p. 11. All further references to this edition will be cited in the text.

11. Leonard Woolf, *Stories from the East*, in *Diaries in Ceylon* (London, 1963), p. 255. All further references to this edition will be cited in the text.

12. Leonard Woolf, *Downhill All the Way*, p. 88.

13. Leonard Woolf, *Stories from the East*, p. 265.

14. Leonard Woolf, "Three Jews," in *Two Stories* (London, 1917), p. 5. All further references to this edition will be cited in the text.

15. Leonard Woolf, *Beginning Again*, p. 91. *The Wise Virgins* was republished in 1979.

16. Ibid., pp. 33–34.

17. Freema Gottlieb, "Reality and Romance: Leonard Woolf's Portraiture of Virginia in Various Early Writings," *Virginia Woolf Quarterly*, Spring 1978, p. 199.

18. Poole, *The Unknown Virginia Woolf*. See chapter six.

19. Leonard Woolf, *Beginning Again*, pp. 91–92.

20. Duncan Wilson, *Leonard Woolf: A Political Biography* (New York, 1978), pp. 11–12.

21. Leonard Woolf, *The Wise Virgins, A Story of Words, Opinions and a few Emotions* (London, 1914), p. 10. All further references to this edition will be cited in the text.

22. See Spater and Parsons, *A Marriage of True Minds*, pp. 61–62, for similar comments by Leonard Woolf and Virginia Woolf.

23. Virginia Woolf, *The Diary of Virginia Woolf, Volume One*, p. 32.

Chapter Three

1. Leonard Woolf, *Beginning Again*, p. 93. All further references to this edition will be cited in the text.

2. Wilson, *Leonard Woolf*, p. 74. All further references to this edition will be cited in the text.

3. Leonard Woolf, *International Government* (London, 1916), p. 15. All further references to this edition will be cited in the text.

4. Leonard Woolf, ed., *The Framework of a Lasting Peace* (London, 1917), p. 9. All further references to this edition will be cited in the text.

5. Leonard Woolf, *The Future of Constantinople* (London, 1917), p. 11. All further references to this edition will be cited in the text.

6. Wilson, *Leonard Woolf*, pp. 103–106.

7. Leonard Woolf, *Empire and Commerce in Africa* (London, 1918), p. 6. All further references to this edition will be cited in the text. For additional discussion of the mandate system, see Woolf's study *Mandates and Empires* (London, 1920).

8. Leonard Woolf, *Economic Imperialism* (London, 1920), p. 8. All further references to this edition will be cited in the text.

9. Leonard Woolf, *Downhill All the Way*, p. 33. All further references to this edition will be cited in the text.

10. Leonard Woolf, *International Economic Policy* (London, 1920), *International Co-operative Trade* (London, 1922), and "Labour and

Foreign Affairs," in *British Labour Speaks*, ed. Richard W. Hogue (New York, 1924), pp. 168–87.

11. Leonard Woolf, *Imperialism and Civilization* (New York, 1928), p. 39. All further references to this edition will be cited in the text.

12. Leonard Woolf, *The League and Abyssinia* (London, 1936), p. 5. All further references to this edition will be cited in the text.

13. Leonard Woolf, *The War for Peace* (London, 1940), p. 46. All further references to this edition will be cited in the text.

14. Leonard Woolf, *The International Post-War Settlement* (London, 1944), p. 16. All further references to this edition will be cited in the text.

15. Leonard Woolf: *Foreign Policy: The Labour Party's Dilemma* (London, 1947), p. 16. All further references to this edition will be cited in the text.

Chapter Four

1. Leonard Woolf, *Downhill All the Way*, p. 87. Woolf shared this view with Beatrice and Sidney Webb. In "Political Thought and the Webbs" (in *The Webbs and Their Work*, ed. M. I. Cole [London, 1949], pp. 251–67), he describes the Webbs as practical politicians who taught members of the Fabian Society to view "all social institutions as the natural genera and species of communal life, to study their dynamic history, and to classify them according to the functions which they performed" (254). Like the Webbs, Woolf saw monopoly capitalism as a system in which communal control was essential because individualism was counterproductive and was quickly becoming impossible. Moreover, the Webbs, like Woolf, were interested in socialism because it offered the possibility of an organized society. Woolf, however, is also quite critical of the Webbs, claiming that they were close-minded and did not allow other views to change theirs, and that "they were so certain of the rightness of the ends which they were pursuing that they did not worry very much about the means which they used to attain them" (258). Nevertheless, he acknowledges that the Webbs made important contributions in the areas of local government and trade unions.

2. Leonard Woolf, *Co-operation and the Future of Industry* (London, 1919), p. 11. All further references to this edition will be cited in the text.

3. Woolf began writing about the Co-operative Movement in the *Co-operative News*. Some articles appeared in the 3, 10, and 17 August

1912 issues, in the 11 and 18 January 1918 issues, and in the 9 and 16 November 1918 issues.

4. Leonard Woolf, *The Control of Industry by the People* (London, 1915).

5. Leonard Woolf, *Education and the Co-operative Movement* (London, 1914).

6. Leonard Woolf, *Co-operation and the War. I: Effects of War on Commerce and Industry* (London, 1915).

7. Leonard Woolf, *Co-operation and the War. II: Co-operative Action in National Crises* (London, 1915).

8. Leonard Woolf, *After the War* (Manchester, Eng., 1918).

9. Leonard Woolf, *Socialism and Co-operation* (London and Manchester, 1921), pp. 6–7. All further references to this edition will be cited in the text.

10. Leonard Woolf, *Downhill*, p. 87.

11. Leonard Woolf, *Quack, Quack!* (London, 1936), p. 28. All further references to this edition will be cited in the text. Woolf had written earlier about the role of writers, artists, and thinkers in a literary review, "Just for the Riband to Stick in Their Coats," which appeared in the *Nation & Athenaeum* 44 (29 December 1928): 468. Reviewing Julien Benda's work *La Trahison des Clercs*, Woolf supports Benda's view that the "clercs," or writers, artists, and thinkers, have "betrayed their trust" by rejecting truth, justice, and humanity, and by turning to unreason, passion, and prejudice. Woolf calls these men "lost leaders" because they serve such "political passions" as patriotism, nationalism, and class prejudice. Nevertheless, Woolf argues that in the twentieth century this "betrayal is not universal"; men like Zola, Bertrand Russell, and Einstein prove that even though there will always be "lost leaders," there will also be men whose work and thought will stand for reason and truth.

12. Leonard Woolf, *Barbarians Within and Without* (New York, 1939), p. 6. All further references to this edition will be cited in the text.

13. Leonard Woolf, *The Hotel* (New York, 1963), p. 5. All further references to this edition will be cited in the text.

14. Leonard Woolf, *International Government*, p. 354.

15. Leonard Woolf, *After the Deluge, Volume I* (New York, 1931), p. v. All further references to this edition will be cited in the text. As early as 1926, Woolf briefly defined communal psychology in a literary review, "The Sum of All Villanies," in the *Nation & Athenaeum* 40 (13 November 1926): 220. In this review, he examines the way a communal

psychology for abolishing the slave trade developed in England. Woolf is particularly fascinated by this because it revealed how the principles of a majority of English people overcame the material interests of a minority who were living in or who had financial interests in the West Indies. Moreover, he felt that this antislavery movement in the late eighteenth and early nineteenth centuries, which emphasized the moral injustice and economic impracticality of the slave trade, could be relevant to the present native labor question in Kenya. Finally, Woolf believed that "it is a curious fact in communal psychology that material or vested interests paralyze the social conscience of the individual," but that history reveals instances when this situation can be reversed.

16. Leonard Woolf, "What Is Democracy?" in *The Modern State*, ed. Mary Adams (Port Washington, N.Y., 1933), p. 56. All further references to this edition will be cited in the text.

17. Leonard Woolf, *Principia Politica* (New York, 1953), pp. v-vi. All further references to this edition will be cited in the text.

18. Leonard Woolf, *Downhill*, p. 26.

19. Leonard Woolf, *The Journey Not the Arrival Matters*, p. 153.

Chapter Five

1. Wilson, *Leonard Woolf*, pp. 50-54, 119.

2. Ibid., p. 122.

3. Leonard Woolf, "The Ideal of a League Remains," *Political Quarterly* 7 (1936): 330-45; 333.

4. Ibid. 2 (1931): 172-85. See also "Educating the Listener-in," *New Statesman & Nation* 2 (1931): 274-75, where Woolf argues that the BBC is beginning to recognize that if it is to provide the kind of adult education suitable for a democracy, it must present all points of view. In "The B.B.C. and Its Critics," *New Statesman & Nation* 7 (1934): 476-77, he points out that the BBC policy is "autocratic and ... heavily class biased... [and] bourgeois, both politically and culturally"; and in "Truth and Public Opinion," *New Statesman & Nation* 30 (1945): 303-304, he comments that newspaper and radio are "terrific engines of obscurantism" (303), yet he writes that democracy would be possible if education, the press, and the BBC were used by democrats for the purpose of educating (304).

5. Leonard Woolf, "From Sarajevo to Geneva," *Political Quarterly* 1 (1930): 186-206.

6. Ibid. 4 (1933): 30-43.

7. Ibid., pp. 504–24.

8. Ibid. 7 (1936): 16–32.

9. Ibid., pp. 330–47.

10. Ibid. 8 (1937): 21–35.

11. Ibid., pp. 337–52.

12. Ibid. 10 (1939): 463–76.

13. Ibid. 11 (1940): 167–82.

14. Ibid., pp. 335–40.

15. Ibid. 13 (1942): 373–83.

16. Ibid. 12 (1941): 367–79.

17. Ibid. 14 (1943): 209–24.

18. Ibid. 16 (1945): 12–20.

19. Ibid. 18 (1947): 199–205. In a book review of E. H. Carr's *Conditions of the Peace, Political Quarterly* 14 (1942): 28–33, Woolf again attacks the typical conservative mind, which he believes is twenty years behind the times, and he comments: "Most of the great social disasters in modern history have been due to conservativism, to the habit of governing classes to reject every truth and deny the need for change" (329). Carr rejects the League and international government because he believes that if nations concentrate on economic recovery, political issues will not be a problem. Woolf counters this view, claiming that unless states have international obligations within a system of international government and collective security, they will put national interests first.

20. Ibid. 20 (1949): 210–18.

21. Ibid. 23 (1952): 230–31.

22. Ibid. 26 (1955): 220–28.

23. Ibid. 27 (1956): 152–62.

24. Ibid. 22 (1951): 396–97.

25. Ibid. 31 (1960): 394–95.

26. Ibid. 37 (1966): 96–97.

27. Ibid. 31 (1960): 89–90.

28. Ibid. 38 (1969): 96–97.

29. Ibid., pp. 315–16.

30. Ibid. 39 (1968): 343–47.

31. Ibid. 14 (1943): 202.

32. Ibid., pp. 289–90.

33. Ibid. 19 (1948): 277–78.

34. Ibid. 27 (1956): 342–43.

35. Leonard Woolf, "The Journalessayist," *Nation* 34 (24 November 1924): 314.

36. Ibid. 35 (12 April 1924): 51.

37. Ibid. 37 (2 May 1925): 136.

38. Ibid. 37 (9 May 1925): 179.

39. Ibid. 26 (15 February 1930): 674.

40. Ibid. 40 (30 October 1926): 148.

41. Ibid. 35 (30 August 1924): 667.

42. Ibid. 38 (12 December 1925): 405.

43. Ibid. 46 (14 December 1929): 402.

44. Ibid. 42 (3 December 1927): 356.

45. Ibid. 44 (23 March 1929): 882.

46. Ibid. 40 (27 November 1926): 304.

47. Ibid. 41 (18 June 1927): 371.

48. Ibid. 42 (3 March 1928): 815.

49. Ibid. 33 (19 May 1923): 226.

50. Ibid. 33 (29 September 1923): 808.

51. Ibid. 35 (17 May 1924): 206.

52. Ibid. 35 (14 June 1924): 354.

53. Ibid. 36 (22 November 1924): 298.

54. Ibid. 38 (3 October 1925): 18.

55. Ibid. 38 (16 January 1926): 554.

56. Leonard Woolf, *Essays on Literature, History, Politics, Etc.* All further references to this edition will be cited in the text.

57. Leonard Woolf, "Books in General," *Nation* 32 (19 October 1946): 285–86.

58. Ibid. 24 (18 July 1942): 39–41.

59. Ibid. 24 (5 December 1942): 375–76.

60. Ibid. 28 (16 September 1944): 188.

61. Leonard Woolf, *Hunting the Highbrow* (London, 1927). All further references to this edition will be cited in the text.

62. Leonard Woolf, *A Calendar of Consolation*. All further references to this edition will be cited in the text.

63. Leonard Woolf, "Words and Things," *Nation* 15 (7 May 1935): 778–80.

64. Ibid. 25 (9 January 1943): 28–29.

65. Ibid. 2 (28 February 1931): 22–24.

66. Ibid. 3 (27 February 1932): 266.

67. Ibid. 16 (10 December 1938): 1014–16.

68. Ibid. 4 (22 October 1932): 485–86.

69. Ibid. 2 (21 September 1931): 645–46.

70. Ibid. 12 (14 November 1936): 784–86.

71. Ibid. 11 (4 January 1936): 19.

72. Ibid. 14 (4 December 1937): 971–72.

73. Ibid. 14 (18 September 1937): 410–12.

74. Ibid. 7 (30 June 1934): 997–98.

75. Ibid. 10 (23 November 1935): 778–79.

76. Ibid. 20 (20 July 1940): 56–57.

77. Ibid. 19 (29 June 1940): 807.

78. Ibid. 20 (17 August 1940): 164.

79. Ibid. 21 (8 March 1941): 253–54.

80. Ibid. 21 (25 January 1941): 76–77.

81. Ibid. 21 (22 March 1941): 304–305.

82. Leonard Woolf, *Essays on Literature, History, Politics, Etc.*, pp. 153–69.

83. Ibid., pp. 170–88.

84. Ibid., pp. 198–211.

85. Ibid., pp. 212–17.

86. Leonard Woolf, "Hitler Speaks," *Nation* 24 (26 September 1942): 208–209. See also 25 (1 May 1943): 294; and 32 (27 July 1946): 68.

87. Ibid. 45 (16 May 1953): 586–88.

88. Ibid. 38 (9 July 1949): 46.

89. Ibid. 55 (4 January 1958): 5–6.

90. Ibid. 55 (24 May 1958): 670.

91. Ibid. 43 (29 March 1952): 377.

92. Leonard Woolf, *Beginning Again.*

93. Leonard Woolf, *Downhill All the Way.*

94. Leonard Woolf, *The Journey Not the Arrival Matters.*

95. John Lehmann, *Thrown to the Woolves* (London, 1978). All further references to this edition will be cited in the text.

96. Virginia Woolf, *Between the Acts* (New York: Harcourt Brace Jovanovich, 1954). See Leonard Woolf's Note.

97. Jane Marcus, "'No More Horses': Virginia Woolf on Art and Propaganda," *Women's Studies* 4 (1977): 265–90, argues that with at least one of Virginia's essays, Leonard chose a less political version for publication.

98. Virginia Woolf, *A Writer's Diary* (New York: Harcourt Brace Jovanovich, 1954). See Leonard Woolf's Preface.

99. See Lucio Ruotolo, ed., *Virginia Woolf Issue, Twentieth Century Literature* 25 (1979), for the published manuscript of *Friendship's Gallery*.

Chapter Six

1. Leonard Woolf, *Sowing; Growing; Beginning Again; Downhill All the Way; The Journey Not the Arrivial Matters*.

2. Virginia Woolf, *The Letters of Virginia Woolf: Volume Two*, p. 83.

3. See Leonard Woolf, *Growing*, pp. 248–52. In *Beginning Again*, Woolf responds to one reviewer's criticism that these letters were boring, and to another reviewer's claim that he did not acknowledge how well the Colonial Office treated him. Woolf defends himself on both charges, arguing that he believed the letters were "interesting as a period piece. They show, I think, the economy and restraint ... considered right and proper in official relations and communications" (53); in addition, he states that the letters did indicate "how decently the Secretary of State treated his subordinate" (53).

4. Lehmann, *Thrown to the Woolves*, p. 152.

Chapter Seven

1. Kingsley Martin, "After the Deluge," *Political Quarterly* 3, no. 1 (1932): 143.

2. H. N. Brailsford, "Quack, Quack!", *Political Quarterly* 6, no. 3 (1935): 435.

3. Barbara Wootton, "Principia Politica," *Political Quarterly* 25, no. 1 (1954): 90.

4. V. S. Pritchett, "Bloomsbury on Safari," *New Statesman & Nation* 62 (3 November 1961): 656.

5. V. S. Pritchett, "What Exactly Do You Mean?", *New Statesman & Nation* 67 (8 May 1964): 726.

6. Noel Annan, "Beginning Again," *Political Quarterly* 35, no. 4 (1964): 469.

7. Kingsley Martin, "A Lost Civilization," *New Statesman & Nation* 73 (12 May 1967): 654.

8. Shelton C. Fernando, "Growing," *Political Quarterly* 33, no. 2 (1962): 218.

9. Noel Annan, "Downhill All the Way," *Political Quarterly* 39, no. 3 (1968): 447.

10. Noel Annan, "The Journey Not the Arrival Matters," *Political Quarterly* 41, no. 1, (1970): 36.

11. Noel Annan, "Beginning Again," p. 470.

12. Barbara Wootton, "Principia Politica," p. 90.

13. V. S. Pritchett, "Grace and Iron," *New Statesman & Nation* 78 (24 October 1969): 577.

14. Ibid.

15. Wilson, *Leonard Woolf*, p. 243.

16. Woolf's comments about Belgium in the 1920s and about tensions in Africa, especially in relation to South Africa, are particularly insightful and appropriate, even today. Moreover, Duncan Wilson claims that Woolf's greatest influence was in the area of the independence of the British colonies (*Leonard Woolf*, 248–49), as well as on post–World War I reparations, rearmament, and the Soviet Union (250).

17. Virginia Woolf, *The Letters of Virginia Woolf, Volume One*, p. 243.

Selected Bibliography

PRIMARY SOURCES

1. Books and Parts of Books

After the Deluge, Volume I. New York: Harcourt, Brace and Company, 1931.

After the War. Manchester: The Co-operative Newspaper Society, 1918.

Barbarians Within and Without. New York: Harcourt, Brace and Company, Inc., 1939.

Beginning Again: An Autobiography of the Years 1911 to 1918. New York: Harcourt Brace Jovanovich, 1963.

A Calendar of Consolation. New York: Funk & Wagnalls, 1967.

The Control of Industry by the People. London: Women's Co-operative Guild, 1915.

Co-operation and the Future of Industry. London: George Allen & Unwin, Ltd., 1919.

Co-operation and the War. I: Effects of War on Commerce and Industry. London: Women's Co-operative Guild, 1915.

Co-operation and the War. II: Co-operative Action in National Crises. London: Women's Co-operative Guild, 1915.

Diaries in Ceylon. London: The Hogarth Press, 1963.

Downhill All the Way: An Autobiography of the Years 1919 to 1939. London: The Hogarth Press, 1968.

Economic Imperialism. London: The Swarthmore Press, Ltd., 1920.

Education and the Co-operative Movement. London: Women's Co-operative Guild, 1915.

Empire and Commerce in Africa. London: The Labour Research Department, 1918.

Essays on Literature, History, Politics, Etc. London: The Hogarth Press, 1927.

Fear and Politics: A Debate at the Zoo. London: The Hogarth Press, 1925.

Foreign Policy: The Labour Party's Dilemma. London: Fabian Publications, 1947.

The Framework of a Lasting Peace. London: George Allen & Unwin, Ltd., 1917.

The Future of Constantinople. London: George Allen & Unwin, Ltd., 1917.

Growing: An Autobiography of the Years 1904 to 1911. New York: Harcourt Brace Jovanovich, 1961.

The Hotel. New York: The Dial Press, 1963.

Hunting the Highbrow. London: The Hogarth Press, 1927.

Imperialism and Civilization. New York: Harcourt, Brace and Company, Inc., 1928.

International Co-operative Trade. London: The Fabian Society, 1922.

International Economic Policy. London: The Labour Party, 1920.

International Government. London: George Allen & Unwin, Ltd., 1916.

The International Post-War Settlement. London: Fabian Publications, 1944.

Introduction. *Letters on India* by Mulk Raj Anand. London: Labour Book Service, 1942.

The Journey Not the Arrival Matters: An Autobiography of the Years 1939 to 1969. New York: Harcourt Brace Jovanovich, 1969.

"Labour and Foreign Affairs." In *British Labour Speaks.* Edited by Richard Hogue. New York: Boni and Liveright, 1924.

The League and Abyssinia. London: The Hogarth Press, 1936.

Mandates and Empire. London: The League of Nations Society, 1920.

"Oil." In *The Encyclopedia of the Labour Movement, Volume II.* Edited by H. B. Lees-Smith. London: Caxton Ltd., pp. 304–308.

"Political Thought and the Webbs." In *The Webbs and Their Work.* Edited by M. I. Cole. London: Frederick Muller Ltd., 1949, pp. 251–67.

Principia Politica. New York: Harcourt, Brace & Company, 1953.

Quack, Quack! London: The Hogarth Press, 1936.

Socialism and Co-operation. London & Manchester: The National Labour Press, Ltd., 1921.

Sowing: An Autobiography of the Years 1880 to 1904. New York: Harcourt Brace Jovanovich, 1960.

Stories from the East (contains "A Tale Told by Moonlight," "Pearls and Swine," and "Two Brahmans"). In *Diaries in Ceylon.* London: The Hogarth Press, 1963.

"Subject Peoples of the Empire." In *The Encyclopedia of the Labour Movement, Volume I,* Edited by H. B. Lees-Smith. London: Caxton Ltd., pp. 257–62.

"Three Jews." In *Two Stories*. London: The Hogarth Press, 1917.
The Village in the Jungle. London: The Hogarth Press, 1961.
The War for Peace. London: The Labour Book Service, 1940.
"What is Democracy?" In *The Modern State*. Edited by Mary Adams. Port Washington, N.Y.: Kennikat Press, 1933.
What Is Politics? London: The Bureau of Current Affairs, 1950.
The Wise Virgins, A Story of Words, Opinions, and a few Emotions. London: Edward Arnold, 1914.

2. Journals
Contemporary Review (1922).
Co-operative News (1913-1917).
International Review (1915-1919).
Nation (1915-1930).
New Statesman (1913-1930).
New Statesman and Nation (1931-1969).
Political Quarterly (1930-1969).

SECONDARY SOURCES

Annan, Noel. "Beginning Again." *Political Quarterly* 35 (1964): 469-71.
_____. "Downhill All the Way." *Political Quarterly* 39 (1968): 447-49.
_____. "The Journey Not the Arrival Matters." *Political Quarterly* 41 (1970): 35-51. Also appears as "Leonard Woolf" in *The Bloomsbury Group*. Edited by S. P. Rosenbaum. Toronto: University of Toronto Press, 1975, pp. 187-93. These reviews emphasize that Woolf's truthfulness and rationalism dominate the autobiography's portrayal of personal and social life.
Bell, Quentin. *Virginia Woolf: A Biography*. New York: Harcourt Brace Jovanovich, Inc., 1972. Bell discusses Leonard primarily in his role as Virginia's husband. The chronology provides useful details about Leonard's life.
Brailsford, H. N. "Quack, Quack!" *Political Quarterly* 6 (1935): 434-36. In this review, Brailsford stresses Woolf's careful thought about political institutions.

Clarke, Peter. "A Peculiar Kind of Socialist." *Times Literary Supplement,* 28 September 1978, p. 1072. In this review of *Leonard Woolf: A Political Biography* by Duncan Wilson, Clarke focuses on Woolf's analysis of social psychology and rationalism which set him apart from other political figures of his time. Clarke also argues that Woolf's liberal socialism was often not an effective way of dealing with social and political problems.

Edel, Leon. *Bloomsbury: A House of Lions.* Philadelphia and New York: J. B. Lippincott Co., 1979. Edel's chapter on Leonard is primarily an analysis of Woolf's personality and life. He relates Woolf's rigid standards and high expectations of people to his emotional insecurities and to his commitment to strict moral values and rationalism.

Elkin, P. K. "Leonard Woolf's Masterpiece." *Journal of Australian Universities Language and Literature* 13 (1960): 46–55. This article discusses *The Village in the Jungle.*

Fernando, Shelton C. "Growing." *Political Quarterly* 33 (1962): 218–20. Fernando focuses on Woolf's approach to the Ceylonese as a colonial administrator and calls him a "benevolent autocrat."

Flood, David H. "Leonard Woolf's *The Village in the Jungle*: A Modern Version of Pastoral." *Virginia Woolf Quarterly* 1 (1973): 78–86. Flood sees the jungle as symbolic of the modern condition of man, yet he also recognizes that the work reflects Woolf's criticism of capitalism and imperialism.

Gervais, David. "Leonard Woolf's Autobiography." *Cambridge Quarterly* 5 (1970): 82–98. This discussion of the autobiography emphasizes Woolf's view of civilization vs. barbarism.

Gooneratne, Yasmine. "Leonard Woolf's 'Waste Land': *The Village in the Jungle.*" *Journal of Commonwealth Literature* 7 (1972): 22–34. Gooneratne sees the novel as portraying the triumph of civilization over instinctive life, and she points out that this work may have influenced T. S. Eliot.

Gottlieb, Freema. "L. W.—The creative writer." *Adam* 364–66 (1972): 66–70.

_____. "Reality and Romance: Leonard Woolf's Portraiture of Virginia in Various Early Writings." *Virginia Woolf Quarterly,* Spring 1978, pp. 199–205. In the first article, Gottlieb claims that Woolf's main intention was to be a creative writer. She therefore focuses on his two novels, discussing how Woolf has taken the facts of his experiences and transformed them into art. The second article discusses *The Wise Virgins* as an autobiographical novel which is the literary expression of Leonard's love for Virginia.

Heine, Elizabeth. "Leonard Woolf: 'Three Jews' and Other Fiction." *Bulletin of the New York Public Library*, Summer 1976, pp. 448–58. Heine analyzes Woolf's use of irony in "Three Jews" and his other works of fiction. The article stresses Woolf's awareness of cultural conflict and his assertion of positive moral values.

Hynes, Samuel. "Mr. and Mrs. Leonard Woolf," *New York Times Book Review*, 25 February 1979, pp. 11, 31. In his discussion of Roger Poole's *The Unknown Virginia Woolf* and Duncan Wilson's *Leonard Woolf: A Political Biography*, Hynes rejects Poole's view of Leonard as a villain figure in Virginia's life. He asserts that Duncan Wilson does justice to Leonard's positive personal values, and gives a thorough picture of Leonard's active role in British politics.

Kennedy, Richard. *A Boy at the Hogarth Press*. London: Heinemann, 1972. Kennedy's account of some of his experiences working for the Hogarth Press presents a rather critical portrait of Leonard as a demanding, authoritarian employer.

Lee, L. L. "The Jungle as the 'Other' in Leonard Woolf's *The Village in the Jungle*." *Modern British Literature* 3 (1978): 122–27.

Lehmann, John. "Leonard Woolf." *Times Literary Supplement*, 30 October 1969, pp. 1258–59.

_____. *Thrown to the Woolves*. London: Weidenfeld and Nicolson, 1978. In his account of his partnership with Leonard and Virginia in the Hogarth Press, Lehmann argues that his working relationship with Leonard was unsatisfactory. Because Leonard rejected most of the new projects and new authors Lehmann wanted the press to publish, Lehmann resigned his partnership.

Ludeking, Leila. "Bibliography of Works by Leonard Sidney Woolf (1880-1969)." *Virginia Woolf Quarterly* 2 (1972): 120–40. This bibliography is a valuable resource tool as it includes published works and some reviews for journals.

Marcus, Jane. "'No More Horses': Virginia Woolf on Art and Propaganda." *Women's Studies* 4 (1977): 265–90. Marcus analyzes the different versions of Virginia Woolf's essay "Professions for Women." She claims that the version Leonard chose to publish in

The Collected Essays of Virginia Woolf is shorter and less angry in its comments about the position of women in society than the original version.

Martin, Kingsley. "After the Deluge." *Political Quarterly* 3 (1932):145–48.

——————. "A Cambridge Apostle." *Political Quarterly* 31 (1960): 391–92.

——————. "A Lost Civilization." *New Statesman & Nation* 73 (12 May 1967): 654. For Martin, *After the Deluge* presents perceptive observations on society and human behavior, while in "A Lost Civilization" he discusses how *Downhill All the Way* reveals Woolf's honesty and courage. And in "A Cambridge Apostle," a review of *Sowing*, he points out that Woolf's rationalism led to his criticism of religion and communism.

Medcalf, Stephen. "The Village in the Jungle." *Adam* 364–55 (1972): 75–79. This article speculates that Thomas Hardy may have been an influence on Woolf's portrayal of nature. Medcalf also emphasizes that Woolf presents the jungle as symbolic of a despairing, destructive world.

Meyerowitz, Selma. "Leonard and Virginia Woolf: An Unfinished Portrait." *Virginia Woolf Miscellany* 11 (1978): 2–3. This review argues that neither Elaine Showalter, in *A Literature of Their Own*, nor Spater and Parsons, in *A Marriage of True Minds*, discusses key elements of the Leonard-Virginia relationship such as the correspondences in their thought and work.

Ozick, Cynthia. "Mrs. Virginia Woolf." *Commentary* 53 (1973): 34–44.

——————. "The Loose Drifting Material of Life." *New York Times Book Review*, 2 October 1977, pp. 7, 40, 41. In the *Commentary* article, Ozick sees Leonard as Virginia's nurse. She also argues that the role of devoted husband created a place for Leonard in Bloomsbury.

Poole, Roger. *The Unknown Virginia Woolf.* Cambridge: Cambridge University Press, 1978. See especially Chapter 6, pp. 74–102. Poole stresses the personal and artistic incompatibility of Leonard and Virginia. In his analysis of *The Village in the Jungle* and *The Wise Virgins,* he focuses on Leonard's treatment of class and race. Moreover, he stresses that the latter novel incorporates autobiographical elements of the Leonard-Virginia relationship, and explores the problem of feeling.

Pritchett, V. S. "Bloomsbury on Safari." *New Statesman & Nation* 62 (3 November 1969): 656.

────────── "Grace and Iron." *New Statesman & Nation* 78 (24 October 1967): 577.

────────── "What Exactly Do You Mean?" *New Statesman & Nation* 67 (8 May 1964): 726. The review of *Growing* emphasizes Woolf's sense of humor and Voltaire-like satire, while the review of *Beginning Again* stresses his honesty and simplicity of style. Pritchett also values Woolf's account of his rejection of the social assumptions of his class and his decision to follow his own conscience. The final review focuses on Woolf's sense of justice and mercy.

Schaefer, Josephine O'Brien. "*Three Guineas* and *Quack, Quack!* Read Together." *Virginia Woolf Miscellany* 7 (1977): 2–3. Schaefer argues that these two works should be read as companion pieces as they both emphasize the barbarism of a class and sexist society. The article further points out that Leonard's perspective is historical, while Virginia's emphasizes a vision of the future.

Showalter, Elaine. *A Literature of Their Own: British Women Novelists from Brontë to Lessing.* Princeton, N.J.: Princeton University Press, 1977. Showalter argues that Virginia's marriage to Leonard had a negative influence on her temperament and literary work. Since Leonard was puritanical and unable to understand Virginia's emotional and physical needs, Showalter believes that he contributed to Virginia's failure to confront her sexuality and achieve identity as a woman.

Spater, George, and Parsons, Ian. *A Marriage of True Minds: An Intimate Portrait of Leonard and Virginia Woolf.* New York: Harcourt Brace Jovanovich, 1977. This work parallels Leonard's life with Virginia's. Some previously unpublished material and photographs are presented; however, there is very little analysis of Leonard's writing.

Wilson, Duncan. *Leonard Woolf: A Political Biography.* New York: St. Martin's Press, 1978. This study is based largely on government documents and some unpublished materials. Wilson presents the only thorough analysis of Woolf's political work and political literature set against helpful background on national and international issues. Although some biographical material and some analysis of Woolf's nonpolitical literature are included, this work is most useful as a complement to Woolf's autobiography.

Woolmer, J. Howard. *A Checklist of the Hogarth Press 1917–1930.* Andes, N.Y.: Woolmer-Brotherson, Ltd., 1976. The introduction provides some history of the press stressing that its two most distinguishing characteristics were individuality and independence. The checklist includes the works published between 1917 and 1938; all of Leonard's works published by the press are listed.

Woolf, Virginia. *The Diary of Virginia Woolf.* Edited by Anne Olivier Bell. New York: Harcourt Brace Jovanovich. Volume One, 1915–1919 (1977); Volume Two, 1920–1924 (1978).

——————— *The Letters of Virginia Woolf.* Edited by Nigel Nicolson and Joanne Trautmann. New York: Harcourt Brace Jovanovich. Volume I: 1880–1912 (1975); Volume II: 1912–1922 (1976); Volume III: 1923–1928 (1977); Volume IV: 1929–1931 (1978); Volume V: 1932–1935 (1979). The diaries and letters are of particular interest because they present Virginia's positive and negative feelings about Leonard and their marriage.

Wootton, Barbara. "Principia Politica." *Political Quarterly* 25 (1954): 88–90. Wootton finds the autobiographical material and discussions of animal behavior and authoritarian discipline particularly interesting. She also acknowledges Woolf's ability to write clearly and honestly about man's political behavior, and to assert civilized values.

Workman, Gillian. "Leonard Woolf and Imperialism." *Ariel* 6 (1975): 5–21. Workman's discussion of Woolf's sympathy for the Ceylonese and his antiimperialist feelings deals with *The Village in the Jungle* and *Stories from the East.* This article emphasizes the use of irony of tone and situation as Woolf's means of criticizing the destructive aspects of both colonialism and native culture.

Index

Allen, Clifford, 129
Amery, Julian, 129
Angell, Norman, 73, 118
Annan, Noel, 201-202
Apostles Society, 3, 23-24, 30, 169, 195
Asquith, Herbert Henry, 147
Auden, W. H., 158
Austen, Jane, 141
Autobiography of Bertrand Russell, The, 130

Bakunin, Mikhail, 148
Baldwin, Stanley, 26, 127
Balfour, Arthur James, 147
Barbarians and Philistines (Worsley), 150
Bell, Clive, 3, 14, 169, 188
Bell, Julian, 12, 158, 190
Bell, Quentin, 19
Bell, Vanessa Stephen, 4-5, 172, 178, 188, 196-97
Bellow, Saul, 160
Bergson, Henri, 102
Berlin, Isaiah, 128
Between the Acts (V. Woolf), 160-61, 192
Birrell, Francis, 12
Bloomsbury Group, 1, 17, 62, 143, 179, 183, 195
Bonaparte, Napoleon, 87
Brailsford, H. N., 73, 200
Brecht, Bertolt, 159
Brennan, Gerald, 130-31

Bunin, Ivan, 156
Butler, Samuel, 137, 145, 169

Canning, Stratford, 152
Carlyle, Jane, 135
Carlyle, Thomas, 102
Carrington, Dora, 12, 183, 190
Case, Janet, 14
Castlereagh, Viscount (Robert Stewart), 152
Ceylon Historical Journal, 31
Chamberlain, Joseph, 129
Chamberlain, Neville, 127
Charpentier, Armand, 148
Chatto and Windus, Ltd., 13, 159
Churchill, Winston, 126
Civilization and Its Discontents (Freud), 104
Clark, R. & R., Ltd., 156
Cobbett, William, 137
Cole, G. D. H., 118, 151
Collective Security (Swanwick), 148
Conrad, Joseph, 135, 137-38
Conservative party, 26, 147, 151
Contemporary Review, 117, 120, 122, 200
Co-operative Movement, 2, 5-6, 18, 63, 83, 93, 94-98, 117, 165, 181, 183, 185, 193, 198, 203
Co-operative News, 9, 117
Craig, Maurice, 180
Culture of Cities, The (Mumford), 150

Daily Mail, 46
Dangling Man (Bellow), 160
Davies, Margaret L., 18
Day to Day, 158
Dickinson, Goldsworthy Lowes, 69, 78, 118
Dickinson, Violet, 14, 21, 196-97
Disraeli, Benjamin, 143, 152
Dostoevski, Fedor, 58
Dreyfus, Alfred, 148-49, 169, 191, 194
Dryden, John, 143

Eberhart, Richard, 158
Edel, Leon, 14
Edwardians, The (Sackville-West), 157
Egoist, 155
Eliot, T. S., 8, 15, 139, 155, 183, 187-88
Empson, William, 158
Ethics (Aristotle), 145
Eugenie of France, Empress, 175

Fabian Society, 5, 6-7, 63-64, 70, 71, 73, 82, 88, 90-91, 181-82, 183, 189, 193, 202, 204
Fernando, Shelton C., 201-2
Fichte, Johann, 102
Forster, E. M., 8, 135, 183
Franklin, Benjamin, 139
Freud, Sigmund, 8, 23, 101, 104, 113, 145, 157, 159, 183, 186
Friendship's Gallery (V. Woolf), 161
Fry, Roger, 133-34, 190, 192
Fyfe, Hamilton, 46

Garrat, G. T., 148
Garvin, J. L., 129

Gladstone, William, 140
Gollin, Alfred M., 129
Gorky, Maxim, 156
Grant, Duncan, 188

Hardy, Thomas, 169
Hazlitt, William, 136-37, 144
Heard, Gerald, 146
Henderson, Arthur, 185
Hindenburg, von, Paul, 125
Historical Inevitability (Berlin), 128
Hitler, Adolf, 28, 100, 104, 106, 114-15, 123-24, 125-26, 144, 150, 151, 153, 159, 188, 190, 194
Hobson, J. A., 73, 118
Hogarth Essays, 157
Hogarth Living Poets, 158
Hogarth Press, 2, 5, 7, 12-14, 17, 32, 53, 61, 81, 85, 117, 142, 154-62, 164, 182-83, 185-87, 193, 203
Holt, Henry, 46
Hyslop, T. B., 180

Ibsen, Henrik, 58, 59, 169
International Review, 2, 9, 119, 122, 200

Jacob's Room (V. Woolf), 185
James, Henry, 135
Jonson, Ben, 136
Joyce, James, 155

Kant, Immanuel, 102
Keynes, John Maynard, 8, 157, 171
Khachaturian, Aram, 127
Koteliansky, S. S., 156

Labour party, 5, 7-8, 12-13, 17, 26, 63, 68-69, 71, 81-82, 86, 88, 90-92, 151, 183, 185, 189, 193-94, 199, 202-4
Landor, Walter Savage, 144
League of Nations, 7, 9, 11, 16, 24, 26, 64-65, 69, 71, 77, 80-88, 92, 118-24, 148, 154, 157, 182, 190, 194
Legrand, Daniel, 68
Lehmann, John, 13, 154, 158-61, 185
Lewis, C. Day, 158
Leys, Norman, 157
Liberal party, 151
Life of Joseph Chamberlain, The (Amery), 129
London Magazine, 161
Lorca, Federico García, 159

Macaulay, Thomas, 144
MacCarthy, Desmond, 181
MacDonald, James Ramsay, 185
Mackinnon, William, 76
Macmillan, Harold, 129-30
Man and Master (Heard), 146
Mannheim, Karl, 149
Mansfield, Katherine, 8, 155, 156, 183, 187
Mao Tse-tung, 194
"Mark on the Wall, The" (V. Woolf), 7, 183
Martin, Kingsley, 200-201
Massingham, H., 9, 64, 185
Master Builder, The (Ibsen), 59
Maynard, John, 130
"Memoirs of a Working Women's Guild" (V. Woolf), 18
Metternich, von, Klemens, 152

Middle Way, The (Macmillan), 129
Montaigne, de, Michel, 29, 202
Moore, G. E., 3, 169, 195, 202-3
Moore, George, 30
Morrell, Ottoline, 187
Morrell, Philip, 187
Mumford, Lewis, 150
Murry, Middleton, 187
Mussolini, Benito, 11, 86, 100, 114-15, 123-24, 194
Myself When Young: Confessions (Waugh), 139

Nation, 9, 16, 64, 117, 131, 136, 145, 185, 200
New Statesman, 7, 9, 63-64, 117, 181
New Statesman & Nation, 9, 13, 117, 131, 140, 145, 200
New Writing, 158, 159
Nietzsche, Friedrich, 102
Night and Day (V. Woolf), 17
Noise of History, The (Lehmann), 159
Northcliffe, Lord, 135

Observer, 129
Observer and J. L. Garvin, The (Gollin), 129
Orwell, George, 176
Our Partnership (Webb), 131
Owen, Robert, 68

Parsons, Ian, 15, 19
Passage to India, A (Forster), 135
Pasternak, Boris, 159
Pétain, Henri Philippe, 125
Plomer, William, 158

Poems (Eliot), 155
Political Quarterly, 2, 9, 13, 85, 117, 122, 125, 127, 129, 131, 189, 200, 201
Pope, Alexander, 143
"Prelude" (Mansfield), 155
Price, F. H., 32
Pritchett, V. S., 201-2
Prokofiev, Sergei, 127
Public Speaking and Debate (Holyoake), 139

Rilke, Rainer M., 159
Rise and Fulfilment of British Rule in India, The (Thompson and Garrat), 148
Robbins, Elizabeth, 197
Robespierre, de, Maximilien, 147-48
Robinson, Rachel, 44-45
Robson, W. A., 117
Roger Fry (V. Woolf), 192
Room of One's Own, A (V. Woolf), 18, 183
Roosevelt, Franklin D., 126
Russell, Bertrand, 24, 118, 130
Russian Peasant, The (Maynard), 130

Sackville-West, Vita, 157, 159, 186, 187-88, 196-97
Sargent, John Singer, 134
Sartre, Jean-Paul, 160
Savage, George, 180
Shakespeare, William, 143, 144
Sharp, Clifford, 64, 181
Shaw, George Bernard, 63, 133, 141, 169
"Shooting an Elephant" (Orwell), 176

Shostakovich, Dmitri, 127
Silone, Ignazio, 159
Smith, Sydney, 144
Smyth, Ethel, 21, 196-97
Snowden, Philip, 185
Spanish Labyrinth, The (Brennan), 131
Spater, George, 15, 19
Spencer, Herbert, 136
Spender, Stephen, 158
Spenser, Edmund, 144
Stalin, Joseph, 153, 191, 194
Stephen, Adrian, 62
Stephen, Leslie, 29, 55, 172
Stephen, Thoby, 3, 4, 14, 169, 171
Sterne, Laurence, 135-36
Strachey, Alix, 186
Strachey, James, 186
Strachey, Lytton, 3, 4, 12, 14, 16, 169, 171, 172, 174, 190
Study of History, A (Toynbee), 128
Swanwick, H. M., 148
Swift, Jonathan, 143
Swinburne, Algernon, 169
Sydney-Turner, Saxon, 3, 20, 169, 170-71

Taylor, Jeremy, 143
Thompson, Edward, 148
Thompson, J. M., 147
"Thoughts on Peace During an Air Raid" (V. Woolf), 18
Three Guineas (V. Woolf), 18, 183
Thrown to the Woolves (Lehmann), 154, 159-61
Times Literary Supplement, 155
Tory party, 92
To the Lighthouse (V. Woolf), 172

Toynbee, Arnold, 128
Trevelyan, George, 30

Ulysses (Joyce), 155
United Nations, 90-91, 126-27, 154

Vaughan, Marny, 63
Voltaire, François, 141
Voyage Out, The (V. Woolf), 17, 62, 180

Wagner, Richard, 179
Walpole, Horace, 144
War and Peace, 69, 117, 118
Waugh, Alec, 139
Waves, The (V. Woolf), 144
Weaver, Harriet, 155
Webb, Beatrice, 6-7, 15-17, 63, 131, 181
Webb, Sidney, 6-7, 16, 63, 69, 181
Wells, H. G., 146
Wilberforce, Octavia, 192, 197
Wilson, Duncan, 56, 202-3
Wilson, Woodrow, 118
Winds of Change (Macmillan), 129
Woolf, Benjamin (grandfather), 166
Woolf, Leonard, life and times, 1-29

WORKS:
After the Deluge, 10, 11, 93, 110-12, 188, 198, 200-201
After the War, 97
Barbarians at the Gate, 191
Barbarians Within and Without, 11, 18, 69, 93, 103-6, 113, 198, 199

Beginning Again, 64, 68, 69, 154, 155, 163-65, 178, 180-81, 183-85, 187, 197, 201
Calendar of Consolation, A, 143
Control of Industry by the People, The, 96
Co-operation and the Future of Industry, 6, 63, 93-94, 96-97, 112, 182, 198
Co-operation and the War, 96-97
Diaries in Ceylon, 3, 30-40, 60, 177
Downhill All the Way, 81, 85, 91, 155-56, 163-64, 183-85, 187-88, 190, 196-97, 201-2
Economic Imperialism, 8, 78-81
Education and the Co-operative Movement, 96
Empire and Commerce in Africa, 8, 73-78, 80, 81, 190, 199
"Espionage, Security, and Liberty," 128
Essays on Literature, History, Politics, Etc., 10, 136
Fear and Politics, 9, 10, 22, 23-28
Foreign Policy, 12, 88, 90-91
Framework of a Lasting Peace, The, 8, 69-71
Future of Constantinople, The, 8, 71-73
"Gentleness of Nature, The," 22
"George or George or Both?", 30
Growing, 31, 32, 34, 38, 39, 44, 46, 51, 61, 163, 172, 174, 176-78, 201, 202

"Hitler's Psychology," 125-26
Hotel, The, 11, 27, 69, 93, 106-10, 200
Hunting the Highbrow, 9, 10, 142-43
Imperialism and Civilization, 8
International Co-operative Trade, 82-83
International Economic Policy, 82-83
International Government, 7, 8, 16, 63-68, 69, 182, 194, 199
International Post-War Settlement, The, 12, 88-90
Journey, Not the Arrival Matters, The, 164-65, 190-95, 197, 202
"Labour and Foreign Affairs," 82, 83
League and Abyssinia, The, 11, 82, 85-87
"Leonard Paper, The," 30
literary reviewing, 131-54, 162
"Music in Moscow," 127
"Pearls and Swine," 4, 44, 46-51
"Please, Sir, it was the other Fellow," 27, 152
"Politics in Spain," 27
Principia Politica, 11, 93, 112-15, 169, 188-89, 198, 199, 200-201
Quack, Quack!, 11, 18, 69, 93, 98-103, 106, 113, 198, 199, 200
Socialism and Co-operation, 6, 63, 93, 97-98, 112, 198
"Something Out of Africa," 128
Sowing, 165, 170, 172, 174

"Statesmen and Diplomatists," 27
Stories from the East, 44, 51, 53, 198
"Tale Told by Moonlight, A," 4, 44-46
"Three Jews," 5, 7, 53-55, 56, 183, 198
"Two Brahmans, The," 4, 44, 51-53
Two Stories (with V. Woolf), 5, 7, 53, 155, 182
Village in the Jungle, The, 4, 5, 16, 22, 30, 35, 39, 40-44, 51, 53, 62, 179-80, 203-4
War for Peace, The, 12, 82, 87-88
"What is Democracy?", 112
"What is History?", 128
Wise Virgins, The, 17, 55-60, 180, 198, 204

Woolf, Sidney (father), 2, 167, 170, 191
Woolf, Virginia Stephen (wife), 1, 4-5, 7, 11, 12-22, 28, 55-56, 60, 62-64, 116, 144, 154-57, 159, 160-62, 164, 172, 178-88, 191-93, 196-97, 201, 203-4
Wootton, Barbara, 201-2
Work, Wealth and Happiness of Mankind, The (Wells), 146
Worsley, T. C., 150
Wright, Maurice, 64
Writer's Diary, A (V. Woolf), 161

Zoological News, 30